HOW TO
SOLARIZE
YOUR HOUSE

HOW TO
SOLARIZE YOUR HOUSE

A Practical Guide to Design and Construction for Solar Heating

THOMAS SCOTT DEAN

with
Jay W. Hedden

Illustrations by John Stephen Lane

WITHDRAWN

Phillipsburg Free Public Library
PHILLIPSBURG, N. J.

Charles Scribner's Sons
New York

Grateful acknowledgment is made to The Franklin Institute
Press, Philadelphia, Pa. for permission to use material from
Thermal Storage by Thomas S. Dean (© 1978 The Franklin
Institute Press). Also available in French as *Accumulation de
Chaleur* (© 1979 SCM, Paris).

Library of Congress Cataloging in Publication Data

Dean, Thomas Scott.
   How to solarize your house.

   Includes bibliographical references and index.
   1. Solar heating.   I. Hedden, Jay W., joint author.
II. Title.
TH7413.D42   697'.78   79-26954
ISBN 0-684-16295-4

1 3 5 7 9 11 13 15 17 19   V/C   20 18 16 14 12 10 8 6 4 2

Printed in the United States of America

CONTENTS

Preface *ix*

1. YESTERDAY, TODAY, AND TOMORROW—AN INTRODUCTION *1*

Passive Systems 5
Active Systems 10
The Solar Future 14

2. FLAT-PLATE COLLECTORS *17*

Principles of Meteorology, Astronomy, and Heat Transfer that You Probably Knew but Forgot 17
Instantaneous Collector Efficiency 25
Materials for Collector Construction 27
Building Your Own Collectors 33

3. THERMAL STORAGE *39*

4. PIPING AND PUMPS *46*

Fittings 50
Pipe Joints 53
Making Solder Joints 56
Making Brazed Joints 59
Testing Joints 65
Design of Piping Systems 65
Pumps 70
Antifreeze Solutions 73
Pump Controllers 74
Other Considerations 75

5. INSTALLING A FLAT-PLATE COLLECTOR SYSTEM *76*

Piping the Array 79
Design of Domestic-Water-Heating Systems 83
Solar Side Design of a Space-Heating System 89
Controls 95

6. USING SOLAR HEAT WITH CONVENTIONAL SYSTEMS *97*

7. SYSTEM PERFORMANCE *109*

8. SYSTEM ECONOMICS *117*

APPENDICES *121*

A-1. Conversion factors 121
A-2. Mean daily solar radiation by month for the United States 122

A-3. Normal daily maximum, average, minimum, and extreme temperatures (°F) by month for the United States   134

A-4. Normal total heating degree days (Base 65°) by month for the United States   146

A-5. Outdoor design conditions—Summer and Winter   148

A-6. Mean percentage of possible sunshine for selected locations   150

A-7. Solar position and insolation values for 24, 32, 40, 48, 56 degrees north latitude   151

A-8. System evaluation chart   157

A-9. Chart for estimating a building's daily, monthly, and annual heating needs   157

A-10. Chart for estimating ΔT_c 158

A-11. Chart for estimating collectable insolation   159

A-12. Chart for calculating solar portion of heating load   159

INDEX   161

To my wife, Jan,
who, despite the skepticism
of our friends,
agreed to build
and live in
a solar house with me

PREFACE

The decision to write this book was not easy for me. Although I have written several book-length manuscripts—two of which have been published—the idea of book authorship remains as ego satisfying to me as to anyone else. Moreover, with regard to the limited scope of my subject, I am probably as competent as the next person to write the book. After all, I have lived in a solar house since early 1975. I have designed many others. I teach courses in solar technology. I serve as an energy adviser to the Kansas Energy Office. I write a regular column on energy for *Workbench* magazine. Furthermore, I am active in research in this area.

My hesitation about writing the book was caused by an awareness of the large number of solar books already on the shelves. Many of these books, unfortunately, reflect more the personal hopes and fantasies of their authors than any technological or practical rationale. This situation is understandable. Architects and engineers of all sorts, chemists, physicists, meteorologists, geographers of several persuasions, inventors, tinkerers, crackpots, nuts, and the just plain stupid have all tried to shape this relatively simple technology to their individual images. Regrettably, many of these persons have written books. More regrettably, some of these have been published.

Among this overabundance of solar books is a handful of excellent volumes. For the general reader, *Other Homes and Garbage,* by Jim Leckie, Gil Masters, Harry Whitehouse, and Lily Young, can hardly be improved upon. Bruce Anderson's *The Solar Home Book* and Don Watson's *Designing and Building a Solar Home* describe general types of solar heating systems in manners understandable to most everyone. Duffie and Beckman's *Solar Energy Thermal Processes* was the first "modern" work to systematically treat the heat-transfer phenomenon associated with solar energy systems. This book was followed by the Meinels'

Applied Solar Energy, in which the authors' exceptional knowledge of optics is displayed. Kreith and Kreider's *Principles of Solar Engineering* contains an especially good chapter on fluid mechanics and heat transfer.

It is necessary to classify these books as modern, because, in fact, solar technology is a relatively mature study. It is certainly more mature than the study of nuclear fission, orbital mechanics, or solid-state physics. These new books draw heavily on the previous work of solar pioneers such as Harry Tabor, George Löf, Eric Farber, Maria Telkes, John Yelliott, and, especially, the work of Hottel and Whillier at MIT, where solar research has been conducted since the 1930s. As a graduate student at MIT in 1949 I recall my daily walk up Memorial Drive past the solar house and Howard Johnson's Restaurant (where I first tasted fried clams) before turning into my barracks apartment in Westgate West.

Despite the work of these researchers, despite the fact that literally thousands of solar installations had already been made, solar applications languished during the 1950s and the early part of the following decade. However, by the 1960s anyone who could read knew of an impending energy crisis. They knew, but they didn't really believe. After all, many utilities during this period were still encouraging their customers not only to use more energy, but to waste it. As the nation experienced a knee-jerk reaction to the onslaught of unbridled pollution, automobile engines grew in size and thirst. Architects and dilettante intellectuals continued to eulogize that energy-devouring urban monster known as the glass office tower.

Nevertheless, two groups of persons heeded the warning. One group, a counterculture that had rejected middle-class materialism, settled by pairs or in communes in such unlikely locations as northern New Mexico or southern Colorado. In this fragile environment, with their own hands they built tepee, soddy, or geodesic dome. Not only a shortage of money, but a disdain for it also, together with an abundance of winter sunshine and an unpolluted atmosphere, encouraged solar experimentation. Recycled beer cans, oil drums, polyethylene film, junked automobile radiators, and many other miscellaneous materials were employed in their systems. Blessed with creativity and daring, but holding low expectations for the performance of their systems, this group designed and built the forerunners of our present solar houses. I think it fair to speculate that more of this group were educated in the arts than in science or engineering, since science and engineering graduates tended to be absorbed into the corporate mainstream. If this be the case, then it may explain the avalanche of books and articles on the subject, many of which contain more hope and faith than fact.

At a considerable philosophical distance, although not necessarily many miles away, another group set to work exploring solar energy. This group, composed of scientists and engineers employed in the dwindling space effort or weapons program, came with impeccable academic credentials. Their employers were already well stocked with the laboratories, equipment, and computers necessary for precise designs, measurements, and simulations. Fortunately for them, they were also in a position to propose and receive research and development grants from the federal government.

If one uses a broad brush, this group might be characterized as cautious to a fault. Although this group has provided us with a mass of welcome data, measurements, and simulations, the same broad brush would paint its members as not particularly sensitive to economic considerations. Accustomed to creating devices capable of operating with an exceptional degree of reliability in any of a number of hostile environments, the group is not especially qualified by experience to design cost-effective solar heating systems. The quality-control standards of an aerospace organization may, and probably do, differ markedly from those available from a local plumber or home craftsman. And stock bins in a local plumbing-supply house may not

compare in either variety or quality with those of a major high-tech corporation.

By the fall of 1974, I knew that my next home would have a solar assist. Armed with books spanning the spectrum of solar writing, attendance at several solar short courses and workshops, my doctorate in engineering, and over twenty years' practice as both architect and engineer, I set forth the following year to bring the house into reality. We had spent 1973 in a small flat near Hampstead Heath in London. The oil embargo, a result of the crisis about which we were warned in the 1960s, occurred in October of that year. London shops darkened. In the shop windows along Regent Street, the sparkle of precious jewels was made visible by the judicious placement of small propane torches. Airline ticket offices where lit by single candles at each agent's station. When riding a bus, the ruby glow through a pub's window or the amber globe marking a pedestrian crossing might be the only light to be seen. We would attend movies wearing pea jackets, watch caps, mufflers, and mukluks. Except for the lack of danger, one could almost imagine the Battle of Britain once again.

We spent the following summer in Palo Alto, where I was fortunate to be a NASA–Stanford Fellow. My particular assignment was to predict the future—an activity risky at best, but more likely to be simply ridiculous. As my research progressed, I was surprised to discover that many of the vectors that are shaping the country's future have already been drawn. Even modest extrapolation of energy reserves and consumption curves led to some chilling conclusions. It was possible to construct some scenarios for the future that ranged from austere to disastrous. It was also possible to construct scenarios in which the quality of life was enhanced, but these latter situations required the development and use of alternate, small-scale energy systems. I returned home determined to devote my total efforts to designing energy-efficient buildings and solar and wind systems, although most of my work already resulted in buildings that were energy-efficient. As a matter of fact, I had designed my first intentionally energy-efficient home in the mid-1950s for a national manufacturer of insulation products (I am again performing research for the same manufacturer), and the lessons I learned on this first effort have not been forgotten. Nonetheless, since my decision in 1974, I have not designed a single home that does not have an active solar-energy heating system in addition to an attached greenhouse for direct passive gain.

(As I write this, the outside temperature is around 15°F (−9.4°C), but it is sunny. Sitting at my typewriter, I gaze through a glass panel into the greenhouse. I see tomatoes, beans, lettuce, and chard in addition to begonias, marigolds, and a variety of tropical plants. A large thermometer on the greenhouse wall tells me that the temperature is about 80°F (26.7°C). A thermostatically controlled reversible fan is moving this warm air into my study.)

My efforts would be limited to designing not only solar-heated buildings, but buildings occupied by the average family. The acceptance of a 55°F (12.8°C) or a 100°F (37.8°C) inside temperature by energy activists—admirable though this acceptance is—is not likely to be endured by the average family. Consequently, I have avoided the purely passive approach. Some, but by no means all, families are willing and able to make a capital investment against the future cost of energy from conventional sources. Even so, in most cases there will be a limit on the size of this investment, and so design compromises are necessary. I do not strive for the "best" system, but for one which is the most cost-effective. To give an example, low-iron-content glass admits about 10 percent more radiation than does ordinary glass. However, if it adds much more than 10 percent to the system cost, then its use might not be a wise choice. It may be reasoned that the kinds of systems I describe are probably not affordable by people whose incomes are at or near the poverty level. Sadly, most other types of systems would not be affordable either. Likewise, these systems might be unacceptable for persons for whom neither cost nor level of performance is a limitation. However, for this group, energy costs are likely to be an insignificant part of the monthly budget. My target is the remaining large portion of our population between these two extremes.

Designing and building my first house with a solar heating system was both exciting and frustrating. I discovered that one class of my reference books was only "about" solar. The other class concentrated on radiation, heat transfer, fluid mechanics, and system simulation, sometimes using inappropriate and often ridiculous data. None of these books considered in detail the actual installation of the piping, fittings, and pumps required for a real system. Fortunately, I often teach these topics, so I was able to fill many of the voids in my references. I learned to ignore my plumber's advice never to use a check valve. When I came up against a particularly vexing problem my wife would suggest that I ask someone for advice. I had to reply that there was no one to ask. I polished up my soldering skills. During the first year of operation, I seemed to be constantly reading thermometers, flow controllers, and watt-hour meters (we have five). I made some mistakes, too. Luckily, none were serious, and I have avoided most of these pesky irritations in my subsequent designs.

I hope that this rambling discussion of my experiences will indicate why I decided to write the book. I wrote it with the hope that it describes "how" in sufficient detail for the average person to incorporate a solar heating system using liquid-cooled flat-plate collectors into a new or existing building. Other types of systems are available, each with its enthusiastic supporters. However, the type of system I describe has a long history of successful applications. For the main part, the components are readily available and relatively inexpensive. I have designed such systems for many buildings and supervised their installation. Furthermore, I have lived with a system of this type for several years while monitoring many of its aspects on an hourly or daily basis. It is the kind of system that can provide one with welcome economic relief in the years to come.

Most of all, this is not a technical book. There are several excellent technical books already in print. I commend them to any interested person. However, architects, air-conditioning and plumbing mechanics, and resourceful craftsmen are not necessarily prepared to digest either the content or the mathematical justifications presented in these books. Yet I feel that this same group of persons may design or install workable solar systems if only the necessary information is available to them in a form that they can understand. Consequently, I have chosen to minimize, insofar as possible, any requirements for an engineering background in order to understand the book. On the other hand, any knowledge of architecture, engineering, or construction will obviously be an asset in the design and construction of one of these systems.

Some readers may have detailed knowledge of the principles of heat transfer and fluid mechanics. For those readers, I hope that my apparent superficial treatment of these topics is not offensive. They are important and deserve serious study, but not by the main readership of this book. I do not feel that any assertions that I have made are in violation of accepted notions.

I have attempted to include suitable references for anyone who desires additional technical information on the several topics. In general, these references are to the few "new" volumes on solar thermal processes. Actually, many of the relationships stated in these books are first published either in standard engineering texts or in specialized journals. However, prior to 1973, many of these journals had a limited circulation, so locating the original source might be difficult. The new volumes, each of which contains an extensive bibliography, appear to be resources more easily located.

At several points throughout the book I have stated various rules of thumb. Most of us have enjoyed the convenience of these shortcuts. But some of us have also been disappointed when, for one reason or another, a rule of thumb did not yield the desired result. In general, rules of thumb work best for the class of situations from which they arose and in the hands of a skilled person, or at least one who is alert.

Some authorities warn against the use of any rule of thumb in the design of a solar energy system. In general, I concur with this position. However, when rules of thumb originate in engineering calculations and are tested under a variety of conditions, then their credibility is considerably enhanced. Of course, one always has the choice of preparing an analytical solution rather than using a shortcut.

I have chosen not to use the "f-chart" method (see page 112) for calculating system performance, although I do not question its accuracy. It seems to me that the calculations it requires may be burdensome for the average person. Consequently, I have used a simpler method devised by Bell and Gossett, which I have modified slightly. When I have used the two methods for analyzing the same system, my results were almost identical.

During the last quarter of this century, the nation is undergoing the painful process of converting from the English to SI (International System of Units or metric system) system of measurement. The metric system is used in most parts of the world. Even in the United States, scientists use SI units, though architects, consulting engineers, and the various trades still mostly use English units. Most new engineering texts use SI units. In the development of solar energy technology, scientists, engineers, architects, and the trades are all making contributions, so that the appearance of both English and SI units must be expected. For example, solar radiation may be expressed as cal/cm^2-min, w/m^2, Btu/ft^2-hr, kJ/m^2-hr, or langleys. Although with my construction background I tend to think of radiation intensity in units of Btu/ft^2-hr, weather stations record it in langleys (1 langley = 3.69 Btu/ft^2). Appendix A–1 contains a chart of conversion factors. I have chosen to express quantities in English rather than SI units for the reason that it is easier to learn one thing (solar-system design) than two things (solar-system design and SI units). On the other hand, I have provided quantities in SI units in parentheses where appropriate.

Finally, I want to express my gratitude to my co-author, Jay Hedden, and my illustrator, Steve Lane. Although I must stand alone in enduring whatever criticism the book may arouse, the actual production of its manuscript was due in no small measure to Jay's genius and diligence in transforming ideas into typescript and attending to the multitude of chores inherent in book production. Steve, a graduate architectural student with several years of office experience, produces most of the working drawings for the solar projects I design. His thorough and practical knowledge of solar heating systems, and his considerable skill as an architectural delineator, have made my task much easier.

—Thomas Scott Dean

CHAPTER ONE

YESTERDAY, TODAY, AND TOMORROW— AN INTRODUCTION

By most any standards our sun is an average star. Its extremely dense interior, at a temperature of millions of degrees, actually is a giant fusion reactor. Temperatures decrease with increasing distance from its center until the photosphere, which lies beneath the corona, chromosphere, and reversing layer, is reached. It is the photosphere, whose temperature is about 10,000°F (6,000 K), that is the source of most solar radiation.

This radiation, a form of energy, travels in all directions. At the outer fringe of the earth's atmosphere, it amounts to about 428 Btu/ft^2-hr (1.35kw/m^2). Radiation having the shortest wavelengths is classified as gamma rays, or X-rays. Luckily for animal life, most of this radiation is absorbed or scattered by carbon dioxide, water vapor, and ozone in the upper atmosphere. Over 90 percent of the sun's energy has wavelengths in the ultraviolet, visible, and near-infrared bands. Despite some absorption and scattering by the atmosphere, most of this radiation reaches the earth. Some of it is reflected, some absorbed. In this latter manner it is converted into longwave infrared or heat energy. Another portion falls upon the green leaves of plants, in which—by the process of photosynthesis—water, carbon dioxide, and nutrients are converted into cellulose and lignin, building blocks of the plant kingdom.

One may imagine that with the discovery of fire, our prehistoric ancestors discovered that somehow the heat energy was locked into wood, leaves, grasses, and other plant material used as their fuel. Indeed, these plant materials, particularly wood,

were humanity's primary heat source until about 200 years ago. It is interesting to note that, technically, the heat derived from a wood stove is solar heat. The wood used as fuel is a thermal-storage device.[1]

Some of the plant materials, instead of decaying on the forest floor or open prairie, were subjected to tremendous pressure and became coal. This pressure largely eliminated the material's moisture and air spaces, so that the resulting coal contained a great deal more heat content than wood does, on either a volume or a weight basis. This increased density of thermal storage allowed for coal's relatively easier collection, shipping, and burning than wood.

Increased use of coal during the last century more or less paralleled industrial growth. Coal-fired locomotives thundered along twin steel rails, inexorably pushing the frontier ever westward. Coal fueled the blast furnaces and engines of industry that made possible both locomotives and rails. Coal-powered oceangoing ships engaged in commerce, travel, and war. Coal fueled boilers not only to heat buildings of all sorts, but also to produce the steam necessary to drive the turbines of a fledgling electric industry. By the end of the last century, coal had replaced wood as our primary fuel.

About a century ago, petroleum was first discovered in Pennsylvania, then Texas, and later in many parts of the world. The first wells were shallow, only a few hundred feet deep, and the oil deposits frequently were accompanied by natural gas. At first this gas was burned at the wellhead as an undesirable by-product. Only later was gas recognized as our most abundant, clean, safe, and inexpensive fuel. Just as coal was easier to collect, ship, and burn than wood, so petroleum and gas enjoyed the same advantage over coal.

A belligerent miners' union, operators unwilling to invest in improved equipment and safety, plus the completion of the "Big Inch" pipeline from Texas to the east in the 1940s assured the demise of coal as our primary fuel. From the end of World War II until the oil embargo of 1973, coal production steadily declined, while this country's consumption of petroleum and natural gas continued to climb.

It is convenient to consider electricity as our primary energy source today, but this concept is valid only for the end user. Some electric power is generated by hydroelectric plants that make use of elevated water reservoirs as energy storage. Neither is it inaccurate to consider hydro power as a solar source, since water flows into the reservoirs as a result of sun-induced weather. Such power generation provokes no adverse atmospheric pollution, but many persons feel that construction of the large water impoundments required by a hydroelectric installation may have catastrophic effects on local ecosystems. Although such arguments are likely to persist, the fact is that most desirable hydroelectric sites in this country already have been exploited and few new hydroelectric plants of this sort will be constructed.

Some electric energy is produced by steam-generating plants driven by light-water nuclear reactors. The lively debate between proponents and opponents of nuclear power is likely to continue. Although the number of applications for new nuclear plants has declined, we may expect and need additional generating capacity from this source, despite the fact that a number of questions regarding nuclear power remain unanswered. The problem of nuclear-waste disposal—a problem bound to become more serious—has not been successfully solved. Although the Nuclear Regulatory Commission estimates nuclear-power generation at about 23 percent efficiency, some antinuclear sources place the efficiency at 7 percent or less. A major unanswered question is the price of nuclear-generated electricity to the consumer. Much of the published favorable-rate information was drawn from data at stations totally or partially subsidized by the federal government, using fuel priced artifically low.

But the fact is, most of our electricity is produced by burning fossil fuels. A considerable body of opinion holds that our supply of these fuels is being rapidly depleted and that actual shortfalls may be expected. Whether or not this is true, it remains that future production of petroleum, natural gas, and coal will be expensive. Gone are the shallow wells of Pennsylvania and Texas. In their stead are giant platforms in the North Sea, the pipeline from Prudhoe Bay, and the offshore drilling along our seacoasts. Some wells are more than 30,000 feet (9,144m) deep. Although the nation has sizable coal reserves, additional safety precautions and capital investment in equipment will increase its cost. The western states hold much of our coal reserves, but this coal has a high sulfur content. An already overpolluted society rightly demands that environmental safeguards be employed when this coal is burned.

Taken together, all these factors conspire to guarantee one significant change—future energy costs will be much higher than they are now. How much? Several utility executives suggest an annual escalation of 15 percent. If allowed to continue, this rate would result in doubling of energy costs in five years, or a whopping 400 percent increase in a single decade. Since the average family's energy budget is about 10 percent of net income, it is unclear how this increase will be met. Clearly, most households do not possess an additional 30 percent of disposable income that can be transferred to their energy budgets. "Normal" inflation and wage increases will soften the impact of increased energy costs for many. Others, however, will view their ten-year future as a time for increased educational expenses rather than increased costs for energy. Or, perhaps, as retirement years with a fixed income—a situation not compatible with rising energy costs.

Many persons still view the energy situation as a conspiracy among the oil producers. Even among those persons not willing to condemn the producers, many still look to the federal or institutional bureaucracies for their salvation. After all, since this country's inception, the prevailing philosophy has been "bigger is better," bigger is more efficient, bigger is more economical. Such an attitude is difficult to change, but change it must, if a rich quality of life is to be maintained. Even the prestigious Office of Technology Assessment that reports only to the Congress concluded, in its report of July 6, 1976, that solar and wind systems were as cost-effective when installed on single buildings as when integrated into central power installations.

A diverse group of persons, large in number but small as a percentage of population, have agreed to accept at least partial responsibility for their future energy costs. The one thread of commonality that binds this group is their conservative prudence. They are willing to subordinate their concern for the lowest initial cost in return for a more favorable lifetime cost. They are willing to invest in the future, a trait that separates the prehistoric farmer, who planted seeds in the spring, cultivated them during the summer, and harvested in the fall, from the prehistoric hunter, who demanded immediate gratification. Even now I am enjoying the fruits of my solar investment made in 1975.

As one makes a tentative commitment to the use of a solar energy supplement, several questions are inevitably raised. The two most commonly asked me—and my answers—are:

1. When will solar technology be sufficiently developed so that it can be employed by the average person?

Actually, solar technology is at least as old as civilization. The ancient Greeks were aware of the principles of passive design.[2] Many primitive peoples acquired the principles perhaps more through experience than design. Montezuma Castle in central Arizona and Mesa Verde in southwestern Colorado are excellent examples of sun-tempered design (Fig. 1–1). These Indian communities of the semiarid Southwest consisted of stone and plaster rooms located beneath overhanging south-facing cliffs. The overhang allowed the low winter sun to irradiate and warm the masonry buildings, but precluded the high summer sun from doing the same.

Modern-day liquid-cooled solar collectors have been around for at least seventy-five years.[3] Roofs in Los Angeles were dotted with collectors as early as 1906 (Fig. 1–2). During the 1920s and '30s an estimated 40,000 solar hot-water heaters were installed in Florida. The availability of inexpensive natural gas and gas-fired water heaters effectively halted their installation at the outset of World War II. Japan, whose climate is less than ideal for solar radiation, had installed an estimated 250,000 solar hot-water heaters by 1960.

In the 1930s the Massachusetts Institute of Technology began serious studies into the use of solar energy for space heating (Fig. 1–3). Since that time a group of solar pioneers, including Maria Telkes, George Löf, Henry Tabor, Erich Farber, and John Yelliott, have devoted their considerable scientific skills to discovering the potential and limitations of solar-assisted space heating. Much to the credit of these pioneers, my own home has performed better than most conventionally heated houses through three of the most severe winters on record.

Yes, we have a sufficiently mature solar technology. This is not to say that additional technology will not be forthcoming. But to ignore what we have while waiting for some ultimate scheme may be courting economic privation. By analogy, the wait-and-see attitude may be equivalent to buyer resistance to Henry Ford's Model T while awaiting the availability of six-way power seats.

2. When will the cost of solar energy decrease?

In my experience, these systems cost more this year than last. In my opinion they will cost more in the future than they do today. The cost of a collector array is less than half the cost of the total system. In addition to on-site labor, a system requires pumps or blowers, pipe or ducts, valves or dampers, controllers, thermometers, and fittings. Each of these is already a "shelf" item for the air-conditioning or hydronics trades. Each has been in use long enough for its manufacturer to have recovered its development costs. Each is manufactured

FIG. 1–1. Restored Indian village at Mesa Verde, Colorado. Built of stone and plaster beneath the brow of a south-facing cliff, the buildings were heated by the low winter sun but shaded from the summer sun. Photo courtesy National Park Service.

FIG. 1–2. A small section of Monrovia, California, showing sixteen day and night solar water-heater installations.

Photo courtesy Ken Butti and John Perlin from *A Golden Thread.*

in large enough quantity that the economies of mass production have been realized. Consequently, we may consider the price of these items as stable, except for increases due to inflation.

Flat-plate collectors are another matter. Even the most advanced of these must be considered an example of intermediate technology. The most technologically advanced industrial giant has no particular advantage over a regional or local fabricator or even the reasonably skilled home craftsman. Compared to other manufactured products, these simple collectors are material-intensive. Furthermore, the materials appropriate for these devices—steel, copper, aluminum, glass, glass fibers, certain plastics—are themselves energy intensive. Their cost increases will parallel increases in the cost of energy.

Even among the fraternity of solar proponents there is a diversity of opinion as to how best to utilize this dilute, nonpolluting, and dependable (in the long run) energy source. Very generally, systems may be classified as *passive* or *active,* with many variations of each.

PASSIVE SYSTEMS

In the purest sense, a passive building is one in which no external energy is necessary to maintain thermal comfort. The building collects solar energy for immediate use. It stores energy for future use, and it excludes radiation when it is not wanted (Fig. 1–4). Obviously, all buildings have some passive characteristics. All buildings should have more of these characteristics.

Such buildings are variously referred to as "sun-tempered" or "solar-assisted." Some designers, such as Malcolm B. Wells, choose to go partially or wholly underground (Fig. 1–5), since the earth is a vast heat sink that approximates the year-round temperature of groundwater—55° to 65°F (12.8° to 18.3°C)—in most parts of the United States.

Architect David Wright, for his home in semiarid Santa Fe, New Mexico, chose to face a large double-glazed south wall to the sun (Fig. 1–6). Other exterior walls are adobe, externally insulated and plastered to serve as a heat sink. Additional thermal storage is provided by water-filled 55-gallon

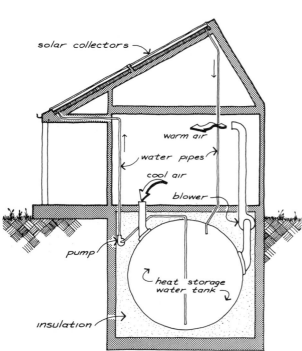

FIG. 1–3. Section through the first MIT house. The 500-square-foot floor area was 100 percent heated by a 360-square-foot collector tilted at an angle of 30°. Thermal storage was in a 17,400-gallon tank.

(208-liter) drums that are plastered and used as bancos (seating) in the dining area. Internal shutters, made of 3-inch-thick (7.62cm) insulation, prevent night heat loss through the large glass area.

Steve Baer's house uses water-filled drums behind plastic glazing to gather and store heat (Fig. 1–7). The Kalwall Corporation produces fiberglass-reinforced cylinders that can be filled with water and used in much the same manner. Architect Doug Kelbaugh's house in Princeton, New Jersey, uses a double-glazed south-facing concrete wall for its heating.

All these schemes are adaptations of a passive design popularized by Professor Felix Trombe. His

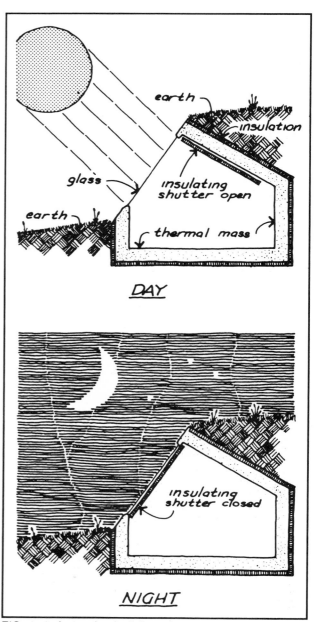

FIG. 1–4. A passive building.

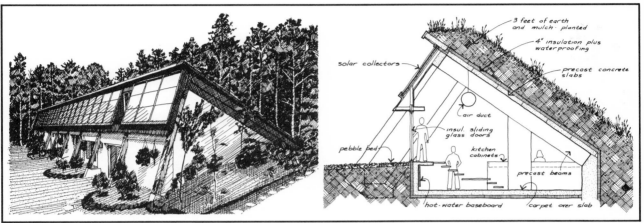

FIG. 1–5. Earth-protected house by Malcolm B. Wells.

FIG. 1–6. Passive house designed by David Wright, Santa Fe, N.M. The adobe walls
are externally insulated and plastered. Insulating shutters cover the glass at night.

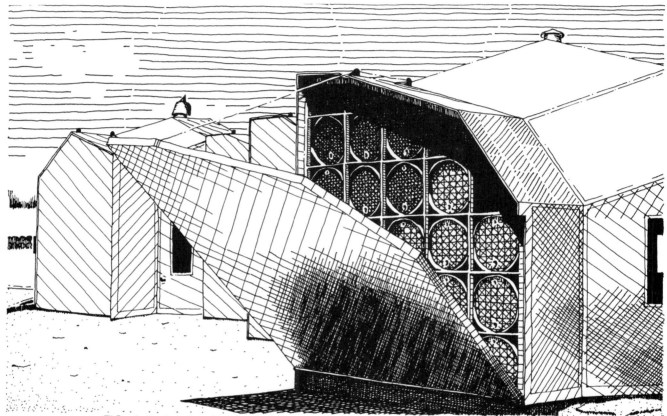

FIG. 1–7. Passive house designed by Steve Baer, Corrales, N.M. Sunlight heats water stored in steel drums. Insulating panel is closed at night.

best-known house was built in 1967 in the mild and sunny Mediterranean climate at Odeillo, France (Fig. 1–8). For this house, the south-facing collector wall has an area equal to 63 percent of the floor area. This wall is made of black-painted poured concrete about 23.5 inches (60cm) thick (Fig 1–9). The external double glazing is separated by a 4¾-inch (12cm) air space. Vents in the wall near the floor and ceiling allow for thermocirculation.[4]

In operation, solar radiation strikes the wall and is transformed into heat energy. As the air between glazing and wall is heated, it rises and flows into the room through the upper openings, causing cooler room air to be drawn into the space near the floor. More important, the temperature of the concrete is raised so that, ultimately, heat is transferred to the room by convection and radiation.

Although this house is about 70 percent solar-heated, Trombe feels that the wall thickness delays heat migration into the room too long. Later houses designed by him had concrete walls about 14½ inches (36.25cm) thick, which he suggests is too thin. Consequently, Trombe suggests walls 15¾ to 17¾ inches (40 to 45cm) thick.

Dr. Douglas Balcomb and his team of researchers at Los Alamos Scientific Laboratory have extensively investigated this type of solar heating.[5] Their thorough research has a three-pronged approach. They built and monitored test rooms having floor areas of 40 square feet (4.65m²). They performed computer simulations using a large volume of meteorological and heat-

FIG. 1–8. Passive house designed by Professor Felix Trombe, Odeillo, France. Heat is stored in the massive south-facing concrete wall.

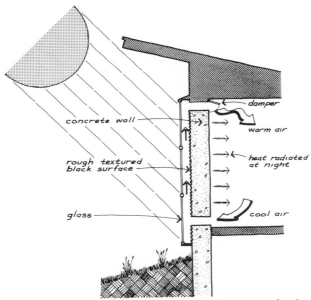

FIG. 1–9. Section through the Trombe wall. Heat transfer is by both convection and radiation.

transfer data. They also monitored several actual buildings, including Doug Kelbaugh's home.

Based on this research, they made the following observations:

1. The concrete wall should be at least 12 inches (30.5cm) thick.
2. Thermocirculation vents should be fitted with dampers to prevent reverse thermocirculation at night.
3. Either double glazing or night insulation is needed. Using both is desirable.
4. On a sunny day, inside temperatures will be 60° to 70°F (15.6° to 21.1°C) above ambient. That is to say, on a freezing but sunny day one might expect inside temperatures in the 90° to 100°F (32.2° to 37.8°C) range.

As a perpetual experimenter, I would like to build a Trombe wall, but hesitate for the following reasons:

1. Any building over one room deep in the north–south direction will require blowers and ducts. Although this might be a low-energy system, it is not completely passive.
2. In many parts of the country the prevailing summer breezes blow from the south. Areas devoted to a Trombe wall decrease the south wall that is available for natural ventilation.
3. I am concerned about summer overheating. Summer shading or external exhaust would solve this problem, but with additional expense and effort.
4. Cost. Using Professor Trombe's experience, a south wall having 63 percent of the floor area would be needed to supply 70 percent of the building's heating needs. Based on my own experience, a solar-assisted heat pump would require a liquid-cooled collector area about 25 percent of the floor area. Using local pricing for poured concrete, glazing, and flat-plate collector systems, the Trombe wall would cost about 20 percent more than my own.
5. Trombe walls provide no real capability for domestic water heating or space cooling.

The Trombe wall is an example of a large, passive element deliberately incorporated into a structure. There also are many other passive strategies which the sensitive designer will incorporate into any structure. The use of proper siting, building proportion, orientation, internal zoning, and trees—both deciduous and coniferous—can affect energy use. So can insulation, multiple glazing, storm doors, weather stripping, the use of airlocks at entrances, well-conceived shadings, and the inclusion of as much insulated thermal mass as is economically justified. Implementation of these strategies, with or without intentionally designed solar systems, will substantially reduce one's dependence on energy from conventional sources.

ACTIVE SYSTEMS

An active solar energy system is one in which specially designed collection and storage elements are employed within the system. Usually, but not always, external (conventional) energy must be supplied to the system in order to move energy from one location to another. Characteristically, such systems utilize products already in use by the plumbing and air-conditioning sectors.

Photovoltaics (solar cells) may be properly considered as active solar systems (Fig. 1–10). So may wind energy systems (Fig. 1–11). Except for wind energy, however, all of these solar sources may be more suitable for a central station than for individual building applications. At the present time, and perhaps for all time, small wind generators are more reliable, efficient, and cost-effective than large wind machines.

Other active systems employ air-cooled and liquid-cooled flat-plate collectors (which may be evacuated or concentrating collectors or both). Each of these collector types has advantages for particular applications.

Concentrating collectors are capable of raising the temperature of the heat-transfer fluid several hundred degrees (Fig. 1–12). Consequently, they are in favor for those systems that provide cooling. Absorption refrigeration machines that use lithium bromide as a refrigerant typically require heat in

FIG. 1–10. A concentrating tracking photovoltaic array. This completely self-contained unit is protected from the elements by a 4-foot-diameter plastic sphere. Peak output is about 60 watts. Such units have efficiencies of 8 to 15 percent.

FIG. 1–11. Wind generator located at the author's home. The 16-foot-diameter wheel is capable of producing 3,200 watts in a 25-mph wind.

FIG. 1–12. A concentrating collector. Although high temperatures may be attained with this sort of collector, they do not necessarily capture more energy than a flat-plate collector. Photo courtesy Solar Kinetics, Inc., Dallas, Texas.

FIG. 1–13. Flat-plate collector array on the author's home. Balancing valves were installed to equalize flow through the unequal arrays.

the 200° to 240°F (93.3° to 115.6°C) range, well within the capability of concentrating collectors. On the other hand, when temperatures less than 100°F (37.8°C) above ambient are required, flat-plate collectors frequently will outperform concentrating collectors.

Concentrating collectors use a mirror, lens, or reflector geometry to concentrate the incoming radiation on an absorber. Since only direct or beam radiation is captured, it is necessary that the collector look at the sun. Depending on collector geometry, this ordinarily is accomplished by moving either the entire collector or the absorber alone. As a result, there will be a need for some sort of tracking mechanism. Because tracking mechanisms require fairly constant attention and maintenance,

concentrating-collector arrays are not advisable for the average homeowner.

Evacuated collectors also are capable of supplying heat in the 200°F-plus (93.3°C-plus) range while still maintaining acceptable efficiencies. Whether of the concentrating or flat-plate type, the space between cover plate and absorber is evacuated of air, thereby decreasing heat losses by convection or conduction. As with concentrating collectors, the efficiency improvement of evacuated collectors when compared with ordinary flat-plate collectors becomes insignificant at low operating temperatures. Obviously, specialized equipment is required in order to pull the necessary vacuum.

Flat-plate collectors are a different matter (Fig.

1–13). Their technology is mature. Although a number of high-quality designs are available through nationwide distribution, their construction is simple enough for the serious hobbyist. Their materials are readily available and no special tools are required for their fabrication. Properly installed, a flat-plate collector array should require almost no maintenance. When used as an alternate to electric energy, even a commercially installed solar water-heating system will amortize itself in four to six years. Depending on the solar tax credits available in the state in which the system is installed, this amortization period may be halved. If some or all of the construction or installation is performed by the homeowner, this period may be reduced even further.

A lively debate continues between proponents of air-cooled systems and those of liquid-cooled systems. The arguments of each side have considerable merit, and it is unclear at this time which side, if either, will emerge victorious.

At least in theory, air systems have an advantage over liquid systems. Air is passed through the collectors, is heated, and subsequently provides heat for the building or is placed in storage. The thermal storage usually is composed of rocks of uniform size, but may be a eutectic salt or containerized water. In any event, air from the collectors and to the heated space flows around elements of the thermal storage, thereby eliminating any need for an additional heat exchanger. Air cannot freeze, causing ruptured piping with attendant drips through the living-room ceiling. In some semiarid climates it even is possible to circulate air through the thermal storage in order to provide some nocturnal cooling.

Ducts are required to transfer energy from the collector array to space heating or storage. Frequently these ducts may be 18 inches (45cm) in diameter, and their installation in existing buildings can present problems. Flow through the collectors, ducts, and thermal storage is provided by a blower, normally of the centrifugal type. Depending on duct size and length, and the geometry of the thermal storage, these blowers may require ¾ horsepower or more.

Some air systems use eutectic salts for thermal storage.[6] These salts, which contain water of hydration, absorb heat as a result of their phase change from solid to liquid. Throughout a limited temperature range they are capable of considerably more thermal storage than either air or water. Glauber's salt (sodium sulfate decahydrate, $Na_2SO_4 \cdot 10H_2O$) is the most widely used of these substances. It is in plentiful supply and its cost is very low. Its melting point of about 90°F (32.2°C), although a little lower than might be desired, is still acceptable.

Unfortunately, these salts have a tendency to precipitate rather than recombine with the water when solidifying. When this happens their heat of fusion is lost. To prevent such an occurrence, thickening and nucleating agents are added. Additionally, the salts usually are packaged in containers whose vertical dimensions are small to discourage precipitation. Cylinders of about 1½ inches (3cm) in diameter and slabs about 1 foot square and 1 inch high are two shapes proved successful. Metal has not proved to be an appropriate material for long-term use, so that most containers are made of plastic. As with many items of our industrialized society, the product is less expensive than the package.

Liquid-cooled collector systems, like all others, have some disadvantages. But they also enjoy some distinct advantages. The most commonly mentioned disadvantage is the possibility of leaks in the system. As with any other plumbing or piping system, this is a real possibility. The danger can be minimized by skilled installation and by performing the usual air-pressure test prior to filling. While the cost of a liquid system frequently is cited as excessive, in my own experience, well-designed air systems and water systems are competitive in cost with each other.

What about the advantages of a water system? A whole variety of advantages become apparent when one realizes that 1 gallon of water will transport or store as much heat as 463 cubic feet (1.04m³) of air. Said differently, water is *3,467 times* as efficient as air for heat transfer on a volume basis. Piping requires far less space than air ducts—a distinct advantage, especially for retrofit installations. For arrays of comparable size, a liquid system might use a ¹/₆-horsepower pump for circulation, while its air-cooled counterpart would require a ¾-horsepower blower.

When air is blown through rock or phase-change storage, no intermediate heat exchanger is necessary. But, on a volume basis, water is about three times better storage than rock, allowing for 30 percent voids in the rock for air passage.

Because of water's excellent heat-transfer characteristics, liquid collectors are the best choice for heating domestic hot water. These systems pay for themselves in the shortest time, since hot water is a year-round need. Liquid systems may be used to drive presently available absorption refrigeration machines (air conditioners) or the expected Rankine turbogenerator.

Although we frequently speak of water collectors, they are seldom filled with pure water. Despite water's high specific heat, low viscosity, safety, and low cost, it has one property that is less than desirable. It freezes at 32°F (0°C). Pure water left continuously in a closed system is suitable only in those areas where the lowest temperature is above 36°F (3°C). (Water in a collector can freeze even though the air temperature is above 32°F (0°C). This is because of radiation to the deep night sky, whose mean radiant temperature may be 4° to 10°F lower.) In other areas, water can be used alone only if provision is made for draining during freezing weather. Otherwise, an antifreeze solution or silicone must be used.

Although water is a better heat-transfer medium and requires less pump energy than either antifreeze solutions or silicone, drain-down systems present some problems. First, since these are open systems, the pump capacity must be capable of overcoming not only pipe and fitting friction, but also a usually large static head. Second, during morning startup, it may require considerable time to refill the system, eliminate any airlocks, and establish uniform flow. For anyone who seeks dependable and attention-free performance, the prudent choice seems to be a closed system incapable of freezing.

THE SOLAR FUTURE

What about the future? If new methods of capturing the sun's energy are not developed it certainly won't be due to lack of technological creativity. For example, the Arthur D. Little Company has performed a feasibility study for an orbiting array of solar cells, several square miles in area, for direct conversion of radiation into electric energy (Fig. 1–14). This energy would be transmitted to a receiving station on earth via microwave. (Heaven protect us from an orbital perturbation!) Major supporters of this scheme include some aerospace manufacturers. Who can blame them?

The idea of solar-driven power plants already has been realized in a prototype near Barstow, California (Fig. 1–15). In this concept a large array of heliostats (fixed mirrors) concentrates available radiation on a boiler mounted atop a tower. The boiler, which may operate at temperatures up to 1,000°F (450°C), supplies steam to drive a turbine and produce electricity.

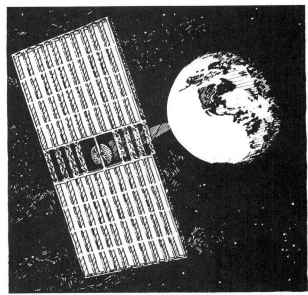

FIG. 1–14. Artist's conception of an orbiting array with an area of several square miles. Energy would be beamed to earth by microwaves.

FIG. 1–15. Photo of a "power tower." A field of mirrors (heliostats) focuses sunlight on a boiler at the top of the tower. Steam drives a generator to produce electricity. Photo courtesy Sandia Laboratories, Albuquerque, N.M.

Following completion of NASA's 125-foot-diameter (38.1m-dia.) wind machine at Sandusky, Ohio (Fig. 1–16), a contract was awarded to Lockheed Aircraft for a feasibility study for a 300-foot-diameter (90m-dia.) machine. A subsequent contract has been awarded for construction of a prototype.

These three hopes for the future share some common elements. Each is aimed at providing electric energy to be distributed through an electric utility's power grid. Each is a government-funded project. Each is performed by a large high-technology corporation.

I don't think anyone questions the scientific capability or resourcefulness of our technological community, although I would prefer that it direct its efforts toward discovering a method to make petro-leum from electricity. Nor would I question these contracts or their amounts, especially since they are insignificant when compared to amounts spent attempting to obtain safe and dependable nuclear energy. Least of all would I suggest that we sacrifice all of our creature comforts made possible by electric energy.

Most of the energy used in our homes is for space and water heating. Necessary temperatures for these purposes are in the 100° to 200°F (37.8° to 75.6°C) range. I certainly do object to using dilute solar or wind energy in highly expensive and complex systems to generate high-quality electric energy—energy that later will be degraded to heat energy. I may not object to a nuclear power station generating sufficient electricity to operate my solid-state stereo, but I absolutely object to this same station's providing energy to heat my water.

In short, I would argue for an appropriate technology, although I realize that this term carries different meanings for different people. We have an appropriate technology today for the production of heat energy—flat-plate solar collectors. They are at least as cost-effective as nuclear plants, whose construction is just beginning. In the one case, an individual makes a one-time fixed commitment. In the other, he tacitly agrees to the same or greater commitment paid through a monthly utility bill.

Flat-plate collectors have a mature technology, their operation places minimum demands on the environment, and their installation frees one from increasingly expensive or (perhaps) unavailable energy from conventional sources. Let us use these devices to free us from international dependence on petroleum, to maintain our energy budgets at their present level, to minimize nuclear waste proliferation, and, most of all, to achieve an enhanced quality of life.

FIG. 1–16. Sketch of the 125-foot-diameter NASA wind generator at Sandusky, Ohio. Peak output is about 100 kilowatts.

NOTES

1. An interesting history of the burning of wood may be found in Jay W. Shelton, *The Woodburners Encyclopedia,* published by Vermont Crossroads Press (Waitsfield, VT). The book also includes authoritative information on the chemistry of the burning of wood and the installation and operation of wood-burning stoves.

2. Xenophon, in his *Memorabilia* (III, viii, 8–14), records some teachings of Socrates (470–399 B.C.): "Again his dictum about houses . . . was a lesson in the art of building houses as they ought to be. He approached the problem thus: 'When one means to have the right sort of house, must he contrive to make it as pleasant to live in and as useful as can be?' And this being admitted, 'Is it pleasant,' he asked, 'to have it cool in summer and warm in winter?' And when they agreed with this also, 'Now in houses with a south aspect, the sun's rays penetrate into the porticoes in winter, but in summer the path of the sun is right over our heads and above the roof, so that there is shade. If, then, this is the best arrangement, we should build the south side loftier to get the winter sun and the north side lower to keep out the cold winds. To put it shortly, the house in which the owner can find a pleasant retreat at all seasons and can store his belongings safely is presumably at once the pleasantest and the most beautiful.'"

3. A. B. and M. P. Meinel, *Applied Solar Energy* (Reading, Mass.: Addison-Wesley, 1976). This book contains an excellent history of solar collectors. It also has a thorough discussion of optics, especially as related to concentrating collectors.

4. F. Trombe, J. F. Robert, M. Cabanat, and B. Sesolis, "Concrete Walls to Collect and Hold Heat," *Solar Age* 2, no. 8 (August 1977).

5. J. D. Balcomb, J. C. Hedstrom, and R. D. McFarland, "Simulation Analysis of Passive Solar Heating Buildings," *Solar Energy* 19, no. 3: 277–82.

6. T. S. Dean, *Thermal Storage* (Franklin Institute Press, 1978), pp. 31–35.

CHAPTER TWO

FLAT-PLATE COLLECTORS

PRINCIPLES OF METEOROLOGY, ASTRONOMY, AND HEAT TRANSFER THAT YOU PROBABLY KNEW BUT FORGOT

As with so many situations in our world, it is necessary to know something about the causes of a situation in order to evaluate the effects. Such is the case at hand, in which a fundamental knowledge of solar radiation will help in understanding the design, construction, and performance of flat-plate collectors.

Our sun emits radiation throughout a fairly wide band of wavelengths, usually measured in angstrom units ($1\text{Å} = 10^{-8}$ meter) or microns ($1\mu m = 10^{-6}m$) (Fig. 2–1). Thus, $1\mu m = 100\text{Å}$. The radiation having the shortest wavelengths includes gamma and X-rays. Luckily for animal life, and some plant life, most of this radiation is absorbed or diffracted by carbon dioxide, nitrogen, ozone, or water vapor in the upper atmosphere. Radiation having wavelengths shorter than $.38\mu m$ is generally classified as ultraviolet, radiation having wavelengths greater than $.38\mu m$ but less than $.78\mu m$ composes the visible spectrum, and radiation with wavelengths between $.78\mu m$ and $3.0\mu m$ is regarded as near-infrared. At the outer fringes of our atmosphere, about 7 percent of the sun's energy is in the ultraviolet range, about 47 percent in the visible range, and about 43 percent in the near-infrared. Of the sun's energy in space, 99.98 percent is associated with wavelengths of less than $15\mu m$.[1]

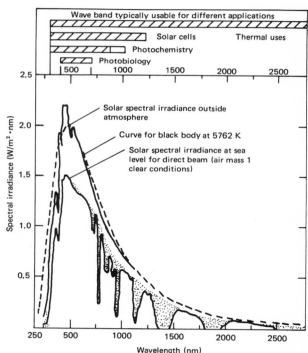

FIG. 2–1. Spectral distribution of electromagnetic radiation from the sun. Most of this energy is in the ultraviolet, visible, and near-infrared regions.

Most of the radiation having wavelengths longer than $2.5\mu m$ is absorbed by carbon dioxide and water vapor in the atmosphere. For all practical purposes, we are concerned with that radiation having wavelengths between $.28\mu m$ and $2.5\mu m$.

This band contains about 95 percent of the total solar energy falling on earth.

The amount of solar energy falling on a unit surface in space normal to the sun in a unit time, and at a distance equal to the earth's mean distance from the sun, is called the solar constant, I_{sc}. Its value is taken to be 428 Btuh/ft² (1,353 w/m²). Because of variation in the earth–sun distance, however, this value varies about 8.5 percent, being greatest in December and least in June.

Even in the band from .28μm to 2.5μm, additional energy is absorbed, depending on the air mass through which the radiation travels and the presence of water vapor, dust, or other particulate material. Some of the radiation is scattered as it passes through the atmosphere but still reaches the earth's surface. Additional radiation is reflected from one surface to another. Thus the total insolation (*incoming solar radiation*) that reaches the surface has three components—direct, diffuse, and reflected. Direct radiation accounts for 88 percent to 95 percent of the total, depending on solar declination, time, and local atmospheric conditions. In regions experiencing severe air pollution the diffuse component may amount to as much as 20 percent of the total.

The ASHRAE solar insolation tables (Appendix A–2) may be used for calculations of solar-energy-system design. They are based on clear, sunny-sky data with a clearness factor of 1.0. It is not difficult to imagine that more sunlight reaches the ground on a high mountaintop than on the seashore. The mountaintop would have a clearness factor greater than 1.0, whereas the seashore location would have a clearness factor of less than 1.0 (Fig. 2–2).

The amount of sunshine available is greatly influenced by the amount and duration of cloudiness. Although tables have been prepared showing percentage sunshine for selected locations throughout the world, the data contained in these tables should be used cautiously. This is due to the method of collecting the data, a method adopted long before it was suspected that the direct use of the sun's energy would achieve its present importance (Appendix A–3).

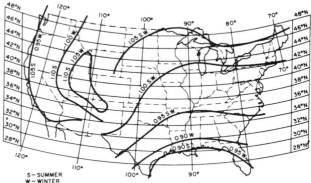

FIG. 2–2. Clearness map of the United States. This map is not valid for localities having significant air pollution. Reprinted with permission from the 1977 Fundamentals volume, ASHRAE Handbook & Product Directory.

The data for this table were gathered by an instrument that records sunshine at any time there is no cloud interference, without regard to the time of day or length of sunny periods. A day might have clear skies in the early morning and late afternoon with a cloudy midday. Although the sun shone 50 percent of the time, there would be little energy to harvest. Likewise, if the sun shone in fifteen-minute intervals separated by fifteen-minute cloudy periods, a collector array might not have time to reach operating temperatures. Consequently, time of day and length of sunny intervals are important parameters in determining the amount of energy collected.

During January 1978, our closest weather station reported 53 percent possible sunshine, yet I had only four days of solar collection. Most of the sunshine was during early morning or late afternoon hours. Federal agencies have acknowledged this problem and taken action to secure additional data that will aid in predicting performance for solar energy systems.

However, the presence of cloud cover does not automatically guarantee no solar collection. Flat-plate collectors gather energy from diffuse as well as direct radiation. A thin cloud cover will diminish energy harvest but not halt it completely. I recall one cloudy winter day when the outside temperature hovered around freezing. Yet a glance at the thermometer on my solar-circuit piping informed me that the liquid temperature was above 100°F (37.8°C).

Galileo Galilei, who lived in a time believing in witchcraft, mysticism, and magic, dared suggest that the earth, in fact, was not the center of the universe. He postulated that the earth revolves around the sun. For these "antitheological" statements he was persecuted by the authorities and barely escaped the Inquisition. Although we now accept the fundamental truth of his postulates, it is still convenient to speak of the sun's rising and setting, and to think of it as moving through our heavens.

The axis of the earth is inclined at an angle of about 23.5° with respect to the normal ecliptic plane. It rotates about the sun once in about 365¼ days. Consequently, in a year's time, we perceive a change of 47° in the sun's altitude at noon. For example, at 40° north latitude on June 21, the sun would rise at about 4:30 A.M. Its position would be about 30° north of east. This direction, measured in a horizontal plane, is called the azimuth, equal to 120° for this time of day, and is always measured from due south. At noon its azimuth would be 0° and its altitude would be 73.5° measured above the horizon. On December 21, however, the sun's azimuth at dawn would be about 60° and its altitude at noon would be only 26.5°.

It is apparent that if we wish to intercept the maximum radiation per unit area of collector, then the plane of the collector should be normal to the incoming radiation (Fig. 2–3). The sun's paths, however, traverse much of the southern hemisphere during a year's time. Since we want a single orientation for our collector, the decision to be made is to choose the *best* one.

Most of the sun's energy comes to us within two or three hours from noon, when its azimuth is zero. Consequently, we shall aim our collector array due south. (Magnetic south may be ascertained with a

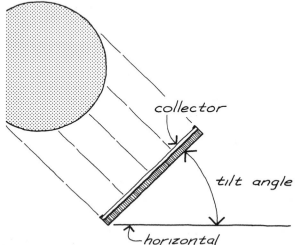

FIG. 2–3. Collector tilt angle.

compass. Due south may then be computed by reference to an isogonic map, Figure 2–4.)

Sometimes it is impossible or at least undesirable to orient collectors due south. For example, topographic features may suggest a variation. Morning clouds or fog may suggest a westward bias. In my own case, a desirable stand of hickory and walnut trees caused me to bias the collector array slightly toward the east. Don't worry! A variation of 20° either way from true south won't impair efficiency too much (Fig. 2–5).

The angle between a collector and a horizontal plane is called the "tilt angle." Since the sun's altitude at noon varies by 47° throughout the year, it is clear that no single tilt angle is best for all seasons. You might be tempted to optimize collection for December 21 (latitude plus 23.5°), but this really would not be optimum. In most parts of the United States our most severe weather occurs not at the solstice, but about a month later. A similar situation exists in summer when the hottest weather occurs in July or August. This is because the earth has tremendous thermal inertia that delays periods of extreme temperatures.

Numerous analyses have been made in order to

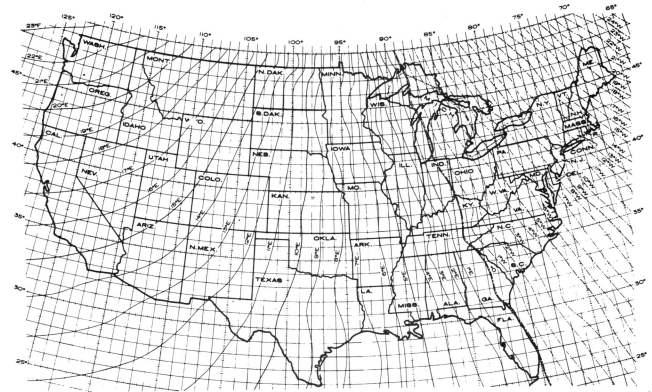

FIG. 2–4. Isogonic map of the United States. For Lawrence, Kans., this chart shows a deviation 8° east of true north. This means that true north will be 8° west of magnetic (compass) north. True south will be 8° east of compass south. From U.S. Department of Commerce, Coast and Geodetic Survey, 1965.

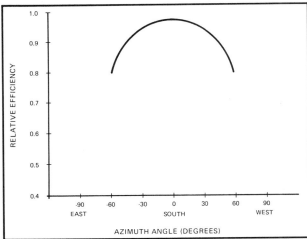

FIG. 2–5. Collector efficiency as a function of azimuth at 40° north latitude. A variation of as much as 20° from true south has little effect on collector efficiency.

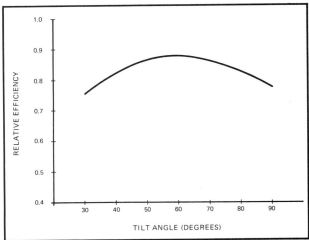

FIG. 2–6. Collector efficiency as a function of tilt angle at 40° north latitude. Even a vertical collector has good winter performance at this latitude.

optimize tilt angles.[2] The general results are as follows:

Season	Tilt Angle
best winter collection	latitude plus 10° to 15°
best summer collection	latitude minus 10° to 15°
best annual collection	latitude

A variation of 5° to 10° from these angles probably would not affect performance noticeably unless the system is well monitored (Fig. 2–6). For my own installation at 40° north latitude, I chose a tilt angle of 45°, since carpenters are familiar with roofs having a 12-in-12 pitch (45°). Also, since snow reflects about 75 percent of shortwave radiation, even a vertical collector can perform well in regions experiencing snow cover.

When solar radiation strikes a material, one or more of three things may occur. The radiation may be *transmitted, reflected,* or *absorbed.* Only transparent or translucent substances are capable of transmission. Opaque objects are capable only of reflection or absorption. Shiny or light-colored objects will reflect more radiation than will dark, matte-finished materials. Real transparent materials transmit a part of the radiation, reflect some of it, and absorb the rest (a small fraction of the total).

When solar radiation, mostly between .28μm and 2.5μm, is absorbed, it changes into longwave heat energy, with wavelengths mostly between 3.0μm and 15.0μm or longer. Much of this heat energy raises the temperature of the absorbing material. In turn, some of it will be emitted to the surroundings as longwave radiation.

Each of these quantities—transmission, reflection, absorption, and emittance—is governed by a physical law. Each may be described by a mathematical expression. Each may be quantified by mathematical analysis or by experiment. Every material, depending on its geometry and surface, has a unique transmissivity, reflectivity, absorptivity, and emissivity. These properties are treated in detail in standard textbooks on heart transfer.[3] We shall examine some of these properties in more detail when considering materials for collector construction.

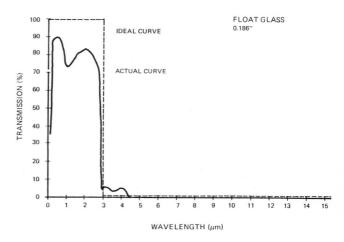

FIG. 2–7a. Transmissivity of high-iron-content glass. This is the glass that is usually available. It is reasonably transparent to shortwave radiation and opaque to longwave (heat) radiation.

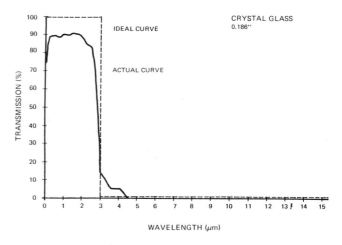

FIG. 2–7b. Transmissivity of low-iron-content glass. This glass admits about 10 percent more radiation than does high-iron-content glass.

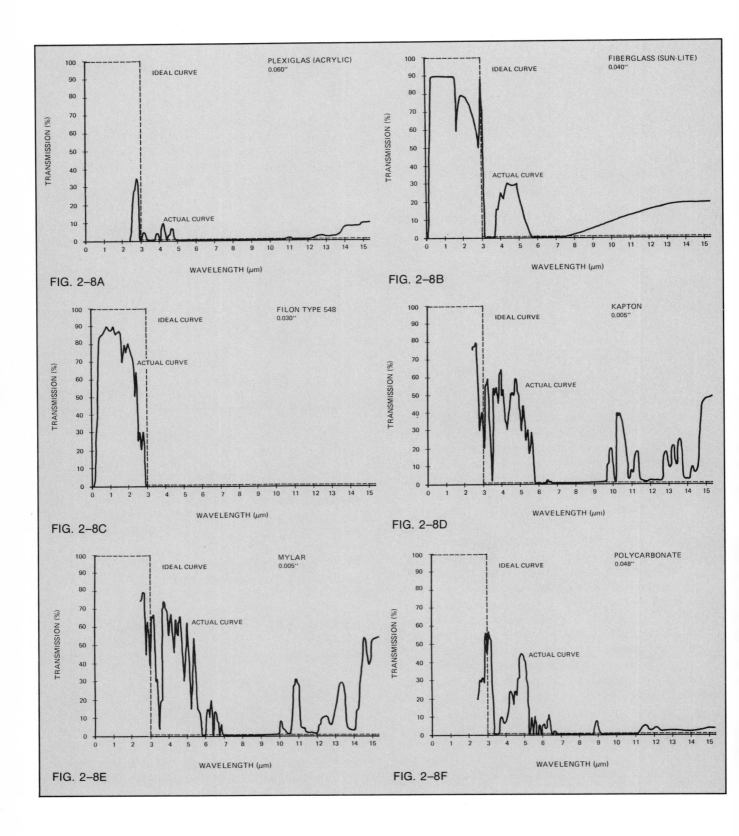

FIG. 2–8A

FIG. 2–8B

FIG. 2–8C

FIG. 2–8D

FIG. 2–8E

FIG. 2–8F

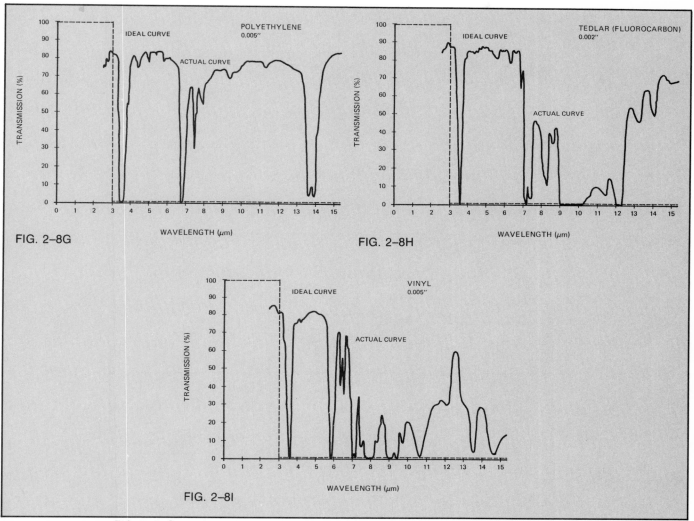

FIG. 2–8G

FIG. 2–8H

FIG. 2–8I

FIG. 2–8. *Opposite and above:* The transmissivity of selected plastics in the long-wave region. Although these plastics are transparent in the shortwave region, some are also transparent to long-wave radiation, making them dubious candidates for a cover plate.

In operation, incoming sunlight strikes the absorber, usually metal with a specially treated surface, and is transformed into longwave heat energy. On the back side and edges, this energy is prevented from escaping by the use of insulation. On the side facing the sun, heat loss is minimized by the use of a cover plate. One of the properties of glass is that while it admits 80 to 90 percent of the incoming shortwave radiation, it is almost opaque to radiation having wavelengths longer than $3.0 \mu m$ (Fig. 2–7). This is the cause of the so-called

greenhouse effect. Some, but not all, plastics share this property (Fig. 2–8). It is not a property that can be determined by visual inspection. Some heat, of course, is lost through the cover plate—not by radiation, but by conduction. The amount of heat lost by conduction through a unit area of a material is a function of the product of the material's conductance (C) and the temperature difference between the two surfaces. Since glass and thin plastics have high conductances, heat loss through the cover can be minimized by using two

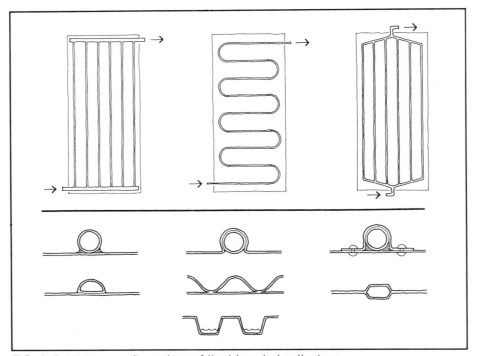

FIG. 2-9. Various configurations of liquid-cooled collectors.

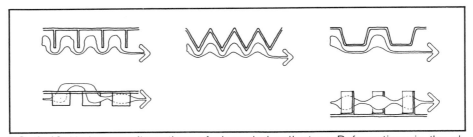

FIG. 2-10. Various configurations of air-cooled collectors. Deformations in the absorber surface create air turbulence to improve heat transfer.

or even three cover plates. This strategy will help maintain higher operating temperatures. It should be remembered, however, that if a sheet of ⅛-inch-thick glass transmits 85 percent of the available radiation, then two sheets will transmit only 72 percent and three sheets only 61 percent.

If the collector simply faced the sun it would become hot—perhaps 300° to 400°F (148.9° to 204.4°C)—but no usable heat would be extracted. This is called the "stagnation" condition. In order to be of any value, the heat must be removed for use or storage. A fluid, usually air or liquid, is circulated through the collector. In doing so, it cools the collector while collecting heat. Fluid flow may be along either front or back of the absorber or through passages attached to or integral with the absorber. Since heat transfer is enhanced by turbulent flow, the absorber surface of air-cooled collectors usually is geometrically deformed (Figs. 2–9 and 2–10).

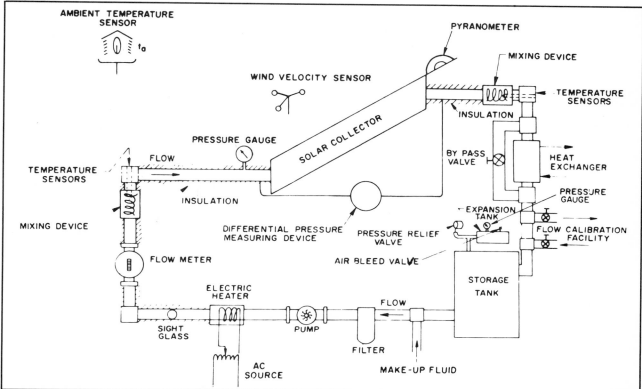

FIG. 2–11. Recommended test arrangement for a solar collector when the heat-transfer fluid is a liquid. Reprinted from ASHRAE Standard 93-77, "Methods of Testing to Determine the Thermal Performance of Solar Collectors," by permission of the American Society of Heating, Refrigeration, and Air-Conditioning Engineers.

INSTANTANEOUS COLLECTOR EFFICIENCY

The efficiency of a collector might be defined in several ways. By common agreement, the collector efficiency, η, is defined as:

$$\eta = \frac{\text{actual useful energy collected}}{\text{solar energy incident upon or intercepted by the collector}}$$

The actual useful energy collected will be a function not only of a collector's materials and geometry, but also of the angle at which radiation strikes the collector, wind velocity, mass flow rate of heat-transfer fluid through the collector, and temperature difference between the heat-transfer fluid and ambient air.

When these factors are taken into account, a collector's instantaneous efficiency may be expressed in mathematical form as:

$$\eta = F_r(\tau\alpha)_e - F_r U_L \frac{(T_{f,i} - T_a)}{I} \qquad \frac{(\dot{m}c_p)(T_{f,e} - T_{f,i})}{A_g I},$$

where:

F_r = solar heat-removal factor, dimensionless
$(\tau\alpha)_e$ = effective transmittance absorption factor, dimensionless
U_L = solar collector heat-transfer loss coefficient, Btu/ft²-hr-°F, (w/m² °C)
$T_{f,i}$ = temperature of the transfer fluid entering the collector, °F (°C)
$T_{f,e}$ = temperature of transfer fluid leaving collector, °F (°C)
T_a = ambient air temperature, °F (°C)
$\dot{m}$ = mass flow rate of the transfer fluid, lbm/hr (kg/s)
C_p = specific heat of the transfer fluid, Btu/lb-°F (J/kg °C)
I = total solar irradiation incident upon the aperture plane of the collector, Btu/ft²-hr (w/m²)
A_g = gross collector area, ft² (m²)

This equation is impossible to solve analytically without estimating values for at least some of the variables. However, a standard test method for experimentally determining the instantaneous efficiency of collectors is described in "Methods of Testing to Determine the Thermal Performance of Solar Collectors," ASHRAE Standard 93-77 (ANSI B198.1—1977). The effective date of this standard was February 1977. Since ASHRAE standards are updated on a five-year cycle, this standard will remain unchanged until at least February 1982. Most manufacturers of collectors have them evaluated by independent testing laboratories and willingly supply the results to prospective users.

Standard 93-77 is based on Interim Report NBSIR 74-635 prepared by the Center for Building Technology, National Bureau of Standards. As you can see from Figure 2–11 (page 25), which shows a typical test configuration, considerable investment in the test setup is required.

In the second equation on page 25, it may be seen that if $\frac{(T_{f,e} - T_a)}{I}$ is considered the independent variable, then the equation plots into a straight line with Y-intercept of $F_r (\tau\alpha)_e$ and a slope of $-F_r U_L$ when $\dot{m}$, C_p, A_g are constant and the collector plane is almost normal with incoming radiation. Actually U_L is a function of the collector and ambient air temperatures. Likewise $(\tau\alpha)$ varies with the incident angle between the collector and incoming radiation (Fig. 2–12).

For liquid-cooled collectors operating under steady-state conditions, a satisfactory expression for the instantaneous efficiency is given by:

$$\eta = F_r(\tau\alpha) - F_r U_L \frac{(\overline{T} - T_a)}{I}$$

where

$\overline{T}$ = average of inlet and outlet temperatures

This expression assumes that U_L is constant and plots as a straight line. The deviation is not significant for normal operating conditions.[4]

The thermal-efficiency curve for a high-quality commercially available collector is shown in Figure 2–13. A number of conclusions can be drawn from a study of this curve. In general, collector efficiency decreases as the available solar radiation decreases. Efficiency decreases as the temperature difference between heat-transfer fluid and ambient air increases. This observation suggests that we operate our collectors at the lowest possible temperature in order to maintain high efficiencies. Most collectors will show an efficiency of 60 to 80 percent for zero temperature rise. However, of more importance is the slope

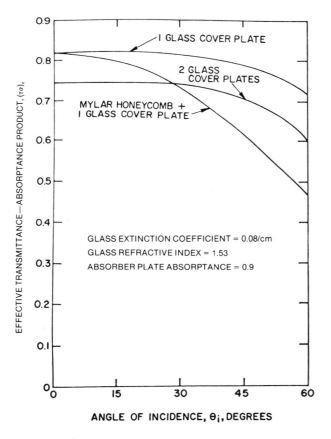

FIG. 2–12. Transmissivity-absorptivity curve. Notice the flatness of the curve near midday. Reprinted from ASHRAE Standard 93-77, "Methods of Testing to Determine the Thermal Performance of Solar Collectors," by permission of the American Society of Heating, Refrigeration, and Air-Conditioning Engineers, Inc.

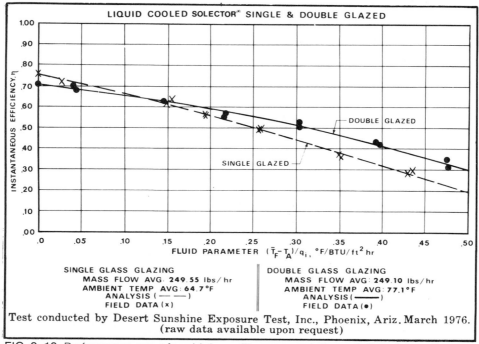

FIG. 2–13. Performance curve for a high-quality commercially made flat-plate collector.

(flatness) of the curve, since this determines the efficiency at fluid working temperatures of interest in actual system design. Note also that single-glazed collectors have higher efficiencies than double-glazed collectors when the fluid parameter $\frac{T_i - T_a}{I}$ is small. Another reason for operating at the lowest possible fluid temperature!

MATERIALS FOR COLLECTOR CONSTRUCTION

ABSORBER PLATE The function of the absorber plate is to capture incoming radiation, convert it into longwave heat energy, and conduct this heat to the coolant fluid. Surface treatment of the absorber is designed to enhance both collection and conversion and to minimize emittance in the longwave region.

During periods of stagnation—times when heat is not being removed from the collector—absorber temperatures may reach 300°–400°F (148.9°–204.4°C). Both the absorber and its coating should be able to tolerate such temperatures without degradation. It is necessary to effect a good heat-transfer bond between absorber and fluid passages.

Of all candidates as absorber materials, probably the best three are the metals commonly used in building construction—copper, aluminum, and steel. Copper has the highest conductivity and steel the lowest. Aluminum is the lightest and copper the heaviest. On a weight basis, copper is the most expensive and steel the least expensive. The fact is, each of these materials is an excellent absorber material. The choice of one of these metals over the other two may depend on several factors, not the least being economy.

An obstacle to fairly comparing these materials is the differing manner in which their thicknesses (and weights per square foot) are measured. Copper usually is measured in weight (in ounces) per square foot of material. Typical weights are 7, 12, 16, 24, and 32 ounces per square foot (2.14, 3.66, 4.88, 7.32, 9.76kg/m²). Several collector manufacturers use 7-ounce (2.14kg/m²) copper, although purchase of small quantities, say 500 to 1,000 square feet (46.5 to 92.9m²), may prove difficult through normal distribution sources.

Aluminum sheet, available in cut sheets or rolls,

is sold by thickness measured in milli-inches. Warehouse stocks frequently will range from .010 to .040 inches (.25mm to 7mm). My own collectors use .025-inch (.64mm) thickness with good results.

Sheet steel is measured by U.S.S. (U.S. Standard) gauge, with 20 to 24 gauge (.0359 to .0239 inches; .91 to .61mm) being most appropriate for absorber application. A mild (low-carbon) steel is desirable because of ease of working.

Copper wins hands down as the best absorber material on either a weight or thickness basis when compared with steel. On a weight basis it loses to aluminum. Especially because of the uncertain availability of 7-ounce (2.14kg/m²) copper to the buyer of small quantities, copper is the most expensive of these three metals.

Typically, fluid passages will be copper tubing that may be soldered to copper or steel. Heat-transfer bond must be accomplished by other techniques when copper tubes are used with an aluminum absorber. When a copper absorber is used, there will be no differential thermal expansion between absorber and tubing.

FLUID PASSAGES Fluid passages may be integral with the absorber or attached to it with an intimate heat-transfer bond.

Integral passages are typified by the Roll Bond panels manufactured by Olin Brass Company. When made of aluminum, these panels are widely used in household refrigerators as evaporators for the refrigerant. Early solar collectors made of aluminum proved unsatisfactory for the average installation because of galvanic action caused by dissimilar metals in the circuit. This problem can be overcome by regular monitoring and chemical control of the heat-transfer liquid, but the effort is hardly justified. These same Roll Bond panels are available in copper as components in commercial collectors or as bare panels for custom installations.

The majority of collectors manufactured in this country use external fluid passages made of copper tubing attached to absorber plates. Various tube configurations are possible, but the most common—and probably the most efficient—is the vertical-riser horizontal-manifold arrangement, in which the manifolds may be pitched slightly to aid in draining. As long as good heat transfer is maintained between tube and absorber, the tube may be placed on either side of the absorber (back or front) with little effect on performance.

Collectors employing the vertical-riser horizontal-manifold configuration will employ risers of ¼-inch or ⅜-inch (6.35mm or 9.52mm) I.D. tubing and manifolds of ¾-inch (19.1mm) I.D. tubing. Manifolds may connect directly into headers. However, a more efficient arrangement is to manifold the collectors one into another in a subarray and to connect the subarrays into headers. Conventionally, heat transfer is by laminar flow into the risers. All connections within the collector should use silver brazing or high-temperature solder.

Collector efficiency is strongly dependent on good heat transfer between absorber and fluid passages. Good heat transfer depends on the thermal conductivity not only of fluid-passage tubing and absorber but also of any intermediate filler material and its area of contact. One of the most proved methods of establishing reliable heat transfer is to attach the riser tubing to absorber with a continuous solder fillet. Certain skills are necessary to establish an intimate and continuous bond without consuming an inordinate amount of solder. Soldering is not possible, of course, between copper and aluminum.

Another method that is gaining favor with manufacturers is a purely mechanical bond between absorber and riser. The absorber first is deformed to provide near-cylindrical passages for the risers, which later are pressed into position. The efficacy of this method is purely a function of the precision of manufacture. Even a small air gap between the tube and absorber, virtually invisible to the naked eye, will significantly impair collector performance.

When aluminum is used for the absorber and copper risers are employed, the best heat-transfer method employs two strategies. Aluminum cleats, either continuous or intermittent, assure that tubing is in proximity to the absorber. Fillets between the tube and absorber and between tube and cleats are filled with a heat-transfer cement of the sort used in industrial processes. As far as I know, no commercially produced collectors use this technique, but it has proved satisfactory on my own installation.

ABSORBER COATINGS   The absorber and fluid passages exposed to radiation should receive a coating that will enhance their absorption of short-wave radiation. Whatever the coating, it should not degrade under periodic thermal environments of 400°F (204.4°C) or thereabouts, it should adhere to the substrate, its long-term performance should be essentially constant, and it should be replaceable.

The ideal surface will absorb most of the incoming shortwave radiation but emit little longwave radiation (Fig. 2–14). Surfaces that approximate this condition are called selective surfaces. This type of surface has received a great deal of study, primarily as a result of the space program.

Most selective coatings are applied by chemical or electrolytic deposition. Consequently, their application requires specialized equipment. Black chrome, one of the most satisfactory selective surfaces, can be applied on a custom basis by a number of companies. Information on long-term performance of these selective coatings is still being gathered.

Actually, flat-black paints frequently have better

absorption than many selective surfaces, but they also reradiate in the region above 3.0μm. Even so, these paints can be used with much success. A satisfactory paint will be one that adheres to metal and withstands maximum collector temperatures without peeling, cracking, or otherwise deteriorating. Flat-black enamel of the sort sold for painting stoves, barbecue pits, or automotive exhaust systems is a satisfactory material. The thinnest possible coat that covers the metal should be applied.

Perhaps the best paint that can be used is Black Velvet Nextel, manufactured by Minnesota Mining and Manufacturing Company. Although this paint is expensive, its relative cost is minor. Used by many collector manufacturers for its excellent optical qualities and compatibility with absorber surfaces, it also is available in small quantities.

INSULATION   Collectors should be insulated to prevent back and edge heat losses. Commercially available collectors usually have about 2 inches (5.1cm) of back insulation and 1 to 2 inches (2.5 to 5.1cm) of insulation around their sides. In reality, side insulation is unnecessary except for the exposed edges of an array.

Unfortunately, closed-cell insulations such as polyurethane or ureaformaldehyde, with their very high thermal resistances, are unsuitable for use in contact with the absorber because of the possible high temperatures. The most suitable insulation is glass- or mineral-wool fiber in a rigid board.

Care must be taken in choosing glass-fiber insulation. Ordinary building insulation contains a binder that may vaporize at stagnation temperatures. The vaporized binder will condense on the first cool surface, which probably is the cover plate. Fogged cover plates will not enhance a collector's performance.

This problem may be avoided by first heating the insulation in an oven in order to drive off the binder before installing it in the collector. But perhaps an easier solution is to purchase "high-temperature" insulation that is manufactured for service temperatures of 800° to 1,000°F (426.7° to 537.8°C). This insulation is made without a binder.

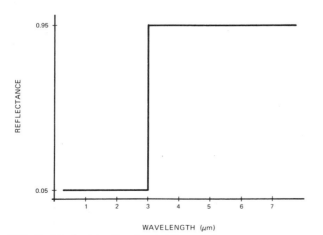

FIG. 2–14. An idealized selective surface.

COVER PLATES Except when collectors operate at temperatures near ambient, cover plates, or windows, are necessary. The typical material for cover plates has been glass because of its many favorable characteristics. A number of plastics also are suitable, but this suitability cannot be visually ascertained, as has already been shown (Fig. 2–8).

Cover plates are subject to severe environmental conditions. Regular bombardment by ultraviolet photons, temperature extremes on the two surfaces, rain, wind, hail, blowing grit and sand, and environmental pollutants all conspire to degrade or destroy cover plates.

Most glass produced in this country has a high iron content. The iron, usually in the form Fe_2O_3, is deliberately introduced in order to enhance the electrical conductivity during manufacture and does not lower the glass quality. It does, however, limit transmittance to about 85 percent for ⅛-inch (3.18mm) thickness. Looked at edge on, high-iron-content glass appears green.

Low-iron-content glass, which appears blue when viewed edge on, has greater transmittance— about 90 percent. Given a choice on an equal cost basis, low-iron-content glass certainly is to be preferred. However, if a premium is to be paid for low-iron-content glass, then some sort of cost-benefit analysis certainly is in order.

Although glass is reasonably transparent to shortwave radiation and opaque to longwave radiation, and although its long-term performance is very acceptable, it suffers from a few shortcomings. Compared to its competitors, glass is heavy. Its coefficient of expansion demands that adequate space be left for thermal movement. Ordinary glass is easily destroyed by impact from falling objects, such as hail or rocks, though its resistance may be improved considerably by tempering (my own tempered-glass cover plates have successfully weathered several storms, one of which had 3-inch (7.62cm) hailstones).

Glass is tempered by heat-treating *after cutting.* Tempered glass cannot be cut without breaking. Although any piece of glass can be cut and subsequently tempered, the cost may be excessive. On the other hand, glass intended for use in sliding patio doors *must,* by federal regulation, be tempered. Consequently, tempered glass in these sizes may be considered stock items and competitive in cost. Common sizes for these door panels are 28 inches (71.1cm), 34 inches (86.4cm), and 46 inches (116.8cm) in width and 76 inches (193cm) high. An examination of collector specifications will indicate the large number of manufacturers who have taken advantage of these standard sizes.

Even though glass is opaque to longwave radiation, it nevertheless is a poor insulator. Heat may be transferred to and from the glass by convection and transferred through the glass by conduction. When the desired temperature for the heat-transfer liquid differs significantly from ambient-air temperature, heat loss through the cover plate may severely impair collector efficiency. In such a case, double or even triple cover plates may be indicated. However, if high-iron-content glass is used, it should be remembered that a double cover plate will admit only 72 percent of the impinging radiation and a triple cover only 61 percent.

Before dismissing ordinary high-iron-content glass as an inferior material, we should remember that at angles of incidence up to about 45°, 8 percent of the incoming radiation is reflected and 6 percent absorbed. The absorbed radiation heats the glass and decreases heat loss through it. About half of the absorbed radiation is regained in output from the system. Additionally, reflective losses can be reduced by providing the glass with an etched surface.

Several plastics have been used as cover plates with varying degrees of success. Like glass, they transmit in the ultraviolet. Unlike glass, many are damaged by these ultraviolet photons and may become discolored or brittle or otherwise degraded. Inexpensive plastics such as polyethylene film have an expected durability of from a few months to a few years.

Some plastic films are very thin and require a supporting frame in which they are mounted in tension. Heavier plastics such as the various fiberglass-reinforced plastics are semirigid in the thicknesses used for cover plates. They too require a supporting frame with intermediate members, but the material is not placed in tension. Other plastics such as Plexiglas (acrylic) or Lexan (polycarbonate) are used in thicknesses sufficient to be self-supporting. For those installations in which the plastic is attached to a frame, considerable attention should be given in mounting the plastic lest the collector be visually disturbing due to stretch marks or ripples.

Plastics are superior to glass in their resistance to breaking and in their light weight. Several plastics also have a cost advantage over glass, being about half as expensive. However, if one must pay for a frame and mounting of the plastic, this advantage can rapidly disappear.

Many plastics degrade rapidly because of ultraviolet radiation. Some manufacturers, such as the Kalwall Corporation and the Filon Corporation, provide their glass-fiber sheets with a Tedlar surface to inhibit degradation.

Perhaps the most severe limitation to the use of some plastics is their transmittance in the infrared (3.0 to 15.0μm) region (Fig. 2–8). Polyethylene, for example, is almost as transparent in the infrared as in the ultraviolet and visible bands. The greenhouse effect is virtually absent when using this material.

COLLECTOR CONTAINERS   Most collectors are sold as individual assembled units. Absorber, insulation, and cover plate are correctly positioned and protected from mechanical damage by a container. Piping connections usually are made outside the container.

These containers may be constructed of a variety of materials, including wood, fiberglass, galvanized sheet steel, or aluminum. Aluminum appears to be the most favored material. Sides and ends are frequently of extruded sections, and backs are of sheet stock.

Amazingly enough, although most collectors are tested for thermal efficiency, few manufacturers supply data on their product's watertightness. In my experience, most persons will tolerate a 5 to 10 percent variation in a collector's thermal efficiency, but they will be opposed to a leak in their living-room ceiling.

The assumption seems to be that the collectors will be mounted in a field array where moisture integrity is of no consequence, or that a finished roofing system will be installed beneath the array. While there is a certain logic in the first assumption, it seems a waste of money to install a roof beneath an array whose individual components could each be suitable for roofing purposes.

Manufacturers normally do not furnish the flashing necessary between individual panels or around the perimeter of an array, although suggested flashing details may be offered. The difficulty in fabricating and installing these flashings, their efficacy, and their relative costs are not usually specified by the manufacturer.

Most collector containers are assembled using mill-finish aluminum. A few manufacturers offer prepainted or anodized boxes at additional cost. These boxes with their attendant aluminum flashings can make a significant visual impact—often a negative one, when presented as a large array on a steeply pitched roof.

The same people who would object to the unbridled use of shiny aluminum on their rooftops may be more than willing to bear the additional expense of a black-glass door on the kitchen oven or dishwasher. In fact, black absorbers beneath clear glass present this same appearance. Their look of luxury is destroyed by a heavy-handed use of utilitarian aluminum.

Nor are these utilitarian and often unsightly containers inexpensive. In most cases, they will cost about as much as the absorber—even a high-quality absorber with black-chrome selective surface. For collectors that must be shipped more than a few hundred miles, the freight charge that must be assigned to containers may amount to 5 percent or more of collector cost.

Obviously, I have a point to make—a point that affects not only the visual quality of a collector array, but its cost as well. When the array is wall- or roof-mounted on a structure, the factory-built container is a needless expense. Curbing of 2 × 6-inch wood works just as well (Fig. 2–15). Flashing can be detailed, which renders the whole array watertight. Furthermore, the flashing can be made of

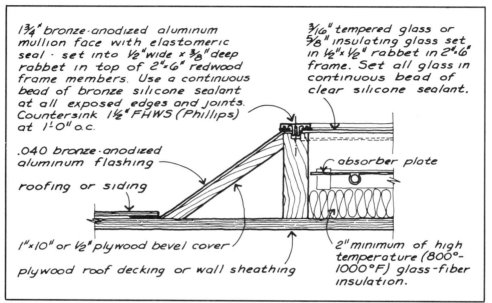

1¾" bronze-anodized aluminum mullion face with elastomeric seal · set into ½" wide x ⅜" deep rabbet in top of 2"x6" redwood frame members. Use a continuous bead of bronze silicone sealant at all exposed edges and joints. Countersink 1½" FHWS (Phillips) at 1'-0" o.c.

.040 bronze-anodized aluminum flashing

roofing or siding

1"x10" or ½" plywood bevel cover

plywood roof decking or wall sheathing

3/16" tempered glass or 5/8" insulating glass set in ½"x½" rabbet in 2"x6" frame. Set all glass in continuous bead of clear silicone sealant.

absorber plate

2" minimum of high temperature (800°-1000°F) glass-fiber insulation.

FIG. 2–15. Detail of wood curb and flashing for a roof- or wall-mounted collector array. Detail may be modified for other situations.

FIG. 2–16. A finished collector array constructed according to the detail in Fig. 2–15.

bronze or anodized gunmetal or fluorocarbon-coated aluminum in a variety of shades. The slight additional cost is more than compensated for by more simple flashing details and the improved visual quality (Fig. 2–16).

A few words of warning for installations that may be made in this manner. If glass is used for the cover plates, allow room for expansion, about ⅜ inch (.95cm) in each direction. Set the cover plate in a high-quality, high-temperature sealant such as silicone. Give the wood curbs and any exposed insulation a thin spray coat of flat-black enamel.

Many manufacturers will sell their absorbers and cover plates as individual items. Moreover, they will frequently provide back, end, or side outlets for little if any additional charge. With this in mind, careful layout of the array can save a substantial amount of field assembly costs and time. Remember, the principal barrier to the use of solar energy is an economic one. Any reduction in initial cost without impairment of performance will result in greatly enhanced lifetime cost benefits.

BUILDING YOUR OWN COLLECTORS

The construction of flat-plate liquid-cooled collectors requires only a minimum of skill and equipment. Although large manufacturers may have a substantial investment in jigs and material-handling equipment, perfectly satisfactory collectors may be assembled using tools found in the average home workshop. As with any other construction project, good planning and attention to detail are at least as important as skill.

Locally built or home-built collectors probably will not have quite the performance of commercially manufactured units, but they may be almost as efficient. The only way to determine the performance of your collector would be to have it tested at an approved testing facility, an expense that hardly seems worthwhile. Most important, you may be able to build collectors for a third of their manufactured price.

A first decision to be made is the materials to be used for construction. If new glass is to be purchased, then one of the standard patio-door sizes

in tempered glass is to be preferred. As already stated, standard sizes are 28 × 76 inches (71.1 × 193cm), 34 × 76 inches (86.4 × 193cm) and 46 × 76 inches (116.8 × 193cm). The 34 × 76-inch size is the best choice.

A bit of judicious shopping may be in order at this point. Glass companies frequently quote installed prices and are accustomed to selling one or two pieces at a time. They usually will have to measure the job before installation. All of these costs are built into their prices.

An inexpensive source of glazing may be so-called "salvage glass." This is glass that has been removed from storefronts because of a crack, hole, scratch, or other defect. Because these sheets, usually ¼-inch (.64cm) polished plate glass, frequently are large, it is often possible to cut one or more cover plates from a sheet of salvage. Most glass companies sell salvage glass for a fraction of the cost of new material.

If you choose plastic for a cover plate, use a well-tested brand such as produced by the Filon Corporation or Kalwall Corporation. Although these materials may be expensive compared with other glass-fiber materials, they are still less than half as expensive as glass. These materials are available in rolls 48 inches (121.9cm) wide. Filon also manufactures a roll 34 inches (86.4cm) wide.

The choice of single or double glazing depends upon the end use of your harvested energy. Double glazing is always desirable when collectors are used to heat domestic hot water. In most parts of the country, double glazing is preferable when space heating is done without a heat pump. In mild climates or where the collectors are used in conjunction with a heat pump, single glazing will be adequate.

In order to arrive at a suitable choice for absorber material and thickness, and tube size and spacing, we might refer to the performance curve shown earlier in Figure 2–13 (page 27). The high-quality collector whose performance is described consists of ¼-inch (.64cm) I.D. copper riser on about 6-inch (15.2cm) centers connected to 1-inch (2.5 cm) I.D. manifolds. The risers are continuously attached to 7-ounce (.010-inch; .25mm) copper

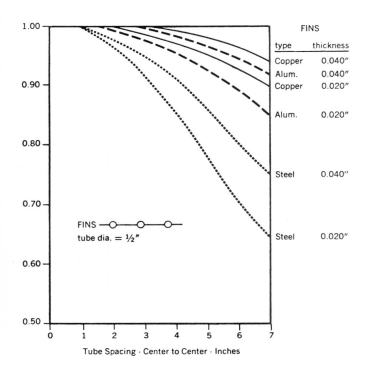

FIG. 2–17. A comparison of copper, aluminum, and steel as absorber materials. Reprinted from *The Solar Home Book,* by Bruce Anderson, Brick House Publishing Co., Inc., 1976, Andover, Mass. 01810.

sheet. Its selective black surface has an absorptivity of 87 to 92 and its emissivity is .07 to .35. The paint that you will use probably will have both higher absorptivity and higher emissivity than this surface.

Obviously, 7-ounce (2.14kg/m²) or heavier copper would be an excellent choice for the absorber material if its cost is not excessive. In order to estimate how other metals might perform, refer to Figure 2–17. Although copper in .010-inch (.25mm) thickness is not indicated in the figure, extrapolation suggests that .025-inch (.64mm) aluminum will be about as efficient. About a 4½-inch (11.4cm) tube spacing with 20-gauge (.0359-inch; .9mm) steel should provide about the same efficiency. Notice that the curves shown in this figure are based on the use of ½-inch (12.7mm) tubing for risers. Other tube spacings can be used. Note that

a closer spacing will improve performance, but not much. With wider spacing the performance falls off rapidly.

The collectors on my own home use .025-inch (.64mm) aluminum absorbers with ½-inch-diameter (12.7mm) risers on about 5¾-inch (14.6cm) centers. This combination, however, was arrived at through analysis and not by comparison with an existing collector.

We shall use drawn (hard-temper) copper tubing for the fluid passages. Type M is the lightest, so we will use it where possible. Manifolds will be ¾-inch (19mm) or 1-inch (25.4mm). For risers, many manufacturers use ¼-inch (.64cm) I.D. tube, but it is not available in Type M. If this size tubing is used, it must be at least as heavy as Type L.

I have a personal hesitancy about using any tubing as small as ¼ inch diameter (.64cm) in a system where access is difficult. With many joints to make, it seems inevitable that droplets of solder will get into a few of them. These droplets, together with normal scaling and the possibility of small bits of foreign matter in the system, could restrict flow. Besides this, you may not be able to purchase ¼-inch-diameter tubing anyway. I couldn't, so I used ½-inch (12.7mm) Type M. The cost penalty is not severe. As a matter of fact, you will discover that tubing and absorber material is not, as you probably thought, the major cost in a collector.

Several methods are available for attaching risers to manifolds. One method consists of building up the manifold of a series of 1 × 1 × ½-inch (25.4 × 25.4 × 12.7mm) tees and short nipples with the riser fitting into the small leg of the tee. This method requires too many fittings and too many sweated joints for my fancy.

Another method was described by Francis de Winter in *How to Design and Build a Solar Swimming Pool Heater.*[5] This method involves drilling and tapping the manifold (remember that tubing cannot be threaded!), inserting a CXM adapter for, at most, one thread, then silver brazing the whole assembly. I have built several collectors according to this scheme. I have the greatest respect for Dr. de Winter at a professional level, but I cannot recommend this technique to my worst enemy.

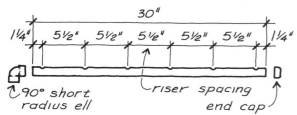

FIG. 2–18. Collector manifold.

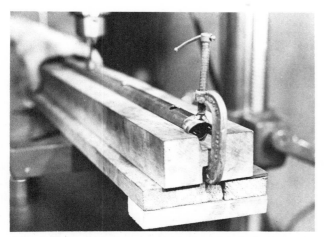

FIG. 2–19. Drilling the manifold. The simple jig is made from a 2 × 4.

FIG. 2–20. Bevel cut on tube end is made by the tubing cutter. This allows for a perfect match with hole in manifold.

My favored method for attaching riser to manifold will be described as we build the collector. Let us assume that the collector size will at least fit 34 × 76-inch (86.4 × 193cm) glazing.

Rigid tubing is available in 20-foot (6.1m) lengths. Purchase two lengths for each collector. Cut each length into three pieces exactly 73⅛ inches (1.86m) long, using a standard tubing cutter.

The risers are connected to the manifolds at each end. Note that inlets and outlets are at opposite ends of the lower and upper manifolds so that the fluid friction through the collector is equal for all possible paths. Cut each manifold exactly 30 inches (76.2cm) long and drill as indicated in Figure 2–18. Use two additional risers with a steel absorber. Use a hole saw with a diameter the same as the inside diameter of the risers. Don't use an ordinary drill bit, because it will bore an oval hole in the curved surface of the manifolds.

A simple wooden jig and a drill press will assure quick and accurate drilling of the manifolds (Fig. 2–19). If you use a standard tubing cutter you will note a 45° bevel on the cut end of each riser (Fig. 2–20). This makes a neat match with the hole in the manifold. These connections, as well as the caps and elbows, are joined with silver solder.

The absorber panels should be exactly 32 × 73 inches (81.3 × 185.4cm). If the absorber is either copper or steel, then the absorber grid may be soldered to it. Use 50-50 ⅛-inch (3.2mm) wire solder and an acetylene, Mapp gas, or propane torch. If a propane torch is used, then one of the larger sizes is advisable. You may wish to practice on scraps in order to develop a technique that does not use too much expensive solder. With practice, you should use about one foot of solder per foot of riser (each side), so be prepared to use lots of solder. If you are assembling more than one or two collectors, consider buying solder in a 50-pound reel rather than the familiar 1-pound coils from the hardware store. The savings can be substantial. When you have finished assembling the grid, I would suggest a pressure test to determine if there are any leaks. Hook up an air compressor and tank, run the pressure up to about 100 pounds per square inch (7.03 kg/cm²), and leave for twenty-four hours. A decrease in pressure will indicate a leak, but a liberal application of soapsuds at each joint will help locate it. A friendly plumbing or air-conditioning contractor may lend you the necessary equipment.

Next, place the absorber panel on a smooth, heat-resistant surface, position the grid carefully on it, and hold it in place with clamps or weights. Begin soldering at the center of the panel and work

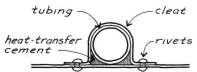

FIG. 2–21. Solder fillet between riser and copper or steel absorber plate. Insufficient heating of tube and absorber will increase throat dimension of fillet, thereby wasting solder.

FIG. 2–22. Use of Thermon heat-transfer cement and cleats to attach copper riser to aluminum absorber.

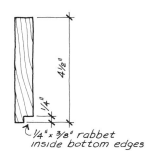

FIG. 2–23. Section through redwood box frame.

toward the manifolds (Fig. 2–21). Unless you have a metal work surface that distributes the heat, you will notice some rippling of the absorber panel. This should not affect collector performance, but it may cause you to use more solder.

If you choose to use an aluminum absorber, the grid is attached by aluminum cleats and heat-transfer cement (Fig. 2–22). The cleats ensure that the grid and absorber do not physically separate, while the heat-transfer cement guarantees an excellent heat-transfer surface. I made full-length cleats from strips of aluminum 2½ inches (6.4cm) wide shaped over a piece of tubing. Intermittent cleats spaced about 12 inches (15.2cm) apart also should work. Place grid and cleats in place and drill at about 12-inch (15.2cm) intervals for attachment. Next, lay beads of Thermon heat-transfer cement along the tube center lines on the absorber plate and along the top sides of the risers. Position the grid on the plate, fit the cleats over the risers, and attach cleats to the plate using "pop" rivets or sheet-metal screws.

Thermon is sold in bulk containers or ¹/₁₀-gallon cartridges. I suggest use of the cartridges, since there will be less waste. The material is fairly expensive, about the same as silicone sealant, but its in-place cost should be no more than solder.

The absorber is now ready for painting. For ease in painting and a more pleasing appearance, I suggest that riser tubes be on the back (insulation) side. For paint, I recommend Black Velvet Nextel, made by the 3M Company, but any flat-back wrought-iron paint is acceptable. Clean and prime or etch the metal according to the paint manufacturer's directions, and apply one coat of paint as thin as possible for complete coverage. Lay the finished absorber plate aside.

If you plan an array for space-heating an entire building, then you may integrate the collector container into the roof or wall construction. However, if you are building only a few panels for domestic water heating, then construction of individual containers is simpler.

Use 1 × 6-inch clear heart redwood, ripped to 4½ inches (11.4cm) and rabbeted as shown in Figure 2–23. Save the narrow strips left over if you plan to use a plastic cover. The container is assembled to the dimensions shown, using waterproof glue and nonrusting brass or aluminum wood screws.

Fiberglass insulation at least 2 inches (5.1cm) thick is placed beneath the collector and the bottom of the container. High-temperature insulation, rated at 1,000°F (538°C), is ideal. If you use ordinary building insulation, heat it in an oven at 400°F

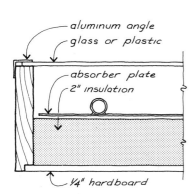

FIG. 2–24. Section through completed box side.

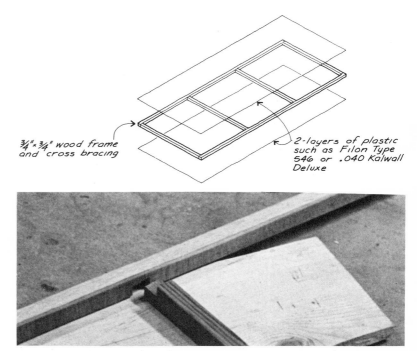

FIG. 2–25. Construction framing for double plastic cover plate.

(204°C) for a few minutes before installing it to drive off the binder. If you don't, you risk fogging the inside of the cover plate after installation, but before the pump is started.

If you choose glass for a cover plate, simply place a 34 × 76-inch (86.4 × 193cm) piece of tempered patio-door glass on a bed of silicone sealer, apply another bead of silicone to the top edges of the glass, and hold in place with lengths of ¾ × ¾-inch (19 × 19mm) lightweight aluminum angles. For a more pleasing appearance, a bronze anodized finish may be used. Cut the angles to fit and screw them to the sides of the container. There will be a ¼-inch (6.4mm) gap between the angles and the edges of the glass for expansion (Fig. 2–24).

If you planned to use a single sheet of glass, you can get a double cover plate and higher water temperatures for about the same cost by using a good fiberglass plastic such as Filon Type 546 and the strips that were ripped from the 1 × 6-inch lumber. Assemble a frame of the strips, but include two intermediate supports for the plastic (Fig. 2–25). Attach the plastic to both faces of this frame with a continuous bead of silicone sealer and nonrusting staples at about 3 inches (7.6cm) on center. A clear, dry day with low relative humidity is ideal for making this assembly. The cover can be attached to the upper edges of the container with additional silicone sealer and rustproof fasteners.

You should read Chapter 4 on circuit piping prior to actually constructing any collectors, since for any specific applications economies of labor or material may be possible. For example, if a four-collector array is to be used for domestic water heating, changing the manifold size to 1 inch (25.4mm) diameter and using side inlets and outlets for parallel flow can simplify installation.

Notes

1. J. A. Duffie and W. A. Beckman, *Solar Energy Thermal Processes* (New York: Wiley-Interscience, 1974), pp. 1–6.

2. A. B. and M. P. Meinel, *Applied Solar Energy* (Reading, Mass.: Addison-Wesley, 1976), pp. 94–100.

3. J. P. Holman, *Heat Transfer* (New York: McGraw-Hill, 1963), pp. 275ff.

4. F. Kreith and J. F. Kreider, *Principles of Solar Engineering* (New York: McGraw-Hill, 1978), pp. 221–23.

5. F. de Winter, *How to Design and Build a Solar Swimming Pool Heater* (Copper Development Association, Inc., 1975).

CHAPTER THREE

THERMAL STORAGE

Unfortunately, periods of maximum heat harvest seldom coincide with periods of maximum heat usage. Such a situation suggests that provision be made for heat storage. If the heat harvest is through south-facing windows, then it is possible that heat storage may be the insulated thermal mass of the building itself—as indeed it should be—although the release of this energy is least subject to control.

If the heat harvest is by several hundred square feet of collectors, a heat-storage system having greater thermal capacity is indicated. Provision also should be made for modulating the rate of heat withdrawal from storage.

When a solar array is used to heat domestic hot water, no additional storage is needed. Water in the tank serves as storage. When a solar array is used for space heating, then separate storage is indicated.

Thermal storage may be in the form of sensible heat in which heat is stored in a material such as rock or water by virtue of its change of temperature. Alternately, it may be stored primarily as latent heat due to a change of state, usually from solid to liquid. Heat is stored or released as heat of fusion.[1] The eutectic salts are examples of materials capable of latent heat storage. Glauber's salt, sodium sulfate decahydrate ($Na_2SO_4 \cdot 10H_2O$), is the best-known and most widely used of these materials. Unfortunately, the melting point of Glauber's salt, the point at which its heat storage is greatest, is only about 90°F (32.2°C), which really is too marginally low for effective space heating.

Conventionally, thermal storage is in the form of sensible heat. The storage system usually is rock or water or, in a few cases, a combination of the two. This latter situation is typified in Dr. Harry Thomason's patented Solaris system, in which a

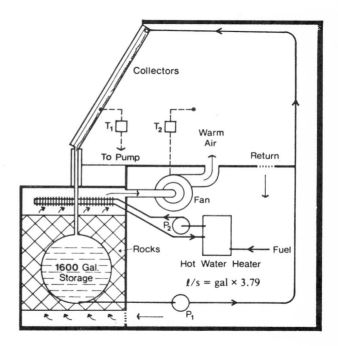

FIG 3–1. The Solaris heating system using trickle collectors and combination water-rock storage. The system is patented by Dr. Harry Thomason.

water-storage tank is surrounded by a rock bed through which room air is circulated (Fig. 3–1).

Of considerable interest is the *specific heat,* C_p, of a substance. This is the amount of sensible heat that will be absorbed or released by a unit mass of a substance corresponding to 1°F change in temperature. For water, $C_p = 1.0$ Btu/lb/°F (4.19 kJ/kg°C). Thus, 1 cubic foot (.028317m³) of water, weighing about 62 pounds (27.026kg) at 100°F (37.8°C), will absorb 62.0 Btu (65.4kJ) for every °F (5/9°C) that its temperature increases. Rock, which weighs about

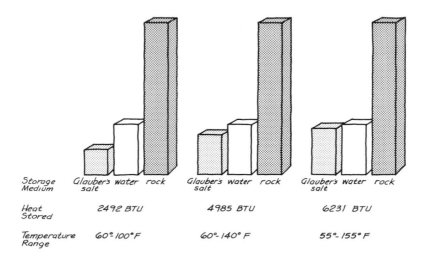

Storage Medium	Glauber's salt	water	rock	Glauber's salt	water	rock	Glauber's salt	water	rock
Heat Stored	2492 BTU			4985 BTU			6231 BTU		
Temperature Range	60°-100° F			60°-140° F			55°-155° F		

FIG. 3–2. Relative volumes necessary to store the same amount of heat in Glauber's salt, water, and rock. Glauber's salt storage includes 50 percent voids and rock storage includes 30 percent voids for air passage. It may be seen that Glauber's salt is most efficient when the temperature variation of storage is the smallest.

150 pounds per cubic foot (2,403kg/m³), has a specific heat of about .20. When 30 percent voids are allowed for air passages, it is seen that the volume of rock required to store the same amount of energy as water is about three times as great (Fig. 3–2).

For all practical purposes, water appears the best choice for thermal storage for a liquid-cooled collector array. It has a high specific heat and is relatively dense. It is cheap, nontoxic, and moderately noncorrosive. It remains liquid through the range of temperatures of most interest. Water's main limitation is its high freezing point and subsequent expansion, which, in most cases, precludes its use as a heat-transfer liquid through the collectors.

A question that perplexes many persons is the optimum size of a thermal-storage system. A large volume of water will store large quantities of energy, but its temperature may be too low to be of use. Furthermore, its temperature at the start of the harvest may still be high enough to degrade collector performance. A small storage capacity will result in a high temperature at the end of a period of energy harvest, but the capacity may not be sufficient to carry over until the following collection period.

Several experimental projects rely on long-term storage. Canada's Provident House, our own ACES (Annual Cycle Energy System) at Oak Ridge, and Denmark's Zero Energy House are examples. The Denmark house was constructed during the spring of 1975 by the Technical University of Denmark.[2] This single-family, one-story dwelling consists of two 645-square-foot (60m²) living spaces joined by a 750-square-foot (70m²) unheated atrium (Fig. 3–3). A vertical south-facing liquid-cooled collector array is mounted on the upper wall of the atrium. Thermal storage is in a 7,900-gallon (30m³) buried steel tank located external to the building (Fig. 3–4). Despite the absence of ground water and 24 inches (60cm) of mineral wool surrounding the tank, 40 percent of the stored energy is lost. Had the storage tank been located beneath the dwelling, most of this wasted energy would actually have been uncontrolled gain for the building.

The value of long-term storage has yet to be

FIG. 3-3. Denmark's Zero Energy House. Photo courtesy Torben V. Esbensen, Technical University of Denmark.

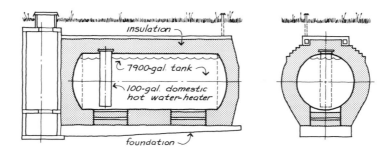

FIG. 3-4. Thermal storage for Zero Energy House.

proved. However, we have a few guidelines for ordinary storage systems. Usable temperature for the thermal storage will be determined by the terminal design. The maximum temperature is determined by the maximum ΔT_c at which the collector operates reasonably efficiently. At the least, the storage should be large enough to store all the energy collected on a sunny day.

One may ask for how long the building can be heated from storage during a succession of cloudy days. This is a question not simply answered, since the heating requirements for two successive cloudy days during early April may be modest compared with the same requirements for one frigid January day. A fairly reasonable requirement is that the storage be capable of storing enough heat to last for one typical January day. Thus, if a building has a heat loss of 12,000 Btu/degree day (12,658kJ/DD), and the average number of degree days/day is 35, then storage should be about 420,000 Btu (443,000kJ). If the system is designed to operate between 100°F (37.8°C) and 140°F (60°C), and remembering that water has a specific heat of unity and weighs 8.33 pounds per gallon, then the required storage is 1,260 gallons (4,770 liters).

Most authorities agree that about 2½ gallons of water storage for each square foot of collector area (102 liters/m²) is a reasonable amount for heating. If maximum storage temperature is 140°F (34.4°C), then each gallon of water will store 333 Btu. If the storage is to be used with existing absorption-refrigeration machines, minimum usable temperature is about 160°F (71.1°C), with a higher temperature desirable. For such a purpose, less water should be stored; about 1½ gallons per square foot (61 liters/m²) of collector.

When the tank is used for off-peak cooling of condensing water, then a larger storage capacity is indicated. Somewhat larger capacities also are desirable when the solar array is used in conjunction with a water-source heat pump. Since the cost of a storage tank is not a linear function of its capacity, and since a tank can be underfilled but not overfilled, prudence suggests that tanks be liberally sized.

Location of the tank is of considerable importance. Placing the tank outside the building plan certainly is one solution. However, in order to fully exploit the earth's relatively constant year-round temperature, the top of the tank must be at least 8 feet (2.44m) below finish grade. Given a choice, a basement or below-grade installation under a building is perhaps a better solution. For either of these cases, most of the heat loss from storage is not a loss at all, but an uncontrolled heat gain.

The heat that is lost by conduction from storage is:

$$Q = UA(t_2 - t_1)$$

where

Q = heat loss, Btuh (watts)
U = overall coefficient of heat transfer, Btuh-ft²/°F (w/m²°C)
A = area of container, ft² (m²)
t_2 = temperature of water in storage, °F (°C)
t_1 = ambient temperature of air or earth surrounding storage, °F (°C)

Heat loss from storage will be less if the tank is well insulated to reduce the U-factor. When the tank is located within or beneath a heated space, I have found that 4 inches (10.2cm) of closed-cell insulation with a U = .20 Btu/ft²-°F·hr is adequate. However, if the tank is buried outside or is in an unheated enclosure, several times this amount may be needed.[3]

Likewise, a compact shape for the tank will reduce the area through which heat may be lost. Although a spherical shape encloses the greatest volume with the least surface area, tanks of this form are seldom used.

Finally, heat loss will be minimized if the storage tank is located within or beneath the space to be heated. For example, a tank in which the water temperature is 130°F (54.4°C) and which is located in a 65°F (18.3°C) basement will lose only half the heat it would if located outside where the temperature is zero. Furthermore, heat loss from the basement-situated tank really is not lost at all, since it serves to heat the basement and perhaps the floor above.

Considerable study has been given to stratification in storage tanks. Duffie and Beckman have simulated two-, three-, and *n*-section tanks and derived expression for the temperature gradients for these models.[4] Their simulations assume that liquid from the collector and to the load enters and leaves at the top of the storage, while liquid to the collector and from the load leaves and enters storage from the bottom. This is a fairly common situation for air systems whose pebble beds have tall vertical dimensions and where stratification enhances system performance.[5] But such a model for water systems would require that the entire storage system be an antifreeze solution. This is an unwarranted and unacceptable expense. Usually, heat exchangers are used between solar-circuit fluid and water in storage.

My own 1,500-gallon (5.68m³) storage tank is 5 feet (1.6m) deep and has a heat exchanger located 6 inches (15.24cm) above its bottom. This tank has been instrumented with thermocouples located at the bottom and every 6 inches (15.24cm) upward. Continuous monitoring is performed by a 12-channel strip chart recorder. From these records, I have discovered that although the temperature at the tank bottom is the lowest, little temperature variation exists from the heat exchanger upward.

Storage tanks can be a major cost item.[6] Obviously, they must be waterproof and possess structural integrity at storage temperatures. Since hot water weighs about 62 pounds/per cubic foot (993kg/m³), the hydrostatic pressure at the bottom of a tank 5 feet (1.6m) deep will be 310 pounds per square foot (1,513kg/m²). This range of pressures requires that storage tanks be structurally designed. Provision should be made for draining a tank. It should not deteriorate, scale, or corrode in the presence of hot water, and its interior surfaces should be easily cleanable. If an internal heat exchanger is employed, then some means of installing and maintaining it should be provided.

Materials suitable for tank construction include steel, fiberglass, and concrete. Steel tanks are customarily prefabricated and installed in a building or buried outside. Some experts recommend an interior coating of silicone, epoxy, vinyl, or fused glass. These tanks are relatively light in weight, although they are fairly expensive. Most available steel tanks will be cylindrical, and it will be necessary to install them with their axis in a horizontal position. This will necessitate some sort of supporting framework. It is difficult to insulate their curved sides using inexpensive insulation. Piping for inlets and outlets can be simply installed below water level by welding, brazing, or by the use of bulkhead fittings.

Fiberglass tanks are supplied by a few manufacturers. Some of these tanks consist of two external surfaces of fiberglass separated by a core of closed-cell insulation so that no additional insulation is required.

Concrete is a relatively inexpensive, easily worked material for tank construction, but it is heavy and requires internal waterproofing. In new construction, one or more basement walls may also serve as tank walls. Precast concrete septic tanks or cisterns are available in many parts of the country. Some of these have circular-plan forms, while others are rectangular. Sizes range from about 750 gallons (2.84m³) to 2,000 gallons (7.75m³), a range that is appropriate for most solar installations. Most of these tanks have a manhole in the top, which makes them especially appropriate for installation under buildings constructed as slab on grade. In most cases, it will be necessary to install some sort of internal waterproofing.

I have never trusted integral waterproofing of concrete to be a completely reliable solution, since the concrete could develop a small crack. Various water-soluble coatings also are available, but I am not personally knowledgeable as to their efficacy. A local contractor coats the inside of tanks with fiberglass-reinforced plastic to a thickness of about .040 inch. This is an excellent coating, but is expensive. Vinyl liners can be custom tailored by fabricators experienced in making tank linings for industry.

My own concrete tank is waterproofed with two coats of high-quality swimming-pool paint. This has proved to be a satisfactory coating for me. However, a word of caution is in order. The vehicle for this paint is extremely volatile and heavier than air. When applied in an enclosed space the fumes settle and displace all oxygen. Be certain that any workers wear respirators (not simple filters) or that a large fan is used to remove these fumes. Despite warnings on the containers and my own emphatic cautions, we filled two ambulances with a professional painter, two would-be rescuers, a subsequent would-be rescuer, and a paramedic—all hallucinating. Luckily, none suffered any permanent physiological damage, but the lesson they learned will not soon be forgotten.

Piping to and from a concrete storage tank can be handled in at least two days. The easiest way is to bring all piping through the top. This scheme effectively eliminates any possible leakage due to pipe penetration. However, it generally requires more fittings and greater pipe length. Additionally, provision must be made for the piping to penetrate the top insulation.

Piping can be brought into poured concrete tanks at any level by the use of swimming-pool flanges. These are available at modest cost from swimming-pool-supply houses in a range of sizes from 1¼ inch diameter upward.

When a solar-energy supplement is added to an existing building, the problem of locating the thermal storage may become extremely troublesome. Even though adequate space may be available in a basement, storage, or utility room, access to these rooms may be restricted by existing door sizes. Since most interior doors are 2 feet 8 inches by 6 feet 8 inches (81.28 × 203.2cm), two of the tank

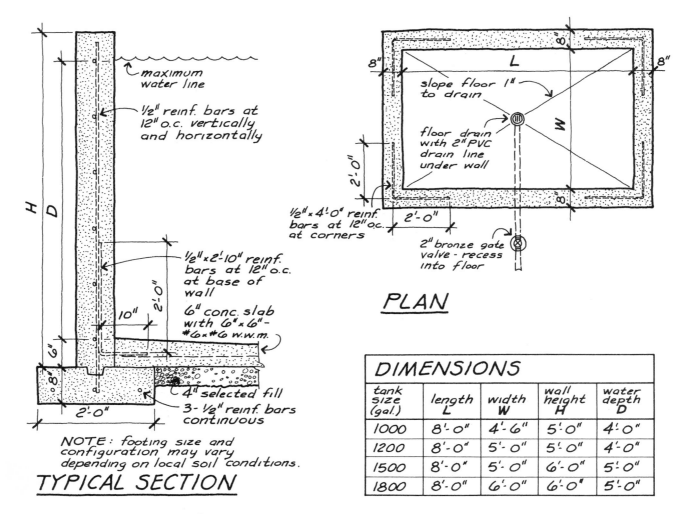

FIG. 3–5. Construction details for 1,000-, 1,200-, 1,500-, and 1,800-gallon cast-in-place concrete storage tanks. Data checked by Dr. W. M. Lucas, Consulting Engineer.

Within the image (TYPICAL SECTION):

- maximum water line
- ½" reinf. bars at 12" o.c. vertically and horizontally
- ½" × 2'-10" reinf. bars at 12" o.c. at base of wall
- 6" conc. slab with 6" × 6" - #6 × #6 w.w.m.
- 4" selected fill
- 3 - ½" reinf. bars continuous
- NOTE: footing size and configuration may vary depending on local soil conditions.
- TYPICAL SECTION

Within the image (PLAN):

- slope floor 1" to drain
- floor drain with 2" PVC drain line under wall
- ½" × 4'-0" reinf. bars at 12" o.c. at corners
- 2" bronze gate valve - recess into floor
- PLAN

DIMENSIONS

tank size (gal.)	length L	width W	wall height H	water depth D
1000	8'-0"	4'-6"	5'-0"	4'-0"
1200	8'-0"	5'-0"	5'-0"	4'-0"
1500	8'-0"	5'-0"	6'-0"	5'-0"
1800	8'-0"	6'-0"	6'-0"	5'-0"

dimensions should not exceed about 30 × 78 inches (76.2 × 198.1cm). The third dimension will be determined by whatever maneuvering might be necessary between doors. A long, shallow tank may be the answer, but it will consume considerable floor space.

When an access problem exists, one solution is to use 30-inch-diameter (76.2cm) by 78-inch-high (198.1cm) corrugated galvanized culvert pipe. A bottom of sheet metal may be welded or brazed to the pipe. Each of these pipes will contain about 250 gallons (.95m³). Two or more can be connected and, if necessary, a small circulating pump installed to maintain all tanks at about the same temperature.

A local contractor produces 1,500-gallon (5.68m³) fiberglass tanks in halves, each of which will pass through an average door. When awarded a contract, he delivers the tank pieces, installs an internal heat exchanger, bolts the halves together, and seals this joint with fiberglass tape and resin. Then he applies a 4-inch thickness of foam insulation. The whole assembly looks like an elongated marshmallow, but seems to work well.

At least two other methods can be used to provide thermal storage in space with restricted access. One of these methods is to cast a concrete tank *in situ*. Its main drawback is the distance that concrete must be moved and its method of movement. A convenient basement window or a concrete pumper can make this type of storage very cost-effective. Moving concrete by wheelbarrows and shovels is labor intensive, however.

There is no reason why wood tanks, properly designed to resist pressures, cannot be assembled within these areas. When fitted with fiberglass or vinyl liners and externally insulated, they should prove as satisfactory as tanks built of other materials. In addition, the material necessary to build a wooden tank may be less than that required to build a form for a concrete tank.

Figure 3–5 shows the suggested construction details for concrete tanks that can be built in place. A tank having a square plan will have both a lower heat loss and lower stresses than one with a rectangular plan. On the other hand, when an immersion heat exchanger is made of rigid tubing, we should like to use the tubing with no waste and the fewest number of fittings. If the tubing is cut into lengths either 5 feet (1.52m) or 6 feet 8 inches (3.03m) long, then one tank dimension should be about 6 feet (1.83m) or 8 feet (2.45m). If soft-temper tubing, at greater tubing cost but lower fitting and fabrication cost, is used, then it may be bent without waste to allow for a square tank.

As with most other components of a solar energy system, the overriding consideration frequently is an economic one. Tanks need to be waterproof, structurally sound, and capable of withstanding internal temperatures of up to 200°F. Any tank that meets these rather simple specifications is acceptable. We seek the tank that meets them with the smallest investment. Because of local variations, no one tank material can be most economical in all geographic locations. Only a design that is sensitive both to system requirements and local construction costs will be best.

NOTES

1. M. Telkes, "Solar Energy Storage," *ASHRAE Journal* (September 1974), pp. 38–44.

2. T. V. Esbenser, and V. Korsgaard, "Dimensioning of the Solar Heating System in the Zero Energy House in Denmark," *Solar Energy* 19:195–99.

3. B. Anderson, *Solar Energy: Fundamentals in Building Design* (New York: McGraw-Hill, 1977), p. 228.

4. J. A. Duffie and W. A. Beckman, *Solar Energy Thermal Processes* (New York: Wiley-Interscience, 1974), pp. 216–27.

5. Ibid., pp. 227–31.

6. E. E. Pickering, "Residential Hot Water Solar Energy Storage," *Proceedings of Solar Energy Storage Subsystems for the Heating and Cooling of Buildings,* ASHRAE (1975), pp. 24–37. This reference reports an exhaustive study of containers for hot water.

CHAPTER FOUR

PIPING AND PUMPS

piping circuit is necessary for the heat-transfer liquid to transport its energy from the collector array to the thermal storage. Usually, an additional circuit is required to transport energy from storage to a space-heating device. In this chapter we will examine various piping materials and fittings, methods of joining, and valves, pumps, and controls. System sizing and economic trade-offs will be considered.

Both pipe and tubing may be suitable for piping. The difference between pipe and tubing is not, as many people imagine, in materials used for their construction. Instead, the distinction between pipe and tubing is in their wall thicknesses. An easy way to distinguish between pipe and tubing is to remember that pipe can be threaded while tubing cannot. Whichever is used, it is convenient to speak of piping.

Both wrought iron and steel are used for piping. Generally, they are galvanized for added corrosion resistance. In addition, wrought-iron pipe contains silicate-slag fibers, which make it more corrosion resistant than steel.

The pipe is made by forming metal sheets into cylindrical shapes that are butt welded to form the joint. In the smaller sizes, steel can be made into tube without a longitudinal joint.

Standard-weight pipe is designated ASTM Schedule 40 and is adequate for most piping applications.

Copper and its alloy, brass, can be formed into either tube or pipe. Red-brass pipe, 85 percent copper and 15 percent zinc, is especially corrosion resistant. Its high cost, however, restricts its use to those applications in which high corrosion resistance is required.

Copper tubing is the piping material against

which all others must be judged. It is lightweight, easily available, easily fabricated, strong, and noncorrosive, and resists the temperatures encountered in both solar-system and heating-system design. ASTM standards require that this tube be at least 99.90 percent pure copper. Most copper used for tubes is deoxidized with phosphorus. It is referred to as Copper No. 122 or DHP Copper.[1]

Copper tube falls into two main classes. The first is called plumbing tube and includes Types K, L, M, and DWV in decreasing order of wall thickness (Fig. 4–1). These types are defined by ASTM standard sizes in which the outside diameter is always ⅛ inch (3.18mm) larger than the standard size (Fig. 4–2). The actual inside diameter depends on tube size and wall thickness. All four of these types are available in drawn temper in straight lengths of 20 feet (6.1m). In the piping trades, drawn temper frequently is called "hard" tube, since it is rigid.

Types K, L, and M also are manufactured in annealed (soft) temper in the sizes and lengths shown in Figure 4–1. Usually, Type M will be locally available only in hard temper.

The Copper Development Association, Inc., a trade association dedicated to promoting widespread and appropriate use of copper tubing, recommends hard-temper Type M or soft-temper Type L for underground water services, Type M or L for small sizes, and Type DWV in larger sizes for chilled-water mains and radiant panels or hydronic heating systems, and Type L for condensate-return lines. Based on these recommendations, it seems both functionally and economically appropriate to employ Type M in the circuit piping for flat-plate solar systems wherever possible.

The other main class of copper tubing is designated ACR and is intended for air-conditioning and

TUBE	DRAWN		ANNEALED	
COMMERCIALLY AVAILABLE LENGTHS				
Type K	Straight Lengths:		Straight Lengths:	
	Up to 8-inch diameter	20 ft	Up to 8-inch diameter	20 ft
	10-inch diameter	18 ft	10-inch diameter	18 ft
	12-inch diameter	12 ft	12-inch diameter	12 ft
			Coils:	
			Up to 1-inch diameter	60 ft
				100 ft
			1¼ and 1½-inch diameter	60 ft
			2-inch diameter	40 ft
				45 ft
Type L	Straight Lengths:		Straight Lengths:	
	Up to 10-inch diameter	20 ft	Up to 10-inch diameter	20 ft
	12-inch diameter	18 ft	12-inch diameter	18 ft
			Coils:	
			Up to 1-inch diameter	60 ft
				100 ft
			1¼ and 1½-inch diameter	60 ft
			2-inch diameter	40 ft
				45 ft
Type M	Straight Lengths:		Straight Lengths:	
	All diameters	20 ft	Up to 12-inch diameter	20 ft
			Coils:	
			Up to 1-inch diameter	60 ft
				100 ft
			1¼ and 1½-inch diameter	60 ft
			2-inch diameter	40 ft
				45 ft
DWV	Straight Lengths:		Not available	—
	All diameters	20 ft		
ACR	Straight Lengths*:	20 ft	Coils*:	50 ft

FIG. 4–1. Standard copper plumbing tube. Courtesy Copper Development Association.

	Nominal Dimensions, inches			Calculated Values, Based on Nominal Dimensions			
TYPE K							
Size, inches	Outside Diameter	Inside Diameter	Wall Thickness	Cross Sectional Area of Bore, sq inches	External Surface, sq ft per lin ft	Internal Surface, sq ft per lin ft	Weight, pounds per lin ft
¼	.375	.305	.035	.073	.098	.080	0.145
⅜	.500	.402	.049	.127	.131	.105	0.269
½	.625	.527	.049	.218	.164	.138	0.344
⅝	.750	.652	.049	.334	.196	.171	0.418
¾	.875	.745	.065	.436	.229	.195	0.641
1	1.125	.995	.065	.778	.294	.261	0.839
1¼	1.375	1.245	.065	1.22	.360	.326	1.04
1½	1.625	1.481	.072	1.72	.425	.388	1.36
2	2.125	1.959	.083	3.01	.556	.513	2.06
2½	2.625	2.435	.095	4.66	.687	.638	2.93
3	3.125	2.907	.109	6.64	.818	.761	4.00
3½	3.625	3.385	.120	9.00	.949	.886	5.12
4	4.125	3.857	.134	11.7	1.08	1.01	6.51
5	5.125	4.805	.160	18.1	1.34	1.26	9.67
6	6.125	5.741	.192	25.9	1.60	1.50	13.9
8	8.125	7.583	.271	45.2	2.13	1.98	25.9
10	10.125	9.449	.338	70.1	2.65	2.47	40.3
12	12.125	11.315	.405	101.	3.17	2.96	57.8
TYPE L							
¼	.375	.315	.030	.078	.098	.082	0.126
⅜	.500	.430	.035	.145	.131	.113	0.198
½	.625	.545	.040	.233	.164	.143	0.285
⅝	.750	.666	.042	.348	.196	.174	0.362
¾	.875	.785	.045	.484	.229	.206	0.455
1	1.125	1.025	.050	.825	.294	.268	0.655
1¼	1.375	1.265	.055	1.26	.360	.331	0.884
1½	1.625	1.505	.060	1.78	.425	.394	1.14
2	2.125	1.985	.070	3.09	.556	.520	1.75
2½	2.625	2.465	.080	4.77	.687	.645	2.48
3	3.125	2.945	.090	6.81	.818	.771	3.33
3½	3.625	3.425	.100	9.21	.949	.897	4.29
4	4.125	3.905	.110	12.0	1.08	1.02	5.38
5	5.125	4.875	.125	18.7	1.34	1.28	7.61
6	6.125	5.845	.140	26.8	1.60	1.53	10.2
8	8.125	7.725	.200	46.9	2.13	2.02	19.3
10	10.125	9.625	.250	72.8	2.65	2.53	30.1
12	12.125	11.565	.280	105.	3.17	3.03	40.4

	TYPE M						
	Nominal Dimensions, inches			Calculated Values, Based on Nominal Dimensions			
Size, inches	Outside Diameter	Inside Diameter	Wall Thickness	Cross Sectional Area of Bore, sq inches	External Surface, sq ft per lin ft	Internal Surface, sq ft per lin ft	Weight, pounds per lin ft
⅜	.500	.450	.025	.159	.131	.118	0.145
½	.625	.569	.028	.254	.164	.149	0.204
¾	.875	.811	.032	.517	.229	.212	0.328
1	1.125	1.055	.035	.874	.294	.276	0.465
1¼	1.375	1.291	.042	1.31	.360	.338	0.682
1½	1.625	1.527	.049	1.83	.425	.400	0.940
2	2.125	2.009	.058	3.17	.556	.526	1.46
2½	2.625	2.495	.065	4.89	.687	.653	2.03
3	3.125	2.981	.072	6.98	.818	.780	2.68
3½	3.625	3.459	.083	9.40	.949	.906	3.58
4	4.125	3.935	.095	12.2	1.08	1.03	4.66
5	5.125	4.907	.109	18.9	1.34	1.28	6.66
6	6.125	5.881	.122	27.2	1.60	1.54	8.92
8	8.125	7.785	.170	47.6	2.13	2.04	16.5
10	10.125	9.701	.212	73.9	2.65	2.54	25.6
12	12.125	11.617	.254	106.	3.17	3.04	36.7
	TYPE DWV						
1¼	1.375	1.295	.040	1.32	.360	.339	.65
1½	1.625	1.541	.042	1.87	.425	.403	.81
2	2.125	2.041	.042	3.27	.556	.534	1.07
3	3.125	3.030	.045	7.21	.818	.793	1.69
4	4.125	4.009	.058	12.6	1.08	1.05	2.87
5	5.125	4.981	.072	19.5	1.34	1.30	4.43
6	6.125	5.959	.083	27.9	1.60	1.56	6.10
8	8.125	7.907	.109	49.1	2.13	2.07	10.6

FIG. 4–2. *Opposite, and above:* Physical characteristics of copper tubing in plumbing sizes. Courtesy Copper Development Association.

refrigeration field service. For this use a sealed, dehydrated tube is provided. Its size is designated by the actual *outside* diameter and it is available in 20-foot (6.1m) lengths in drawn temper or 50-foot (15.24m) coils of soft temper. It is appropriate for use in any portion of a flat-plate solar-system circuit.

Of the many plastics from which pipe and tubing are made, only a few are in widespread use in the plumbing trade (Fig. 4–3). Polyvinyl chloride (PVC) pipe is the most universally used plastic, although its use is limited to applications where the fluid temperature is below 150°F (65.6°C). Chlorinated polyvinyl chloride (CPVC) pipe, with a service temperature limit of 170°F (76.7°C), sometimes is used for domestic hot-water piping. This limit is too low for most solar circuits, where liquid temperature may be 200°F (93.3°C) or more.

Size, inches	Nominal Dimensions, inches			Calculated Values, Based on Nominal Dimensions			
	Outside Diameter	Inside Diameter	Wall Thickness	Cross Sectional Area of Bore, sq inches	External Surface, sq ft per lin ft	Internal Surface, sq ft per lin ft	pounds per lin ft
⅛	.125	.065	.030	.00332	.0327	.0170	.0347
3⁄16	.188	.128	.030	.0129	.0492	.0335	.0577
¼	.250	.190	.030	.0284	.0655	.0497	.0804
5⁄16	.312	.248	.032	.0483	.0817	.0649	.109
⅜	.375	.315	.030	.0780	.0982	.0821	.126
⅜	.375	.311	.032	.0760	.0982	.0814	.134
½	.500	.436	.032	.149	.131	.114	.182
½	.500	.430	.035	.145	.131	.113	.198
⅝	.625	.555	.035	.242	.164	.145	.251
⅝	.625	.545	.040	.233	.164	.143	.285
¾	.750	.666	.042	.348	.196	.174	.362
⅞	.875	.785	.045	.484	.229	.206	.455
1⅛	1.125	1.025	.050	.825	.294	.268	.655
1⅜	1.375	1.265	.055	1.26	.360	.331	.884
1⅝	1.625	1.505	.060	1.78	.425	.394	1.14
2⅛	2.125	1.985	.070	3.09	.556	.520	1.75
2⅝	2.625	2.465	.080	4.77	.687	.645	2.48
3⅛	3.125	2.945	.090	6.81	.818	.771	3.33
3⅝	3.625	3.425	.100	9.21	.949	.897	4.29
4⅛	4.125	3.905	.110	12.0	1.08	1.02	5.38

NOTE: Sizes shown in bold face type are available in annealed temper only; sizes shown in italics are available in hard temper only, all others in both.

FIG. 4–3. Physical characteristics of copper tubing in air-conditioning and refrigeration sizes. Courtesy Copper Development Association.

Both of these pipes are manufactured to meet the specifications of ASTM Schedule 40. Their light weight, low cost, and ease of fabrication make them desirable substitutes for either steel or copper where temperatures permit. However, their low flexural strength and brittleness require additional support and protection from mechanical damage.

Although, strictly speaking, they are neither pipe nor tube, some plastic hoses are used in solar systems, especially for joining adjacent collectors in the array. Since plastic hose is attached by hose clamps, it offers the advantage of easy and nondestructive disassembly. Polyethylene hose should not be used for such purposes, since the hydrogen–carbon bond is destroyed by ultraviolet photons, but silicone tubing is an excellent choice. Except for its cost, this tubing could be used throughout the circuit.

FITTINGS

A wide variety of fittings is available for joining pipe and tubing and for altering the direction and sizes (Fig. 4–4). A *coupling* is used for joining two consecutive lengths. Short pieces of pipe and tubing are called *nipples*. When two pieces of threaded pipe are joined and neither can be turned, a *union* is used. This fitting consists of two halves; one end is threaded to mate with a pipe and the other end has a ground seat. The two halves are joined by a nut that pulls the two halves together and forms a compression joint. Even in tubing circuits, unions frequently are installed at pumps, valves, and heat exchangers to allow for their easy removal for repair or replacement. Other fittings include *elbows* of 45°, 90°, 180° to allow

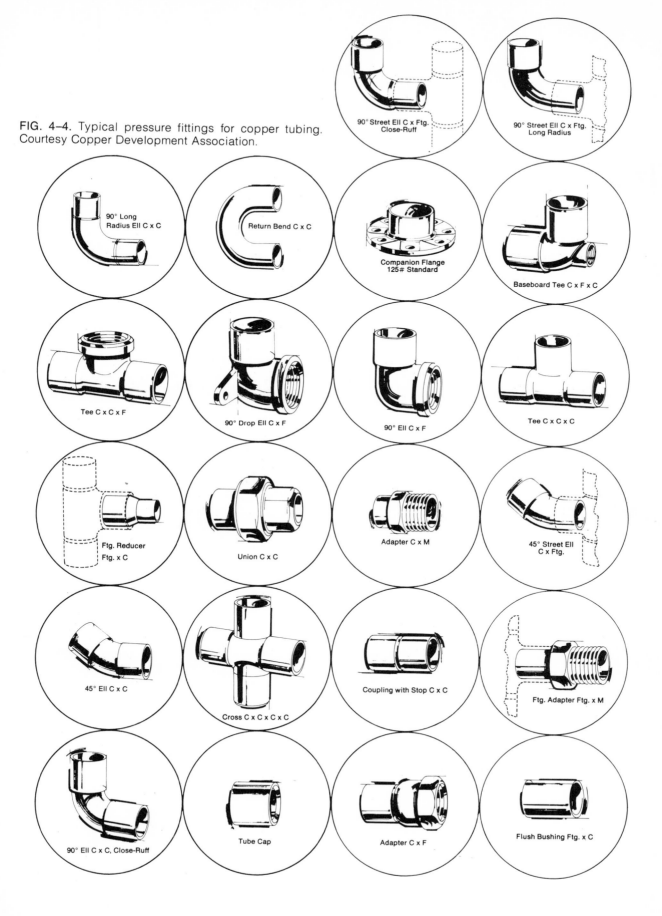

FIG. 4–4. Typical pressure fittings for copper tubing. Courtesy Copper Development Association.

90° Street Ell C x Ftg. Close-Ruff

90° Street Ell C x Ftg. Long Radius

90° Long Radius Ell C x C

Return Bend C x C

Companion Flange 125# Standard

Baseboard Tee C x F x C

Tee C x C x F

90° Drop Ell C x F

90° Ell C x F

Tee C x C x C

Ftg. Reducer Ftg. x C

Union C x C

Adapter C x M

45° Street Ell C x Ftg.

45° Ell C x C

Cross C x C x C x C

Coupling with Stop C x C

Ftg. Adapter Ftg. x M

90° Ell C x C, Close-Ruff

Tube Cap

Adapter C x F

Flush Bushing Ftg. x C

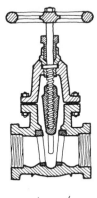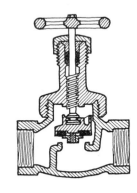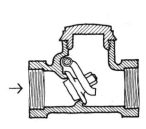

gate valve   globe valve   check valve

FIG. 4–5. Typical valve types.

change of direction, as well as *tees, crosses,* and *reducers,* or combinations. *Caps* and *plugs* also are available. *Adapters* are used to allow tubing to be joined to threaded connections.

Valves are employed to control the flow of liquid in piping systems (Fig. 4–5). *Gate valves* are used in those instances in which the flow is full on or completely off. For this valve, the body contains two seats arranged so their faces form a small angle. The gate, which is wedge-shaped with a similar angle, lowers against these faces to stop the flow completely. A handle on a threaded screw raises and lowers the gate. The handle itself may or may not rise during operation, depending on design.

Globe valves are used to modulate the amount of flow. Liquid makes two 90° turns while passing through the valve body. Between these two turns is the valve seat, against which a washer on the end of the valve stem can mate. Raising or lowering the washer controls the liquid flow. Other types of globe valves are available, including a 90° pattern, and one in which a drilled spherical gate is employed.

Check valves control the direction of flow of liquid. Reversal of flow during nonsunshine hours can waste thermal energy in storage, so that their use is mandatory for our systems. These valves are made in several patterns, but the swing check valve may serve as an example. It has a hinged disk mounted in a straight bore. When liquid flows in the desired direction, it rises in a vertical arc to allow passage. When the flow is reversed, gravity allows it to swing shut. An arrow on the valve body indicates direction of flow, and valves *must* be installed correctly. Some check valves operate only when installed in horizontal piping, while others may be installed in any position.

Flow-control valves are usually necessary in solar systems to control the flow to predetermined specifications. Sometimes it is necessary to adjust the flow in two or more branches served by a single supply. Various flow-control valves are available to meet this need.

The Thermoflo balancer, manufactured by Bell and Gossett, is one such device (Fig. 4–6). It is available in ¾-inch (19.1mm) size for flow rates of 0 to 5 gpm (gallons per minute) (18.9 liters/min), and 1-inch (25.4mm) size for flow rates of 0 to 10 gpm (37.85 liters/min). The device consists of a calibrated glass tube through which flow rates can be observed, and a slotted-head valve that controls the flow. An advantage of this device is the ease with which flow rates can be visually deter-

FIG. 4–6. Thermoflo control valve.
Courtesy Bell and Gossett.

FIG. 4–7. Circuit Setter flow-control valve.
Courtesy Bell and Gossett.

FIG. 4–8. Flow-control valve with rate preset at the
factory. Courtesy Griswold Controls.

mined. An inherent disadvantage is the inaccuracies that may be introduced because of scale buildup in the internal components of the device.

Other flow-control devices are more accurate, but in general cannot be read directly. Bell and Gossett manufactures one that can, the Circuit Setter (Fig. 4–7). This device consists of an accurately broached cylindrical orifice in a spherical gate whose angular position may be ascertained by an external pointer. Pressure taps on either side of the valve and a handy circular "slide rule" allow one to calculate flow rates to a high degree of accuracy. A necessary adjunct to this device is a special instrument for detecting differential pressures.

A similar device is offered by Griswold Controls

as its automatic pressure-compensating constant-flow control valve (Fig. 4–8). Although no special equipment is required to monitor its flow, it is necessary to prespecify size of piping, flow rate, and temperature, viscosity, and specific gravity of the fluid.

Similar devices are offered by other manufacturers. None of these costs enough to preclude its inclusion in any solar energy system.

PIPE JOINTS

Pipe may be joined by bolted flanged connections, by butt welding, or by the use of screwed fittings. The first two methods are ordinarily used only on pipes of large diameter. Screwed joints are made with American National Pipe Taper Thread (NPT). When pipe is threaded, a burr is left on its inner edge. This burr must be removed before joining so there is minimum resistance to flow.

Pipe is not used very often for small solar applications. Copper or brass pipe is very expensive. Since most collectors have copper fluid passages, the use of ferrous pipe requires the inclusion of dielectric unions. Pipe is much heavier than tubing. Threaded joints are more expensive than soldered joints.

None of these remarks should be taken to mean that systems using tubing will not also include some threaded joints. Many pumps are built with threaded suction and discharge ports. Threaded wells for in-line temperature sensors or thermometers may be needed. Some valves are available only with threaded joints.

Threaded joints may be incorporated into a tubing system by the use of adapters, either C × M or C × F as appropriate. All threaded joints should be sealed. Pipe-joint compound was formerly used for this purpose. Now it has been replaced by Teflon tape. At least three loops of the tape should be placed around the male threads of a joint and pressed into them before completing the joint.

Although it is not done very often, copper tube can be joined without the use of fittings by butt welding. Mechanical joints utilizing compression (flared) fittings may be employed for joints that may have to be disconnected or where a fire hazard may be present so that heat cannot be used. Otherwise, tubing is joined by soldering (sweating) or brazing (often incorrectly called silver soldering).

SOLDERS Soldered joints depend on capillary action drawing free-flowing molten solder into the gap between the fitting and the tube. Flux, applied first, acts as a cleaning and wetting agent and, when properly applied, permits uniform spreading of the molten solder over the surfaces to be soldered. Capillary action is most effective when the space between the surfaces to be joined is between .002 and .004 inch (.05 and .13mm).

The selection of a solder depends on the operating pressure and temperature of the line. As a general guide, all tube joints within the collector and joints between collectors should be brazed, and other joints made with 50-50 tin-lead or 95-5 tin-antimony solder. Consideration also should be given to the stresses on the joint caused by thermal expansion and contraction. Stresses due to temperature changes, however, should not be significant in two commonly encountered cases—when the tube lengths are short, or when expansion loops are used in long tube runs.

Rated internal working pressures for soldier-fitting joints made with 50-50 tin-lead solder and 95-5 tin-antimony solder are listed in Figure 4–9. For the average flat-plate solar system, pressure and temperature relief valves are set for 10 to 20 psi (pounds per square inch).

The 50-50 tin-lead solder is suitable for moderate pressures and temperatures. For higher pressures, or where greater joint strength is required, 95-5 tin-antimony solder should be used. For continuous operation at temperatures exceeding 250°F (121.1°C) or where the highest joint strength is required, brazing filler metals should be used.

Solder of 40 percent tin and 60 percent lead has been used for plumbing applications with a reasonable degree of success. It is, however, somewhat less easy to use than the more popular 50-50 solder. The 95-5 tin-antimony solder is more difficult to use, as it melts at a slightly higher temperature than does the 50-50 solder and has a very narrow solidification range.

Solder generally is used in wire form, but paste-type solders also are available. These are finely granulated solder in suspension with a paste flux. When using a paste-type solder, observe these four rules:

1. Wire-type solder must be applied in addition to the paste to fill the voids and assist in displacing the flux; otherwise, the surfaces may be well tinned and yet there may not be a good joint with continuous bond.
2. The paste mixture must be thoroughly stirred if it has been standing in the can for a time,

Alloy Used for Joints	Service Temperature, °F	Environment					
		Water and Non-Corrosive Liquids and Gases					Saturated Steam
		Tube Size, Types K, L and M (in inches)					
		¼ to 1 Incl.	1¼ to 2 Incl.	2½ to 4 Incl.	5 to 8 Incl.	10 to 12 Incl.	All
50–50 Tin-Lead Solder(a)	100	200	175	150	130	100	—
	150	150	125	100	90	70	—
	200	100	90	75	70	50	—
	250	85	75	50	45	40	15
95–5 Tin-Antimony Solder(a)	100	500	400	300	270	150	—
	150	400	350	275	250	150	—
	200	300	250	200	180	140	—
	250	200	175	150	135	110	15
Brazing Alloys (Melting at or above 1000 F)	100–150–200	(b)	(b)	(b)	(b)	(b)	—
	250	300	210	170	150	150	—
	350	270	190	150	150	150	120

NOTE: Ratings up to 8 inches are those given in ANSI Standard B16.22 "Wrought Copper and Bronze Solder-Joint Pressure Fittings" and ANSI B16.18 "Cast Bronze Solder-Joint Pressure Fittings."

(a) Solder alloys are covered by ASTM Standard Specification B32.
(b) Rated internal pressure is that of tube being joined; see Tables 9 and 10.

FIG. 4–9. Rated internal working pressure for copper-tube joints. Courtesy Copper Development Association.

as the solder may settle to the bottom.
3. The flux cannot be depended on to clean the tube. Cleaning should be done manually as is recommended for any other flux or solder.
4. Remove any excess flux.

Solders are available containing small amounts of silver or other additives to impart special properties. Such solders may require special fluxes. The manufacturer's recommendations should be consulted regarding proper procedures and fluxes for such solders and the expected properties.

The functions of the soldering flux are to remove residual traces of oxides, to promote wetting, and to protect the surfaces to be soldered from oxidation during heating. The flux should be applied to clean surfaces, and only enough should be used to lightly coat the areas to be joined.

An oxide film may re-form quickly on copper after it has been cleaned. Therefore, the flux should be applied as soon as possible after cleaning.

The fluxes best suited to the 50-50 and 95-5 solders are mildly corrosive liquid- or petroleum-based pastes containing chlorides of zinc and ammonium.

Most liquid fluxes are so-called self-cleaning fluxes and their use involves a risk. Some paste-type fluxes are also identified by their manufacturers as "self-cleaning," and there is similar risk in their use. There is no doubt that a strong corrosive flux can remove some oxides and dirt films. However, when highly corrosive fluxes are used this way, there is always an uncertainty as to whether or not uniform cleaning has been achieved and whether corrosive action continues after the soldering has been completed.

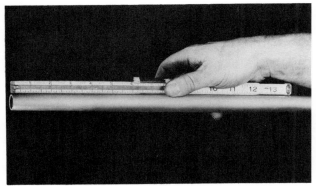

FIG. 4–10. Measuring the tube.

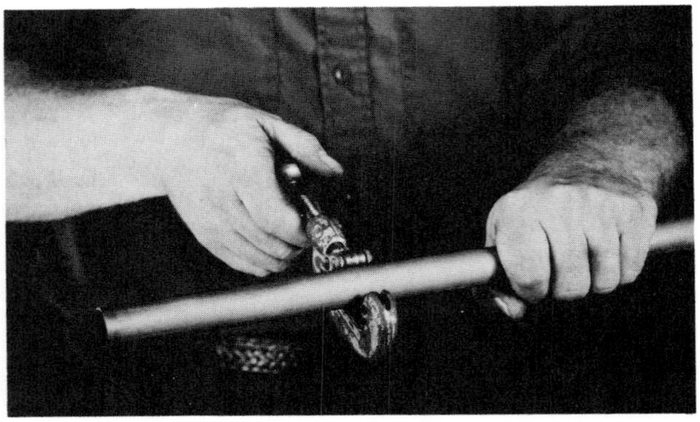

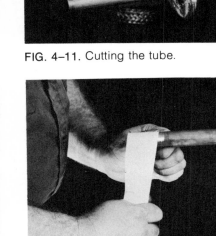

FIG. 4–11. Cutting the tube.

FIG. 4–12. Reaming the cut end.

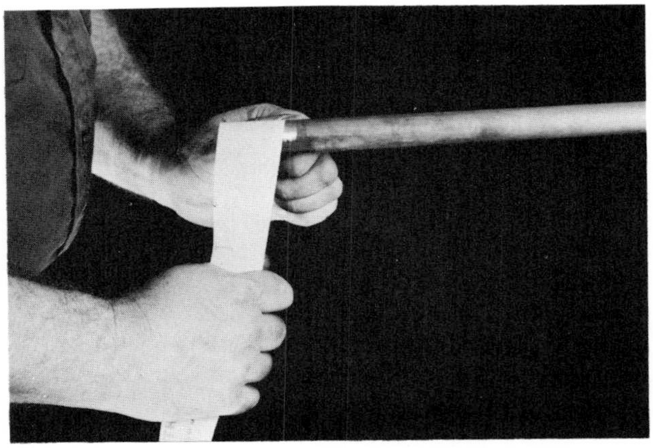

FIG. 4–13. Cleaning tube end.

MAKING SOLDER JOINTS

There are twelve simple steps in making a solder joint:

1. Measure length of tube
2. Cut tube square
3. Ream cut end
4. Clean tube end
5. Clean fitting socket
6. Apply flux to tube end
7. Apply flux to fitting socket
8. Assemble
9. Remove excess flux
10. Apply heat
11. Apply solder
12. Allow joint to cool

Although these operations are simple in themselves, they make the difference between good joints and poor ones. Most of these steps take less time to perform than to describe. For best results none should be omitted.

MEASURING   Measuring the length of the tube is actually a preliminary to the soldering job, but inaccuracy can affect joint quality. If a piece of tube is too short, it will not reach all the way into the socket of the fitting and a proper joint cannot be made. See Figure 4–10.

CUTTING   Tube should be cut to exact length with a square cut. Tube cutters (Fig. 4–11) generally are used for sizes up to about 1½ inches (3.8cm). Large-size cutters for tube up to 8 inches (20.3cm) are available. An alternate, but more laborious, method is to cut with a hacksaw or abrasive cutoff saw.

REAMING   The tube cutter will leave a small burr on the end of the tube, which should be removed, using the reamer attached to the cutter (Fig. 4–12) or some other appropriate tool. If the tube is cut with a hacksaw, there may be both burrs and slivers, both of which should be removed.

If the tube is out-of-round, as may happen when a soft-temper tube coil has been straightened, it can be brought to true dimension and roundness with a sizing tool, which consists of a plug and sizing ring.

CLEANING Surfaces to be joined must be clean and free from oil, grease, and heavy oxide. The end of the tube should be cleaned for a distance only slightly more than is required to enter the socket of the fitting (Fig. 4–13). Fine emery cloth (2/0), cleaning pads, or special wire brushes may be used. Rub hard enough to remove the surface film or soil, but not hard enough to remove metal. Tube and fittings are made to close tolerances, and abrasive cleaning should not remove a significant amount of metal. If much metal is removed during cleaning, the capillary space may become so large that a poor joint will result. If the cleaning is done on work in place, care should be taken that particles of materials do not fall into the tube or fitting.

The socket of the fitting should be similarly cleaned, and the same precautions observed (Fig. 4–14).

FLUXING As soon as possible after cleaning, the surfaces to be joined should be covered with a thin film of flux (Figs. 4–15 and 4–16). The preferred flux is one that is mildly corrosive, containing zinc and ammonium chlorides. In some paste fluxes the chemicals have a tendency to settle during long standing, so the paste should be stirred thoroughly when a new can is opened, or when an opened can has been standing more than a few hours. The flux can be applied with a small brush or clean rag. Since rags are apt to pick up dirt, they should be changed frequently. Avoid using your fingers to apply flux. The flux could accidentally be carried to your eyes and prove very harmful. Particular care should be exercised to avoid leaving excess flux inside the completed joint.

FIG. 4–14. Cleaning fitting socket.

FIG. 4–15. Fluxing tube end.

FIG. 4–16. Fluxing fitting socket.

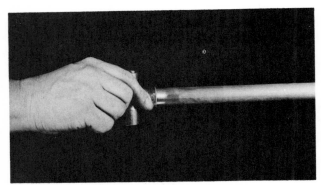
FIG. 4–17. Assembling fitting and tube.

FIG. 4–18. Removing excess flux.

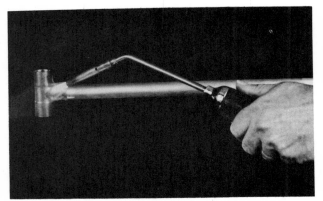
FIG. 4–19. Heating the assembly.

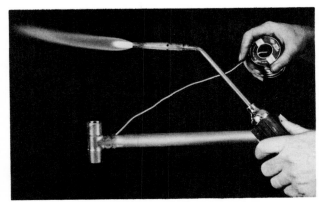
FIG. 4–20. Applying solder.

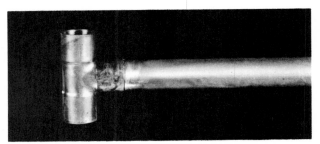
FIG. 4–21. The finished joint. All photos courtesy Copper Development Association.

ASSEMBLING Assemble the joint by inserting the tube into the fitting socket, making sure that the tube is firmly against the end of the socket (Fig. 4–17). A twist will help spread the flux over the two surfaces. Remove excess flux with a rag (Fig. 4–18). The joint now is ready for soldering.

It frequently is the practice to clean, flux, and assemble a series of joints before soldering. However, assembling joints more than two or three hours ahead of soldering should be avoided. The fluxed assembly should never be left overnight before soldering.

APPLYING HEAT AND SOLDER Heat usually is applied with a propane, butane, or Mapp gas torch, or with an air-acetylene or an oxyacetylene torch. Small propane torches sold in hardware and discount stores perform well for small tube diameters and may be used for tube sizes as large as 1 inch (2.54cm). A larger torch, however, or one that

Tube Size, inches	Solder Required,* pounds	Flux Required,* ounces
¼ – ⅝	½	1
¾ & 1	¾	1½
1¼ & 1½	1	2
2	2	4
2½	2½	5
3	3	6
3½	3½	7
4	4	8
5	7	14
6	10	20
8	16	32

FIG. 4–22. Typical consumption of 95-5 tin-antimony solder per 100 joints. Includes an allowance of 100 percent to cover wastage and loss for tube sizes up to 2 inches and 25 percent for tube sizes 2½ inches and larger. Courtesy Copper Development Association.

burns at a high temperature (Mapp gas or acetylene), will prove a definite time-saver for most installations.

The flame is played on the fitting and moved in order to heat as large an area as possible (Fig. 4–19). Do not point the flame into the socket. Avoid overheating, which will burn the flux and destroy its effectiveness. If the flux has been burned, the solder will not enter the joint, and the joint must be opened, recleaned, and refluxed. Cast fittings should not be overheated, because they might crack.

When the joint is hot enough, the solder will melt on contact with the tube and the flame should be moved away (Fig. 4–20). If the solder does not melt, remove it, continue to heat the tube, then try again. For large fittings, a multiple-tip or ring-type torch may be useful. After the initial application of solder, complete penetration and filling of the joint can be effected by alternating applications of heat and solder. The completed joint is shown in Figure 4–21.

Opinions differ as to when a solder fillet is necessary or desirable. Unless specifications require fillets, they should be omitted.

If the metal is properly cleaned and fluxed, capillary action should draw all the solder needed into the joint. Pretinning is not necessary and generally is not recommended for the tube sizes ordinarily used in our kind of solar installations. Pretinning

actually may interfere to some extent with the capillary action.

Remember that soldered joints depend on capillary action drawing free-flowing molten solder into the narrow clearance between the fitting and the tube. Flux, applied first, acts as a cleaning and wetting agent and, when properly applied, permits uniform spreading of the molten solder over the surfaces to be soldered. As previously stated, capillary action is most effective when the space between the surfaces to be joined is between .002 and .005 inch (.05 and .13mm). A certain amount of looseness of fit can be tolerated, but a loose fit can cause difficulties with large-size fittings.

For joining copper tube to solder-cup valves, follow the manufacturer's instructions. The valve should be in the full-open position before applying heat, and the heat should be applied to the tube only.

The amount of solder consumed when adequately filling the capillary space between the tube and either wrought or cast fittings may be estimated from Figure 4–22. The flux requirement usually is 2 ounces per pound (125 gram/kg) of solder.

MAKING BRAZED JOINTS

All tube connections within the collector should be brazed. Sometimes it is necessary to join two tubes

MANUFACTURER	AWS CLASSIFICATION							
	BCuP-2	BCuP-3	BCuP-4	BCuP-5	BAg1*	BAg2*	BAg5	BAg7
Air Products	Air Products BCuP-2	Air Products BCuP-3	—	Air Products BCuP-5	Air Products BAg-1	Air Products BAg-2	—	—
Airco Welding Products	Airco Phos-Copper Rod	Aircosil 5, Airco Phos-Silver 6M	Airco Phos-Silver 6	Aircosil 15	Aircosil 45	Aircosil 35	Aircosil G	Aircosil J
All-State Welding Alloys Co., Inc.	All-State No. 21, All-State Silflo 0	All-State Silflo 5	All-State No. 29	All-State Silflo 15	All-State No. 101			All-State No. 155
Alloy Ring Service, Inc.	Ag 0	Ag-5	Ag-6	Ag-15	Ag-45	Ag-35	Ag-45-3	Ag-56
Allweld Equipment Corporation	Phos-Braze No. 0	Phos-Braze No. 6	Phos-Braze No. 6A	Phos-Braze No. 15	Phos-Braze No. 45	Phos-Braze No. 35	—	Allweld No. 56
American Brazing Alloys Corp.	Ambraze Phos Sil 0	Ambraze Phos Sil 6	Ambraze Phos Sil 6F	Ambraze Phos Sil 15	Ambraze 45 Sil Solder	Ambraze 35 Sil Solder	—	—
American Platinum & Silver Div. of Engelhard Ind., Inc.	—	Silvaloy 5	Silvaloy 672	Silvaloy 15	Silvaloy 45	Silvaloy 35	Silvaloy A-18	Silvaloy 355
American Smelting & Refining Co.	Asarco No. 1300	Asarco No. 1220-5	Asarco No. 1220-6	Asarco No. 1180	Asarco No. 45	Asarco No. 35	Asarco No. 145	—
Anchor Alloys Co.	Shurbond -0	Shurbond -5	—	Shurbond -15	Shurbond -45	Shurbond -503	Shurbond A-25	Shurbond 301
Aufhauser Bros. Corp.	Aufhauser BCuP-2	Aufhauser BCuP-3	Aufhauser BCuP-4	Aufhauser BCuP-5	Aufhauser BAg-1	Aufhauser BAg-2	Aufhauser BAg-5	Aufhauser BAg-7
Belmont Smelting & Refining Works Inc.	—	Sil-Fos 5	—	Sil-Fos	Easy-Flo 45	Easy-Flo 35	Braze-DE	Braze 560
Canadian Liquid Air Ltd.	Fos-Flo	Sil-Fos 5	—	Sil-Fos	Easy-Flo 45	Easy-Flo 35	Braze DE	Braze 560
Fusion Inc.	SP-2-1300	SP-5-1300	SP-6-1300	SP-15-1300	STD-1000	STD-1100	STD-1250	STD-1205
Gases Agamex, S.A.	AGA-SUTEC Var 282	AGA-SUTEC Var 283	—	AGA-SUTEC Var-283-15	AGA-SUTEC Var 2800	AGA-SUTEC Var 2601	—	—
Goldsmith Div. National Lead Co.	GB No. 1300	GB No. 5	GB No. 6	GB No. 15	GB No. 45	GB No. 35	GB No. 145	GB No. 56
Handy & Harman	—	Sil-Fos 5	—	Sil-Fos	Easy-Flo 45	Easy-Flo 35	Braze DE	Braze 560
J. W. Harris Co. Inc.	Stay-Silv 0	Stay-Silv 5	—	Stay-Silv 15	Stay-Silv 45	Stay-Silv 35	—	—
Marquette Corp.	—	—	—	No. 1300	No. 1175	No. 35	No. 145	No. 56
National Cylinder Gas Div. of Chemetron Corp.	—	Sil-Fos 5	—	Sil-Fos	Easy-Flo 45	Easy-Flo 35	—	—
Pacific Welding Alloys Mfg. Co.	Pacific BCuP-2	Pacific BCuP-3	Pacific BCuP-4	Pacific BCuP-5	Pacific BAg-1	Pacific BAg-2	Pacific BAg-5	Pacific BAg-7
Perma-Latem Welding Alloys, Inc.	Perma-Loy 291	—	Perma-Loy 294	Perma-Loy 299	Perma-Sil No. 3	Perma-Sil No. 4	Perma-Sil No. 16	Perma-Sil No. 19
Special Chemicals Corp.	Speksolder 1485	Speksolder 1300	—	Speksolder 1300P	Speksolder 1145	Speksolder 1295	Speksolder 1370	Speksolder 1205

FIG. 4-23.

MANUFACTURER	AWS CLASSIFICATION							
	BCuP-2	BCuP-3	BCuP-4	BCuP-5	BAg1*	BAg2*	BAg5	BAg7
Super Tecnica, S.A.	SUTEC-VAR 282	SUTEC-VAR 283	—	SUTEC-VAR 283-15	SUTEC-VAR 2800	SUTEC-VAR 2601	—	—
Tricon Brazing Alloys	—	SF No. 5	—	SF No. 15	EF No. 45	EF No. 35	DE	560
United States Silver Corp.	Unibraze Phos Sil -0	Unibraze Phos Sil -6	Unibraze Phos Sil -6F	Unibraze Phos Sil -15	Unibraze 45 Sil-Solder	Unibraze 35 Sil-Solder	—	—
United States Welding Alloys Corp.	US Copper Phos 0	US Silver Phos 5	US Silver Phos 6	US Silver Phos 15	US Silver 45	US Silver 35	US Silver 150	US Silver 156
United Wire & Supply Corp.	Phoson 0	Phoson 5	Phoson 6-7	Phoson 15	Sil Bond 45	Sil Bond 35	Sil 45	Silver 56T
Welco Alloys Corp.	—	—	—	—	—	Welco 204 FC	Welco #201	Welco #200
Westinghouse Electric Corp.	Phos-Copper	Phos Silver 5	Phos Silver 6	Phos Silver 15	Co Silver 45C	Co Silver 35C	Co Silver 45	Co Silver 56

SOURCE: AWS A5, 0-66 "Filter Metal Comparison Charts," American Welding Society, Miami, Florida.

The information in this comparison chart has been obtained from the manufacturer or supplier of the particular filler metal at the time of issue. Neither the American Welding Society nor the Copper Development Association Inc. assumes responsibility for the accuracy of the listings. Filler metals are not "approved" by the American Welding Society or by the Copper Development Association Inc. The manufacturer or supplier should be consulted regarding his guarantee of compliance to specifications.
*WARNING: BAg1 and BAg2 contain cadmium. Heating when brazing can produce toxic fumes. Avoid breathing fumes. Use adequate ventilation.

FIG. 4–23. *Opposite, and above:* Trade names for brazing filler metals. Courtesy Copper Development Association.

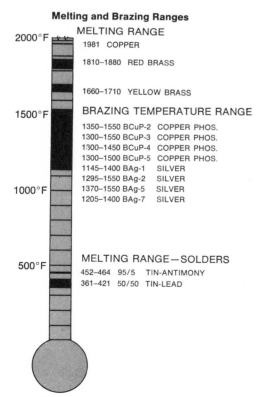

Melting and Brazing Ranges

FIG. 4–24. Brazing parameters. Courtesy Copper Development Association.

without a fitting or to repair a hole in the tube. These operations also can be performed by brazing.

Brazed connections for copper tube may be made by brazing with filler metals that melt at temperatures in the range between 1,100° and 1,500°F (593°–816°C). Brazing filler metals sometimes are referred to as "hard solders" or "silver solders"—confusing terms that should be avoided.

The temperature at which filler metal starts to melt on heating is known as the solidus temperature; the liquidus temperature is the higher temperature at which the filler metal is completely melted. The liquidus temperature is the minimum temperature at which brazing will take place. The difference between solidus and liquidus is known as the melting range and may be of importance when selecting a filler. It indicates the width of the working range for the alloy and the speed with which the alloy will become fully solid after brazing. Narrow ranges require more care and solidify more quickly. The melting ranges of common brazing alloys are shown in Figure 4–24.

Brazing filler metals suitable for joining copper tubes are of two classes: alloys containing 30 to 60 percent silver (the BAg series) and copper alloys that contain phosphorus (the BCu series), as shown in Figure 4–23. The two classes differ in their melting, fluxing, and flowing characteristics, and these should be considered in the selection of a filler metal. For joining copper tube, any of these metals will provide the necessary strength when used with standard solder-type fittings.

The strength of a brazed copper-tube joint does not vary much with the different filler metals, but depends mainly on maintaining the proper clearance between the outside of the tube and the socket of the fitting. Copper tube and solder-type fittings are accurately made for each other, and the tolerances permitted for each assure that the capillary space will be within the limits necessary for a joint of satisfactory strength. The rated internal working pressures for brazed lines are shown in Figure 4–9. These pressure ratings, however, should be used only when a fitting made to close tolerances has been used and the correct capillary space has been maintained.

In preparing to braze a joint, the preliminary steps of tube measuring, cutting, removing burrs, and cleaning are identical to the steps in the soldering process. Tube ends and sockets must be thoroughly cleaned before beginning the brazing operation.

Best results will be obtained by the step-by-step brazing procedure that follows.

FLUXING Fluxing should be done in accordance with the recommendations of the manufacturer of the brazing filler metal being used. The flux is applied with a brush to the cleaned area of the tube end and the fitting socket (Fig. 4–25). If the outside of the fitting and the heat-affected area of the tube are covered with flux, it will prevent oxidation and greatly improve the appearance of that joint. Avoid getting flux inside the tube itself.

Flux may be omitted when joining copper tubes to wrought-copper fittings with copper-phosphorus alloys (BCu series), which are self-fluxing on copper. Fluxes are required for joining to cast (bronze) fittings.

The filler metals most commonly used in plumbing, piping, and air conditioning are BCuP-4 (for

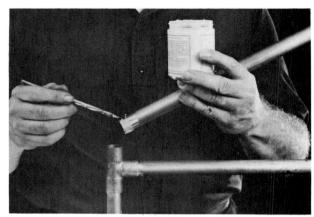

FIG. 4–25. Fluxing the tube.

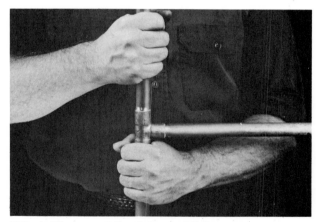

FIG. 4–26. Assembling tube and fitting.

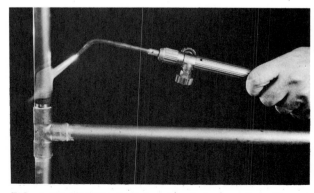

FIG. 4–27. Heating the tube. All photos courtesy Copper Development Association.

close tolerances), BCuP-5 (where close tolerances cannot be held), and BAg-1. Since BAg-1 contains cadmium, brazing with it can produce toxic fumes. Use adequate ventilation.

ASSEMBLING Assemble the joint by inserting the tube into the socket hard against the stop and turn it if possible (Fig. 4–26). The assembly should be firmly supported so that it will remain in alignment during the brazing operation.

APPLYING HEAT AND BRAZING Proceed as follows:

1. Apply heat to the parts to be joined, preferably with an oxyacetylene flame. Air-acetylene sometimes is used on smaller sizes. A slightly reducing (excess acetylene) flame should be used, with a feather on the inner blue cone; the outer portion of the flame should be white. Heat the tube first, beginning about an inch from the edge of the fitting, sweeping the flame around the tube in short strokes at right angles to the axis of the tube (Fig. 4–27). It is very important that the flame be in motion continuously and not remain on any one point long enough to damage the tube. The flux may be used as a guide as to how long to heat the tube; continue heating the tube until the flux becomes quiet and transparent, like clear water. The behavior of the flux during the brazing cycle is described in Figure 4–28.

2. Switch the flame to the fitting at the base of the cup (Fig. 4–29). Heat uniformly, sweeping the flame from the fitting to the tube until the flux on the fitting becomes quiet. Avoid excessive heating of cast fittings.

3. When the flux appears liquid and transparent on both tube and fitting, start sweeping the flame back and forth along the axis of the joint to maintain heat on the parts to be joined, especially toward the base of the cup of the fitting. The flame must be kept moving to avoid burning the tube or fitting.

4. Apply the brazing wire, rod, or strip at a point where the tube enters the socket of the fitting (Fig. 4–30). When the proper temperature is reached, the filler metal will flow readily into the space be-

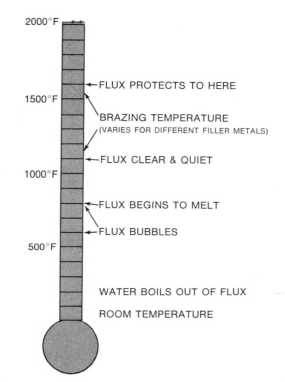

FIG. 4–28. Behavior of flux during brazing cycle. Courtesy Copper Development Association.

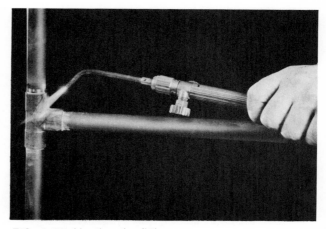

FIG. 4–29. Heating the fitting.

tween the tube and the fitting socket, drawn in by the natural force of capillary attraction. Keep the flame away from the rod or wire itself as it is fed into the joint. The temperature of the joint itself should be hot enough to melt the filler metal. Keep both the fitting and tube heated by moving the flame back and forth from one to the other as the filler metal is drawn into the joint. Stop feeding as soon as the joint is filled. Figure 4–22 is a guide for estimating how much filler metal will be consumed, along with the torch-tip sizes and gas settings.

For 1-inch (25.4mm) tube and larger it may be difficult to bring the whole joint up to temperature at one time. It frequently will be found desirable to use a multiple-tip torch to maintain the proper temperature over the large area. A mild preheating of the whole fitting is recommended for larger sizes. Heating then can proceed as outlined in the steps above. If difficulty is encountered in getting the entire joint up to the desired temperature at one time, a portion of the joint can be heated and brazed at a time, proceeding by segments progressively all around the joint.

HORIZONTAL AND VERTICAL JOINTS When making horizontal joints it is preferable to apply the filler metal first at the bottom, then at the two sides, and finally at the top, making sure the operations overlap. On vertical joints it is immaterial where the start is made. If the opening of the socket is pointing down (Fig. 4–31), care should be taken to avoid overheating the tube, as this may cause the brazing alloy to run down the outside of the tube. If this happens, take the heat away and allow the alloy to set. Then reheat the cup of the fitting to draw up the alloy.

REMOVING RESIDUE After the brazing alloy has solidified, clean off flux residue with a wet brush or swab (Fig. 4–32). Wrought fittings may be chilled quickly; however, it is advisable to allow cast fittings to cool naturally to some extent before wetting. You can see what the completed brazed joint looks like in Figure 4–33, on the next page.

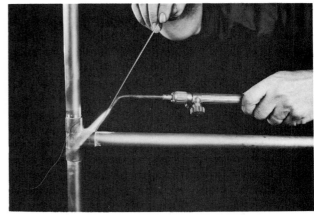

FIG. 4–30. Feeding brazing alloy to horizontal joint.

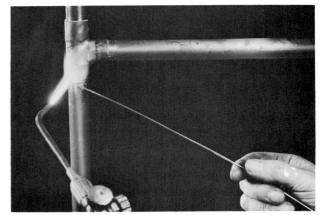

FIG. 4–31. Feeding brazing alloy upward into vertical joint.

FIG. 4–32. Removing residue.

FIG. 4–33. Completed brazed joint. All photos courtesy Copper Development Association.

GENERAL HINTS AND SUGGESTIONS If the filler metal fails to flow or has a tendency to ball up, it indicates oxidation of the metal surfaces, or insufficient heat on the parts to be joined. If work starts to oxidize during heating, there is too little flux. If the filler metal does not enter the joint and tends to flow over the outside of either member of the joint, it indicates that one member is overheated and the other is underheated.

TESTING JOINTS

Any prudent person will test a joint before attempting to put it into service. An ideal situation would be one in which each joint could be tested immediately after it was completed. Unfortunately, such a procedure is impractical. However, it may be prudent to test individual subassemblies before incorporating them into the whole system.

For example, if collectors are locally fabricated, then the riser-manifold assembly should be tested before attaching it to the absorber sheet. Likewise, if a heat exchanger is locally fabricated, then later inconvenience may be avoided if it is tested before inclusion in the circuit.

A large number of connections is necessary for any flat-plate solar-energy collection or distribution system. It is unrealistic to assume that even the most skilled person will make all of these connections without experiencing failure of at least one joint.

If liquid is used for testing, the first filling should be only tapwater, since it is probable that some or all of the liquid will be wasted. If leaks are present, then their locations are easily detected by visual observation. It may be necessary, however, to drain the system before any corrections can be made.

A preferred method is to pressurize the system with air or some inert gas such as nitrogen. Test pressures usually are in the 100 psi (45kg/6.5cm²) range, and the circuit should maintain this pressure for about twenty-four hours. If a drop in pressure is observed, then the leak location can be identified by applying a soap-and-water solution to each joint. The advantage of this method is that leaks may be corrected immediately without waiting for liquid to drain from the system.

DESIGN OF PIPING SYSTEMS

The design of a solar circuit piping system will require deciding the following:

1. Choice of fluid path through the collector array
2. Piping sizes and locations
3. Selection of pump(s), heat exchanger, valves, and controls
4. Location of valves, vents, and drains for easy maintenance and operation
5. Physical location of each of these elements for minimum interference with architectural requirements and adequate accessibility

STATIC HEAD Water weighs about 62.4 pounds per cubic foot (999.5kg/m³) at room temperature (Fig. 4–34). Therefore, a column of water 1 foot (.30m) high and 1 inch square (6.5 cm²) exerts a pressure of $\frac{62.4}{144} = .434$ psi (.031kg/cm²) on its base. Notice that columns of water 1 foot (.30m) high and ½ inch (12.5mm) round or 100 feet (30.5m) square also will exert a pressure of .434 psi (.031kg/cm²) on their bases.

As an example, suppose it is necessary to lift water in an open system from a basement storage location to the top of a roof array 32 feet (9.6m) above the storage (Fig.4–35). Then the pump must

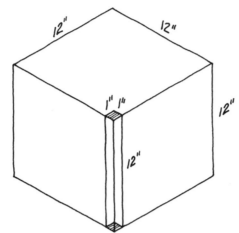

FIG. 4–34. A column of water 1 foot high exerts a pressure of .434 psi on its base.

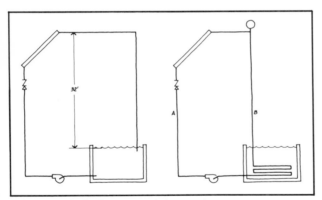

FIG. 4–35. *Left:* An open piping system.
FIG. 4–36. *Right:* A closed piping system.

supply a pressure of P = 32 ft × .434 psi/ft = 13.89 psi (.976kg/cm²), in order to lift the water this high. Additional pressure will be required to initiate and maintain flow at this height.

Notice that if this were a closed system as shown in Figure 4–36, then no pressure would be required in order to overcome the static head due to elevation. Since water is incompressible, for every drop of water being pushed upward at point A, there also is a drop at point B pushing downward. In other words, in a closed system there is no static head due to elevation. This explains why closed systems have lower pumping requirements, and therefore lower energy inputs, than open systems.

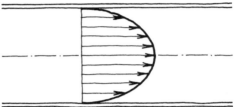

FIG. 4–37. Velocity profile for laminar flow.

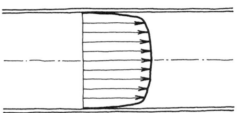

FIG. 4–38. Velocity profile for turbulent flow.

DYNAMIC HEAD When liquid flows through a pipe, the liquid film in contact with the inside surface of the pipe is, of course, at rest. Consequently, a shear force is set up in the liquid. This shear force is called pipe friction. Its magnitude is a function of the pipe length and diameter, the condition of its inside surface, and the velocity of flow, as well as the viscosity of the liquid.[2] Velocities in copper tubing should not be greater than about 8 feet per second (2.44m/sec) to assure that erosion will not be a problem.

When flow through a pipe is smooth, it is said to be laminar, and its velocity profile might appear as illustrated in Figure 4–37. At the other extreme, flow may be turbulent, in which case its velocity profile might appear as indicated in Figure 4–38. Flow between these extremes is said to be transitional. Laminar flow requires the least pumping energy, while turbulent flow provides the best heat transfer. In general, the more turbulent the flow, the better the heat transfer. Nevertheless, there comes a point of diminishing return when the additional heat transfer is offset by the extra energy required for pumping.

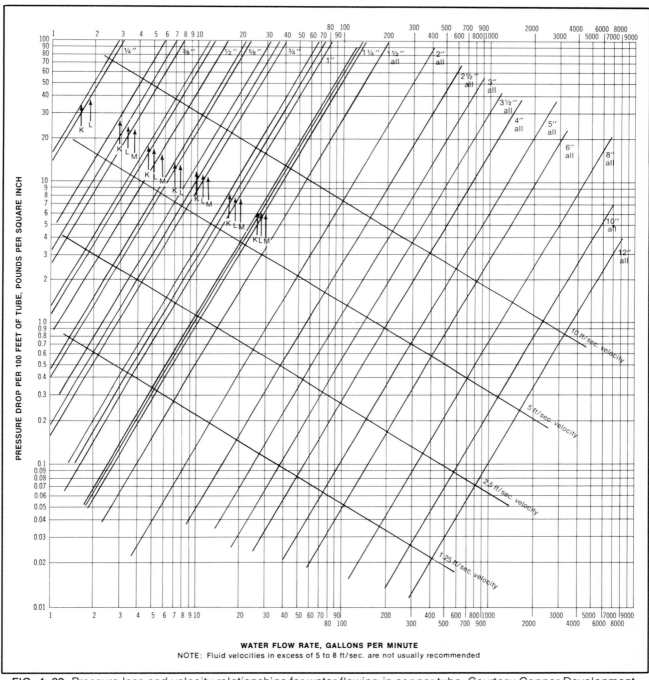

FIG. 4–39. Pressure loss and velocity relationships for water flowing in copper tube. Courtesy Copper Development Association.

Flow, gpm	Pressure Loss per 100 Feet of Tube, psi											
	Standard Type M Tube Size — inches											
	⅜	½	¾	1	1¼	1½	2	2½	3	4	5	6
1	2.5	0.8	0.2									
2	8.5	2.8	0.5	0.2								
3	17.3	5.7	1.0	0.3	0.1							
4	28.6	9.4	1.8	0.5	0.2							
5	42.2	13.8	2.6	0.7	0.3	0.1						
10		**46.6**	8.6	2.5	0.9	0.4	0.1					
15			17.6	5.0	1.9	0.9	0.2					
20			**29.1**	8.4	3.2	1.4	0.4	0.1				
25				12.3	4.7	2.1	0.6	0.2				
30				**17.0**	6.5	2.9	0.8	0.3	0.1			
35					8.5	3.8	1.0	0.4	0.2			
40					11.0	4.9	1.3	0.5	0.2			
45					**13.6**	6.1	1.6	0.6	0.2			
50						7.3	2.0	0.7	0.3			
60						10.2	2.7	1.0	0.4			
70						**13.5**	3.6	1.2	0.5	0.1		
80							4.6	1.6	0.7	0.2		
90							5.7	2.0	0.9	0.2		
100							**7.5**	2.7	1.0	0.3	0.1	
200								**8.5**	3.6	1.0	0.3	0.1
300									**8.0**	2.0	0.7	0.3
400										**3.3**	1.2	0.5
500											1.7	0.7
750											**3.6**	1.5
1000												**2.5**

NOTE: Numbers in bold face correspond to flow velocities of just over 10 ft per sec.

FIG. 4–40. Pressure loss due to friction in Type M copper tube based on Fig. 4–39. Courtesy Copper Development Association.

The type of flow that may be expected can be determined by a dimensionless parameter called the Reynolds number. It may be defined by $Re = \dfrac{\rho V D_H}{\mu}$ where

ρ = density of fluid, lbm/ft³ (kg/m³)
V = average fluid velocity, fps (m/sec)
D_H = hydraulic diameter, ft (m). For a circular tube, D_H is the tube diameter.
μ = fluid viscosity, lbm/fps (kg/m/sec)

Using this parameter, the flow is laminar when R_e is less than 2,100. For values between 2,100 and 6,000, the flow is transitional, while Reynolds numbers above 6,000 indicate turbulent flow.

Pipe friction may be determined from the relevant equations of fluid mechanics, from experiment, or—most simple of all—by reference to such charts as Figure 4–39.

On this chart, tubing sizes and types are shown by straight lines slanting upward to the right. In the larger sizes, inside diameters are essentially the same for all types, so only one line is shown for each diameter. Flow rates in gallons per minute are indicated along the horizontal axis, and pressure drops per 100 feet of tube are indicated along the left-hand vertical axis. Dashed straight lines sloping down to the right indicate velocities. Figure 4–40 expresses pressure drops in tabular form. It

Fitting Size, inches	Equivalent Length of Tube, feet						
	Standard Ells		90° Tee		Coupling	Gate Valve	Globe Valve
	90°	45°	Side Branch	Straight Run			
⅜	0.5	0.3	0.75	0.15	0.15	0.1	4
½	1	0.6	1.5	0.3	0.3	0.2	7.5
¾	1.25	0.75	2	0.4	0.4	0.25	10
1	1.5	1.0	2.5	0.45	0.45	0.3	12.5
1¼	2	1.2	3	0.6	0.6	0.4	18
1½	2.5	1.5	3.5	0.8	0.8	0.5	23
2	3.5	2	5	1	1	0.7	28
2½	4	2.5	6	1.3	1.3	0.8	33
3	5	3	7.5	1.5	1.5	1	40
3½	6	3.5	9	1.8	1.8	1.2	50
4	7	4	10.5	2	2	1.4	63
5	9	5	13	2.5	2.5	1.7	70
6	10	6	15	3	3	2	84

NOTE: Allowances are for streamlined soldered fittings and recessed threaded fittings. For threaded fittings, double the allowances shown in the table.

FIG. 4–41. Allowance for friction loss in valves and fittings expressed as equivalent length of tube. Courtesy Copper Development Association.

was derived from Figure 4–39. As an example of the use of this chart, suppose that a flow rate of 16 gallons per minute (60.6 liters/min) is required through 1¼-inch-diameter (31.8mm) Type M tube. Then the friction loss would be about 1.9 psi per 100 feet (.44kg/cm² per 100m) of length and the liquid would have a velocity of about 4.5 fps (1.37m/sec). Had the pipe length been 50 feet, then the friction loss would be only .95 psi. For a pipe length of 300 feet, the friction loss would be $3 \times 1.9 = 5.7$ psi. For all these cases the velocity would remain at 4.5 fps.

Additional frictional resistance is encountered when the liquid flow passes through a fitting or valve. Flow through a globe valve makes two 90° changes in direction, a situation that obviously increases pipe friction. As a simple method for accounting for these situations, frictional losses for fittings and valves have been tabulated as the equivalent losses through lengths of straight tube

(Fig. 4–41). These tabulations make the calculations of pressure drops through a circuit a simple matter.

For the sensitive designer this process may include two or even more iterations. Tubing length generally can be estimated rather accurately. As a general rule, fitting friction will be about 50 percent of tubing length, but this estimate must be verified later. Flow rates are prespecified as suggested in the next chapter. A tentative tube size is selected and the total pressure drop calculated. This pressure drop and the flow rate will determine the required pump size. If the pump size appears excessive, then a larger-diameter tube may be proposed. The whole design sequence becomes one of balancing higher initial costs resulting from larger tube sizes against long-term costs for pumping energy. Several combinations of tube size and pump capacity may be necessary before a "best" combination can be specified.

FIG. 4–42. A small high-performance pump.

FIG. 4–43. An in-line bronze circulating pump.

FIG. 4–44. A ⅓-horsepower base-mounted pump.

PUMPS

In order to overcome the frictional resistance due to piping and the static head (if any), it is necessary to provide a solar circuit with a pump. Pumps may be of the reciprocating or centrifugal type, with the latter type the overwhelming favorite for circulating systems, since it is both quiet and relatively maintenance-free (Figs. 4–42 and 4–43).

Pumps up to about ¼ horsepower usually are mounted "in-line" and the piping supports the pump. Larger sizes are fitted with a base that must be bolted to an appropriate support (Fig. 4–44). I have found that an 8 × 8 × 16-inch

(20.3cm × 20.3cm × 40.6cm) concrete block, the cells of which have been filled with concrete, makes a suitable support for pumps up to ½ horsepower. This support should be isolated from the floor in order that noise and vibration be minimized. A faucet washer placed under each corner of the block serves the purpose adequately.

Pump bodies and internal parts usually are made of iron, bronze, bronze fitted, or stainless steel. Bronze or stainless steel are recommended for all applications and should always be used in circuits containing fresh water. Iron and bronze-fitted pumps may be used in closed loops.

Care should be taken to disturb liquid flow into and out of a pump as little as possible. Excessive turbulence will cause cavitation (small regions in which there is no liquid), which results in lowered pump efficiency, increased noise and vibration, and internal erosion of the pump. Cavitation may be minimized by installing the last fitting at least five tube diameters from a pump's suction and discharge ports. Sometimes it is difficult or impossible to exactly align a base-mounted pump with the piping. However, considerable variations are possible if flexible pump connections are used.

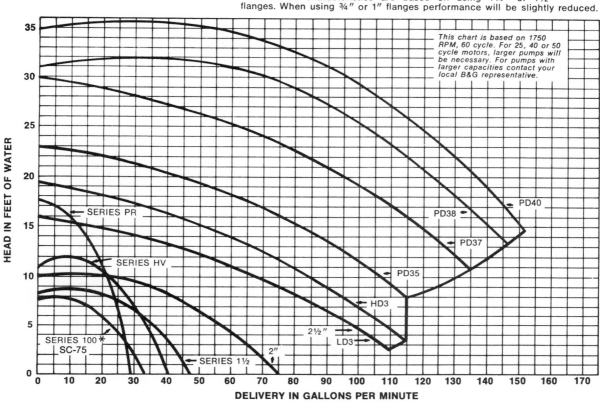

FIG. 4–45. Performance curves for some Bell and Gossett in-line booster pumps.

These connections not only compensate for mis-
alignment but also control vibration, reduce noise,
and allow for thermal expansion. Isolation valves
installed on both sides of the pump will allow for
maintenance, repair, or replacement without draining the entire system. Their use is recommended.

A pump's capacity is described by its "performance curve," on which the delivery rates are plotted on the horizontal axis (head is plotted along the
vertical axis). Remember, however, that flow friction is calculated in pounds per square inch. For
conversion:

1 ft head = .434 psi
and 1 psi = 2.30-ft head

In Figure 4–46, which is the performance curve
for a small high-quality variable-head pump widely
used in solar applications, heads from 8 to 20 feet
are possible with no flow, and flow from 16 to 30
gpm may be maintained if there is no head. Real

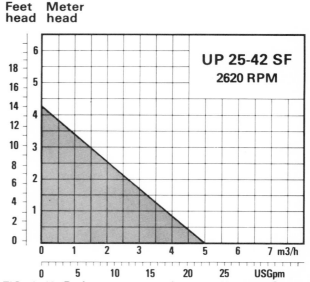

FIG. 4–46. Performance curve for a small pump. Courtesy Bell and Gossett.

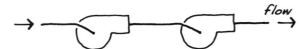

FIG. 4–47. Two pumps installed in series.

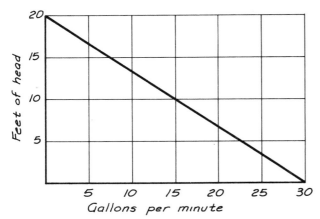

FIG. 4–48. Performance curve for a single pump.

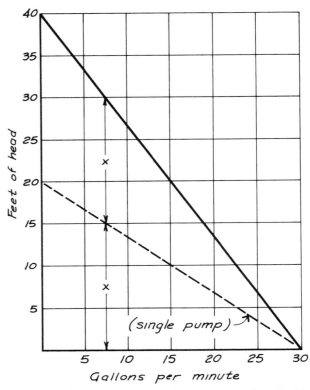

FIG. 4–49. Performance curve for two pumps installed in series.

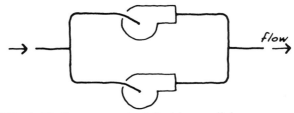

FIG. 4–50. Two pumps installed in parallel.

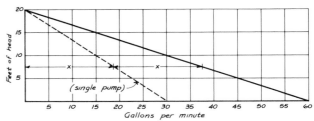

FIG. 4–51. Performance curve for two pumps installed in parallel.

applications fall somewhere between these two extremes. For example, this pump will deliver 10 gpm against a head of 14 feet (6.08 psi).

Some pump manufacturers show the performance curves for a number of pumps on the same chart (Fig. 4–45). With this chart the designer may select two or more pumps for closer scrutiny to see which best fits his need.

It sometimes is possible that a pump has either the necessary lift or the necessary delivery, but not both. For such instances, two or more pumps may be combined in series or parallel arrangements to achieve the desired performance.[3]

When two pumps are piped in series (Fig. 4–47), the combination yields twice the head of one pump, but flow remains the same as for a single pump. Figure 4–48 is the performance curve for an energy-conserving 1/20-horsepower pump. The performance curve for two of these pumps in series is shown in Figure 4–49.

On the other hand, these same two pumps could be piped in a parallel arrangement (Fig. 4–50) to double the flow of one pump, but not increase the head. For this arrangement the performance curve will be as shown in Figure 4–51. Although more than two pumps could be employed in either of these arrangements, it is unlikely that their use would be economically justified.

Fluid Temperature °F	Flow-Increase Need for 50% Glycol as Compared with Water
40	1.22
100	1.16
140	1.15
180	1.14
220	1.14

FIG. 4–52. Increased flow requirements for same heat conveyance. A 50 percent glycol solution compared to water.

Fluid Temperature °F	Pressure-Drop Correction Flow Rates Equal	Combined Pressure-Drop Correction: 50% Glycol
40	1.45	2.14
100	1.1	1.49
140	1.0	1.32
180	.94	1.23
220	.9	1.18

FIG. 4–53. Pressure-drop correction factors. A 50 percent glycol solution compared to water.

ANTIFREEZE SOLUTIONS

Tables indicating pipe friction and the performance curves for pumps assume that the circuits are filled with pure water. Except for isolated instances in solar circuits, however, an antifreeze solution must be employed. Inasmuch as such a solution will have both a specific heat and a viscosity different from those of water, suitable modifications should be made in pipe sizes, flow rates, and pump sizing.

Three materials are commonly used to prevent freezing in solar circuits: ethylene glycol and water, propylene glycol and water, and Dow-Corning Q2-1132 silicone heat-transfer liquid. Each of these materials has some advantages and some disadvantages.

Ethylene glycol is the familiar antifreeze used in automobiles. Its cost is modest, it is slightly heavier than water, and it has a boiling point of 387°F (197.2°C). Although pure ethylene glycol freezes at 8.6°F (−13°C), when mixed with water on an equal-weight basis, the freezing point of the mixture is about −33°F(−36.1°C). This material is toxic, however, so precautions should be taken to prevent contamination of potable water.

Propylene glycol is less readily obtainable than ethylene glycol and its cost is a little higher. It is nontoxic. It also is slightly heavier than water, has a boiling point of 369.4°F (187.4°C), and a 50-50 mixture (by weight) with water freezes at about −26°F (−32.2°C).

Recall that the specific heat of water is 1.0 Btu/lb°F. This fact qualifies water as one of the best heat-transfer liquids. For comparison, the specific

heats of ethylene glycol and propylene glycol are .56 and .59 Btu/lb-°F (cal/gm-°C), respectively.

This situation means that a mixture of either of these glycols and water will require a higher flow rate than for water alone in order to transfer the same amount of heat. Of equal concern are the viscosities of the glycols, since viscosity is a measure of the resistance to flow. Consequently, a high viscosity requires a greater pumping effort. Although at high temperatures their viscosities compare with that of water, at 100°F (37.8°C) they are three to four times as much. At lower temperatures their viscosities increase dramatically.

Glycol/water mixtures will require a greater flow rate and cause a greater pressure drop than pure water. The increased flow rates required for a 50 percent glycol mixture are shown in Figures 4–52 and 4–53.

As an example of the use of these tables, suppose that a system has been calculated to require 12 gpm at a 22-foot head for water at 140°F. From Figure 4–52, a 50 percent glycol mixture at the same temperature requires 1.15 times the flow of water, so that the adjusted flow rate is 12×1.15 or 13.8 gpm. From Figure 4–53, the pressure-drop factor is 1.32, so that the adjusted head is 22×1.32 or 29 feet. Using these new values, 13.8 gpm and 29-foot head, standard performance curves can be used for pump selection.

In a pure state, both of these glycols are less corrosive than water. When mixed with water, however, the solution assumes the corrosivity of water, which may become progressively worse with use. This corrosivity may be minimized or eliminated by the addition of inhibitors or stabilizers. Most commercially available ethylene glycol contains inhibitors. The effectiveness of the inhibitors generally will decrease with time. An important consideration is to prevent the liquid from becoming acid. Regular monitoring two or three times a year (especially during the first year) and maintenance are recommended. Most of all, glycols should not be expected to have an indefinite service life.

Dow-Corning Q2-1132 silicone heat-transfer liquid possesses both advantages and disadvantages when compared with the glycols. This material is noncorrosive and is not likely to boil in most collector arrays. With care it may last the life of the system. Maintenance is not ordinarily required, but periodic monitoring is in order for any heat-transfer liquid.

The major barrier to its widespread use is cost. On a volume basis, silicone is about ten times the cost of ethylene glycol. Silicone is used without dilution, so that when compared with a 50 percent glycol solution, its cost actually is about twenty times greater.

Silicone's specific heat is lower than both water and the glycols, whereas its viscosity is greater than these materials. Consequently, its manufacturer suggests that if water/glycol systems be changed to Q2-1132, the following modifications be made:

1. Increase all pipe sizes in the system by one size. Example: from ½ inch (12.7mm) to ¾ inch (19.1mm).
2. Increase the pump size to accommodate twice the flow rate and ten times the viscosity. Heat exchangers must be increased in the same manner.

There is one other point of consideration that is extremely important when silicone is contemplated as a heat-transfer fluid. Since its surface tension is much lower than that of either water or glycol, extreme care must be exercised that no flaws exist in any joints. Otherwise, leaking systems can result. At silicone prices, these leaks cannot be afforded.

PUMP CONTROLLERS

In a solar-energy collector system, we want the pump to operate when a solar harvest is available. By the same token, we do not wish that energy be withdrawn from storage only to be reradiated when no solar surplus is available. Operation of the pump is governed by a controller.

In its most simple form, the controller consists of a suitably designed electronic circuit activated by two thermistors (Fig. 4–54). One is located at the outlet of the collector array and the other at the storage outlet. When the temperature of the liquid at the collector outlet is sufficiently above that of the liquid in storage—usually a temperature difference of about 20°F (11.1°C)—then the pump is ac-

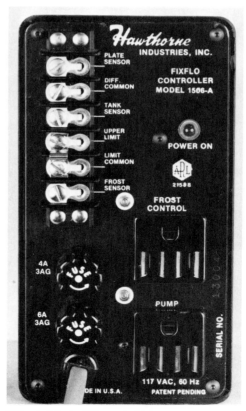

FIG. 4–54. A differential controller.

tivated. When collector outlet temperature approaches storage outlet temperature—usually a difference of about 3°F (1.7°C)—then the pump stops. A built-in hysteresis loop prevents unnecessary pump cycling. Some controllers have an integral high-limit control to prevent overheating of domestic-hot-water storage tanks. Other functions may be controlled by one of these devices.

In general, the cost of these pump controllers is modest. However, as additional functions are added to the controller's responsibility, its cost can increase almost without limit. On a recent project on which I was a consultant, for which the client required total electronic control of all its aspects, the control system cost more than the collector array.

OTHER CONSIDERATIONS

Although it may not seem of importance while a piping system is being installed, it is of considerable importance not to have low points in the system. Such points can prevent a system from draining completely if such draining is ever necessary. Such low points may also cause airlocks when filling the system.

An air valve should be installed at the high point of an array. This may be a simple manual valve that should be opened when filling or draining the system. Additionally, a pressure- and temperature-relief valve (PRV) should be installed to protect the system against excessive pressures which could occur, for example, during a pump malfunction or electric-power outage on a sunny day.

An expansion tank is necessary for any closed system. If this tank is located above the collector array, then the air valve and pressure-relief valve may be mounted directly on it. The tank should have a capacity equal to the volume of liquid contained in the collectors (but not the circuit piping) plus a little more. (The capacity of most collectors is about ½ gallon per panel.)

Inasmuch as a closed system generally requires much less pump capacity than an open system, the circulating pump on a closed system may not have enough capacity to fill the system. In this event it is necessary to fill the system through an upper air valve or the expansion tank. An alternate method that I have found very convenient is to use a small high-capacity auxiliary pump. Since the operation takes only a few minutes, a rental pump, which costs only a few dollars a day, is my choice for this operation.

The inclusion of thermometers in the solar circuit is, in general, an optional matter. I have found, however, that two or three thermometers, strategically located, serve an inquisitive, if not practical, need.

NOTES

1. *Copper Brass Bronze Product Handbook*, Copper Development Association, Inc., 405 Lexington Avenue, New York, N.Y. 10017. Much of the information on copper tubing is taken from this publication. Single copies of the handbook are available at no cost from the association.

2. F. Kreith and J. F. Kreider, *Principles of Solar Engineering* (New York: McGraw-Hill, 1978), pp. 85–93.

3. *Parallel and Series Pump Application*, Bulletin No. TEH–1065, Bell and Gossett, 1965.

CHAPTER FIVE

INSTALLING A FLAT-PLATE COLLECTOR SYSTEM

In this chapter we will discuss how to design and install a flat-plate collection system and suggest alternate methods for arriving at satisfactory performance.

With regard to design, a first decision to be made is the size of the array. The size will be influenced by domestic-hot-water requirements and space-heating needs and the portion of these needs expected to be supplied by solar, as well as the local climatic conditions and the end use of the solar contribution.

In general, it is not practical to rely solely on solar energy for these needs, since periods of cloudy and cold weather would require a collector area and storage volume far in excess of average requirements. A usual strategy is to make the collector array and its associated thermal storage large enough to provide 50 to 75 percent of the building's heating needs for the average season. As a rule of thumb, if a building is insulated such that its walls have R-20, ceiling R-30, and basement walls R-15, then a collector array of 25 percent of the building's floor area will supply 60 to 70 percent of the heating needs. For example, a building of 1,600 square feet (148.6m²) insulated in this manner would require 400 square feet of collector area to meet 60 to 70 percent of its heating needs. This rule of thumb is less accurate for commercial and institutional buildings.

In my opinion many authorities suggest collector arrays that are too small. This is because we often refer to a system's cost at a price per square foot, but in fact, the actual collector cost will be only 20 to 50 percent of the system cost. Investment pumps, piping, thermal storage, and contr relatively constant over a range of a Therefore, a modest increase in cost the effect of reducing the square-foot cost of the in stalled system.

Collector size for domestic-water-heating requirements is subject to a number of variables. Personal water use, the presence of a dishwasher, whether or not hot water is used for clothes washing, and the temperature of the incoming water all affect array size. As a general rule, I have found that one panel of 17 to 18 square feet (1.58 to 1.67m²) and 20 gallons (75.7 liters) of storage per family member is a very healthy assist.

Frequently, several options are available for collector location. For a new building, the array may be incorporated into its roof. Since the array may have an area of several hundred square feet, and since it will be inclined at a steep angle, such a decision will have a significant impact on the building's form and appearance.

When the building has a flat roof, collectors may be mounted on it and often concealed by keeping them well away from the edge, or by the use of a raised fascia. Since the total weight of the array and its piping will be in the range of 3 to 5 pounds per square foot (14.65 to 24.41kg/m²), no significant additional structural strength will be necessary.

Although rooftop locations are the most widely used for collectors, there may be valid reasons for placing them elsewhere. They may be incorporated in south-facing sloping walls. If one is willing

FIG. 5–1. Solar home of Ian Mackinley, FAIA, North Lake Tahoe. Vertical collectors serve as the south wall of the house. Heavy snow cover in the winter reflects additional radiation to the double-glazed collectors. Architect: Mackinley Winnacker McNeil, AIA, and Associates. Photo: Mort Beebe.

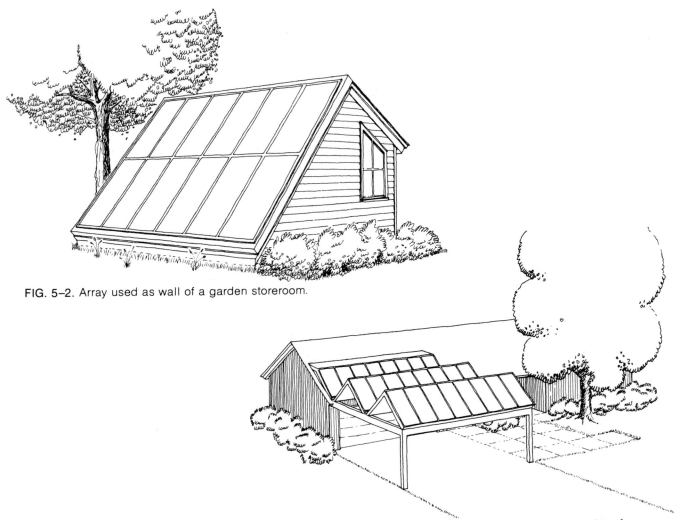

FIG. 5–2. Array used as wall of a garden storeroom.

FIG. 5–3. Use of array as terrace or carport roof.

to sacrifice a little efficiency (and add to the size of the array), they actually may be installed in a vertical south wall for winter use only (Fig. 5–1).

A number of large systems employ field-mounted arrays. While such an arrangement allows for easy inspection and maintenance (little of which should be required), it does require quite a lot of ground area. Furthermore, many persons object to its appearance. For a residence, a better approach for an isolated array may be to enclose the space beneath an array for use as a storeroom (Fig. 5–2).

When an array is to be installed on an existing building, a multitude of obstacles may present

themselves. Roof slopes may be low or face other than south. Trees, gardens, or terraces may restrict location of the array. Shadows cast by neighboring buildings or large trees may rule out an otherwise desirable location. (From a practical viewpoint, I do not feel that shading before 9:00 A.M. or after 3:00 P.M. has much effect on collector performance.) Overcoming these obstacles may demand non-traditional design approaches. For example, lack of ground space may suggest that the array be incorporated into a new carport or terrace roof (Fig. 5–3).

Many persons object to the appearance of a collector array, wherever it is located. But as I have

FIG. 5–4. Array used as a side wall. All flashing and trim are bronze-anodized aluminum. Designed by the author.

pointed out earlier, the clear glass over a black absorber gives the appearance of black glass, a rich look for which one pays extra when it is in an oven or dishwasher door. The primary objection, I think, is to the mill-finish aluminum collector boxes and associated flashing that usually are silver or gray. Care in designing and installing the array may overcome this objection. I recently have been specifying bare uncoated absorbers manufactured by one of the nation's leading producers. These are installed in a grid constructed of redwood. The entire array and framing is painted with 3M's Black Velvet Nextel paint. Trim members are standard storefront extrusions in a bronze finish, while flashing is .040-inch bronze-anodized aluminum. Although these materials are expensive, the system's costs are less than if complete collectors had been purchased. Furthermore, the end result is one that suggests richness and luxury (Fig. 5–4).

PIPING THE ARRAY

The desired goal in piping an array is to assure equal flow through each riser. For simple arrays, equal flow may be guaranteed by requiring that every possible liquid path has exactly the same length and same tubing diameters as any other. This is the same condition that requires a collector's inlets and outlets to be on opposite ends of its headers. A simple four-panel array piped in this manner is shown in Figure 5–5. Notice that which-

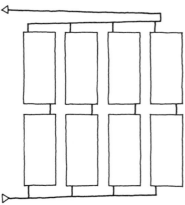

FIG. 5–5. Two-panel-high collector array. This layout guarantees equal flow through all collectors.

ever path the liquid follows, exactly the same lengths of ½-, ¾-, and 1-inch (12.5, 19.1, and 25.4mm) tubing will be traversed. This type of piping arrangement, called a "reverse return," works well, provided the array is not too large. For larger systems, say over 600 square feet (55.7m²), the supply manifold may be decreased in size and the return manifold increased in size according to the actual flow at a point, so that pipe friction remains relatively constant.

When a system for space heating is designed, it is often desirable to arrange the collectors two or more panels high. Figures 5–5 and 5–6 illustrate how this may be done using a reverse return. No-

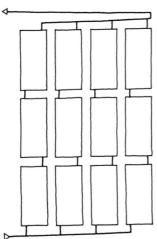

FIG. 5–6. Three-panel-high collector array. Top and bottom rows are identical, while manifold connections on middle row are reversed.

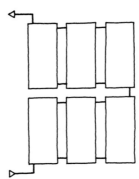

FIG. 5–7. Method of joining six collectors into a single module when 1-inch headers are used.

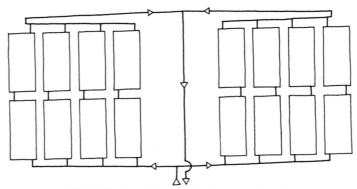

FIG. 5–8. A split array having equal parts.

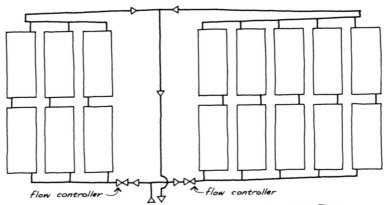

flow controller — — *flow controller*

FIG. 5–9. A split array having unequal parts. Flow-control valves should be used for this arrangement.

tice that inlets and outlets are reversed for panels in the middle row of Figure 5–6.

Some field piping and connections may be eliminated if the collector panels are constructed or purchased with 1-inch-diameter (25.4mm) instead of ¾-inch-diameter (19.1mm) headers. In such a case, usually about four to six panels may be joined directly before connecting to the manifolds (Fig. 5–7).

Depending on the array configuration, it may be possible to bring supply and return headers up the axis of the array and feed to each side (Fig. 5–8). For such a system to have balanced flow, the array must be symmetrical with respect to the risers.

Many times the array must be divided into two or more unequal areas. In such an instance, flow controllers installed in each branch will properly regulate the individual flows (Fig. 5–9).

Air vents should be installed at the high points of all arrays for assistance in filling or removing trapped air. These vents may be automatic or a simple manual type. If the expansion tank is mounted at the system's high point, then the air vent may be installed in it. In many cases, the system's high point will occur near a roof ridge that normally would require that the vent penetrate deck and roofing. This problem can be avoided by attaching a line of ¼-inch (6.4mm) soft-temper tubing to a high point and then routing this tubing to a location where a manual valve can be conveniently installed (Fig. 5–10).

Once the heat is harvested it must be transferred to the thermal-storage tank. A liquid-to-liquid heat exchanger is used for this purpose. Various designs are available from a number of manufacturers. One of the most common of these is the shell-and-tube design in which a bundle of tubes containing one of the liquids is surrounded by a cylinder containing the other liquid. Another type utilizes a coiled tube placed inside a larger closed-end tube. The deformations serve to create turbulent flow for better heat transfer. A schematic drawing showing how these heat exchangers are placed in the circuit is shown in Figure 5–11. Notice that an additional pump is required to circulate water from the storage tank through the heat exchanger.

Most of these readily available heat exchangers were developed for use in conventional heating and cooling systems. In these systems it is possible to prespecify not only the flow rates, but also the entering temperature of both liquids. Such is not the case for either a solar circuit or storage-tank water whose temperatures may fluctuate widely. Furthermore, the catalog performance data furnished for commercial exchangers frequently is presented for a liquid whose temperature is 140°F (60°C), 160°F (71.1°C), or even 180°F (82.2°C). While these temperatures are attainable in a solar circuit during much of the year, higher collector efficiencies can be maintained by operating at lower temperatures during severe weather. In short, commercially available heat exchangers operate in a satisfactory manner at lower temperatures, but in

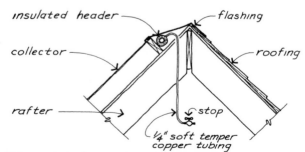

FIG. 5–10. Location of air vent below high point.

FIG. 5–11. A shell-and-tube heat exchanger. Mounted external to storage. Courtesy Bell and Gossett.

order to ascertain an appropriate size and performance, you will have to request these values from the manufacturer's representative. Ordinarily, this information is freely given.

The heat exchange between water in turbulent flow and copper is quite high. Even the heat transfer between copper and water whose only flow is by thermocirculation is relatively good. Consequently, it is possible to self-construct a heat exchanger for tank installation. In all cases, the heat exchanger should be located near the tank bottom so that thermocirculation within the tank is encouraged.

One should recognize that the temperature of liquid in the collector loop might vary from 80° or 90°F (26.7° or 32.2°C) to above 200°F (93.3°C). Likewise, the temperature of water in storage may vary from 60°F (15.6°C) to 140°F (60°C) or more, so that any heat exchanger must be chosen to perform adequately over a wide range of temperatures.

Dr. Jerald Parker, a heat-transfer expert from Oklahoma State University, and I have devised a simple heat exchanger that performs with reasonable efficiency for many systems. This exchanger employs .20 feet (6.1cm) of 1-inch-diameter (25.4mm) Type M tubing for each square foot (.09m²) of collector area. This tubing must be in a continuous circuit—not in a header arrangement. (A header arrangement could result in laminar flow and poor heat transfer.) When so installed, on a collector array of 400 to 600 square feet (37.2 to 55.7m²), Reynolds numbers remain in the turbulent region, aiding good heat transfer.

This is the heat exchanger that is used in my own home. It has performed reasonably well. However, in order to construct a heat exchanger comparable to commercially available heat exchangers, and to maintain an approach temperature of about 10°F (−12.2°C) when the temperature difference between circulating fluid and tank is 20°F (−6.7°C), it is necessary to double the heat-transfer area. A satisfactory rule of thumb for this case is to allow 1 square foot of heat transfer area for every 10 square feet of collector. The external surface area of the copper tubing may be obtained from Figure 4–3.

Type M copper tubing is available in 20-foot

(6.1m) lengths. If a length is cut into thirds, each 6 feet 8 inches (2.03m) long, then there is no waste. The easiest way to join consecutive lengths is by using a 90° standard elbow and a 90° street elbow. Two standard elbows may be used, but an additional copper nipple and an additional soldered joint will be necessary. A 180° elbow could be used, but this fitting is not usually in local supply. Furthermore, a 180° elbow costs appreciably more than a 90° standard elbow, a 90° street elbow, and one additional joint. Tubing also can be cut into 5-foot (1.52m) lengths without waste, but with an additional number of fittings required for joining the pieces. Likewise, tubing may be cut into 10-foot (3.05m) lengths, with a decrease in the number of fittings required, but with an overall tank length that may be unmanageable.

When 6 foot 8 inch (2.03m) lengths of tubing are joined in a serpentine manner to make a heat exchanger, the overall exchanger length is about 7 feet 2 inches (2.18m). This length suggests that one dimension of the thermal storage tank be about 8 feet (2.44m). If 100 feet (30.5m) of tubing is cut into lengths of 6 feet 8 inches (2.03m) and assembled into a serpentine in one plane, its finished width will be about 4 feet (1.22m), which could almost cover the floor of a storage tank. The only objection to this arrangement is that very little space

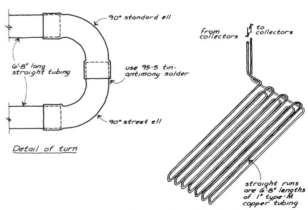

FIG. 5–12. Simple job- or shop-fabricated heat exchanger. This heat exchanger is installed about 6 inches above bottom of tank.

is left for standing when one needs to get into the tank for cleaning or maintenance. It is just as simple to assemble the heat exchanger in two rows as shown in Figure 5–12. As a precautionary measure, install the heat exchanger with unions and isolation valves.

Capacity of the thermal storage tank can vary between wide limits, with many authorities suggesting between 10 and 18 pounds of water for each square foot of absorber surface (48.9 and 87.8 kg/m²), or between 1½ and 2½ gallons of water per square foot (61.1 and 101.8 liters/m²) of absorber. The smaller volume will result in higher tank temperatures, but less total thermal storage or lower collector efficiency. When a tank is being constructed for a specific installation, remember that additional volume can be had at a minimum cost. Also, although it is impossible to overfill a tank, it may be underfilled with few problems. In the next chapter I will indicate how this thermal storage may be used to good advantage with an ordinary heat pump or summer air conditioner. Additional storage will improve this advantage.

Whether or not another heat exchanger should be placed in the top of the tank and included in the space-heating circuit depends on the quality of the water in storage. Mild scaling of piping, radiators, and coils from this water can be tolerated, but its iron content and degree of acidity or alkalinity should be controlled. Since hot water lends itself to algae formation, mild chlorination is in order. Household bleach added several times during the season may suffice. It also will help control the iron content. When storage-tank water is circulated through a heating terminal of any sort, the system is referred to as an open system. Regardless of advice from any written source, consultation with a qualified water-quality engineer is desirable before such a system is put into operation. The difference in water quality from one location to another simply is too variable to allow for any sort of blanket recommendation.

DESIGN OF DOMESTIC-WATER-HEATING SYSTEMS

The simplest domestic-water-heating circuit is one that does not use a pump at all. Instead, flow is caused and maintained by the difference in density of water at different temperatures (thermocirculation). For this circulation to take place, it is necessary for the storage tank to be higher than the collectors. A usual rule is that the bottom of storage must be at least 12 inches (30.5cm) above the top of collectors. Collectors mounted at ground level and the storage tank on a building's upper floor or attic would be one example of the geometry for a system of this sort (Fig. 5–13). So would a south-facing slope adjacent to the building (Fig. 5–14).

Since the driving force for the circulation is a modest temperature difference, piping lengths should be as short as possible and the piping should be oversized to minimize pipe friction. Use 1-inch (2.54cm) tubing as a minimum.

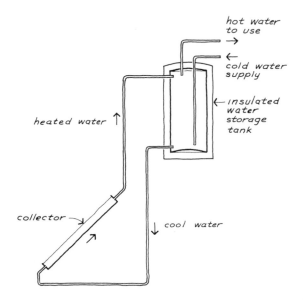

FIG. 5–13. Simple thermocirculation system with ground-mounted collectors and storage tank in attic or second floor.

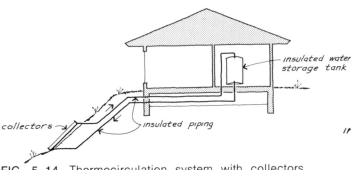

FIG. 5–14. Thermocirculation system with collectors mounted on slope below floor level.

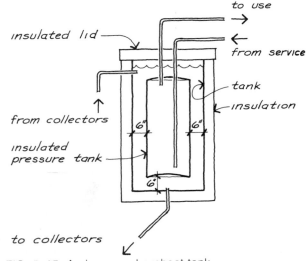

FIG. 5–15. An immersed preheat tank.

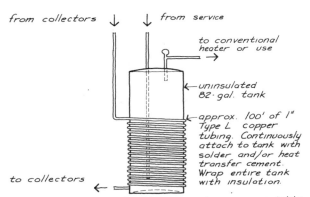

FIG. 5–16. Preheat tank with heat exchanger on outside.

It is possible to construct the preheat tank for a system of this sort. First, secure an uninsulated pressure tank of adequate size. Construct or purchase an open tank with a diameter 8 to 12 inches (20.3 to 30.5cm) greater than the pressure tank and mount them as shown in Figure 5–15. The exterior should be insulated with at least 4 inches (10cm) of glass fiber.

Before the advent of easily available solar storage tanks, I made my own. I purchased an 82-gallon (310-liter) uninsulated pressure tank and 100 feet (30.5m) of 1-inch (2.54cm) soft-temper Type L copper tubing. The tubing was wound around the tank in a spiral and was attached with continuous solder and heat-transfer cement (Fig. 5–16). The whole assembly was wrapped with 6 inches (15.2cm) of glass fiber insulation, and this was covered with 1 inch (2.54cm) of vinyl-faced glass fiber of the sort used to wrap air-conditioning ducts. It worked very well.

A number of solar water heaters are now available from the major manufacturers (Fig. 5–17). Various heat-exchanger configurations are employed and single or dual immersion heaters usually are installed. Some manufacturers offer complete systems, including collectors, pumps,

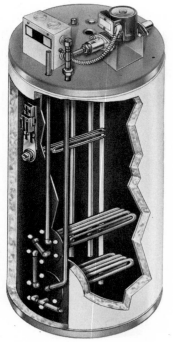

FIG. 5–17. Cutaway drawing of commercially available solar water heater. Courtesy A. O. Smith.

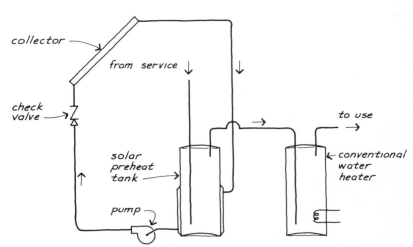

FIG. 5–18. Domestic-water-heating system using preheat tank.

and controls. I deplore this practice, since it locks the purchaser into a system that one may not consider optimum.

From long experience I have learned to respect the water heaters offered by certain manufacturers. The credibility of these same manufacturers as solar designers has not been demonstrated. Some manufacturers sell 4 × 8-foot (1.22 × 2.44m) collector panels—a difficult size to integrate into a space-heating array of 3 × 7-foot (.76 × 2.13m) panels. Some manufacturers use plastic film glazing. Some of these systems use distilled water in a drain-down manner. When I attempted to purchase the solar heater only from an experienced manufacturer, I was told that its warranty was void unless I also purchased the manufacturer's collectors. Frankly, I was less concerned about the heater's warranty than I would have been about the collectors, but I chose another brand anyway.

A word of caution. One manufacturer offers a series of solar storage tanks. One of these is described as a solar storage tank intended for replacement use. It has four piping connections on its top—collector in, collector out; cold water in and hot water out. I installed one of these units, only to discover that antifreeze solution was mixed with potable water. A call to the factory confirmed that this tank has no heat exchanger! True, the catalog sheet for this item did not mention a heat exchanger, but cutaway drawings of other heaters in the series indicated its presence, and four piping connections certainly suggested a heat exchanger. Obviously, it was necessary to remove this tank.

Ordinarily, circulation through the array is by means of a small in-line pump. For a four-panel array, adequate flow usually may be maintained by a 1/20-horsepower pump if 3/4-inch (19.1mm) circuit piping is employed. A schematic of such a system as generally suggested is shown in Figure 5–18. While this scheme works, it can be improved. In order to understand how this improvement can be made, it is necessary to recall a few facts about hot-water use and automatic control.

The hottest water needed for domestic purposes is required by an automatic dishwasher at 140°F (60°C). A booster heater within the machine further raises the water's temperature to a sanitizing level of 180°F (82.2°C). All other water in a home is used at a lower temperature. The temperature of water used for baths, showers, and shampoos is a matter of personal preference. Usually the desired temperature is slightly above that of the human body, about 100° to 105°F (37.8° to 65.6°C). This temperature ordinarily is achieved by mixing at the faucet. The thermostat setting on most water heaters may be varied between 120° and 160°F (48.9° and 71.1°C). Setting the thermostat below 140°F, however, does not decrease hot-water usage, since less cold water will be mixed with the heated water at the point of use.

The adequacy of a water heater depends not only on the size of its storage tank but also on its "recovery rate." The recovery rate is the number of gallons per hour whose temperature can be raised 100°F (37.8°C). An electric heater with a single 4,500-watt heating element has a recovery rate of about 18 gallons (68 liters) per hour.

Whether or not the water needs to be heated 100°F (37.8°C) depends on geographic location, time of year, and the depth of the water main or supply well. Frequently, wintertime-supply water temperature is taken to be 40°F (4.4°C), although in some locations it might be a few degrees cooler. In this case, a heater's published recovery rate would be fairly accurate. During the late summer and early fall, however, the temperature of the supply water might increase to 60° or 70°F (15.6° or 21.1°C), so that a heater could provide a greater quantity of water at 140°F (60°C).

A frequently overlooked energy use is that required to overcome "standby" losses. Even if no hot water is actually used, heat must be supplied to replace that which is lost from storage. When the

Heater "Set" Temperature	Standby Heat Loss, BTU/Hr.	30 Day Month Standby Heat Loss, BTU/Month
160	1,980	1,425,000
150	1,935	1,390,000
140	1,540	1,100,000
130	1,320	950,000
120	1,100	790,000
110	880	635,000
100	660	475,000

FIG. 5–19. Standby losses for typical 40-gallon water heater tank.

water heater is located within a heated portion of the building, this loss is recaptured as an uncontrolled gain. Such a situation is desirable during heating months, but undesirable during the summer. In either event, additional heat must be supplied to storage to compensate for this loss.

Most water heaters manufactured in this country are built for lowest initial cost. Consequently, the amount of insulation used in them is minimal. The standby heat loss for a typical currently available 40-gallon (151.4-liter) heater using fossil fuel is shown in Figure 5–19. A larger tank will have greater losses, one with more insulation, smaller losses.

Let us now return to Figure 5–18 and describe a possible water-heating and water-use situation. By 4:00 P.M., solar radiation has heated water in storage to 150°F (65.6°C). After dinner, the dishwasher is used so that storage temperature drops to 135°F (57.2°C) and the thermostat activates the heating element in order to raise tank temperature to 140°F (60°C). If it were not for the thermostat, bathing during evening hours might drop the tank temperature to 105°F (40.6°C). Tank temperature, however, is maintained at 140°F (60°C) not only during the evening hours, but during the ensuing sixteen to eighteen hours when there may be al-

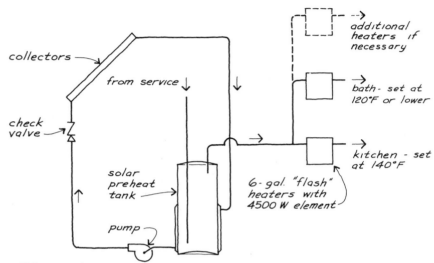

FIG. 5–20. Improved domestic-water-heating system using flash heaters.

most no hot-water usage at all. Furthermore, the next day's heat harvest begins with water already at service temperature, so that collectors operate with reduced efficiency.

From an energy-use viewpoint, this system may be improved as shown in Figure 5–20. A solar storage tank is still used, but its capacity is increased. Its heating element, if present, is activated only during periods of inclement weather or an excessive number of house guests. Small "flash heaters" are located near point of use, usually beneath cabinets or in cupboards. These flash heaters have small storage tanks, with a capacity of 6 to 15 gallons (22.7 to 56.8 liters), which minimizes standby losses, but they are fitted with 4- or 5-kilowatt heating elements, so their recovery rates are equal to larger heaters. A flash heater serving a dishwasher might have its thermostat set on 140°F (60°C), while one serving a bath might have its thermostat set at 120°F (48.9°C). For that matter, a bath heater might be turned off completely during most of the year, since 105°F (40.6°C) water for bathing is available from solar storage most of the time. The convenience of these flash heaters can be improved by installing switches to control their heating elements near their points of use.

Choosing the proper size of flash heater de-

pends on one's bathing habits. Conversely, if a particular size is chosen in advance, it is possible that one's bathing habits might change. Personally, I favor the smaller sizes, since standby losses will be less. Let's look at an extreme example.

Suppose that a 6-gallon (22.7-liter) heater with a 5,000-watt element is used and its thermostat is set at 140°F (60°C). Assume that incoming cold water has a temperature of 40°F (4.4°C). If a water-saving shower head having a flow rate of 3 gallons per minute (11.4 liters/min) is used, then the maximum length of a comfortable shower will be about three minutes. With the large element, water in the tank will be at service temperature again in 20 minutes. A four-minute shower would be possible if the thermostat were set at 160°F (71.1°C) a few minutes before the water is used. Of course, a 10- or 15-gallon (37.9- or 56.8-liter) tank could have been used, but standby losses would be larger. Remember that during much of the year the heater will be turned off completely and that the 6-gallon (22.7-liter) heater wiii provide comfortable water at the shower head more quickly.

Creature comfort in the form of longer showers still can be maintained during these extreme periods. Continue to use the 6-gallon heater, but

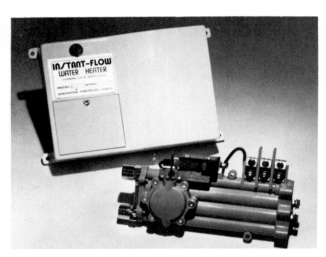

FIG. 5–21. Instantaneous electric heater. Courtesy Chronomite Laboratories, Inc.

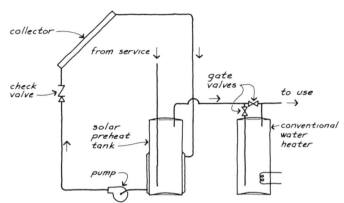

FIG. 5–22. Bypass valves used to reduce energy consumption.

set the thermostat on the storage-tank heater to a minimum level of 110°F or 120°F (43.3° or 48.9°C). This will minimize tank losses, and the flash heater now serves only as a booster.

Instead of installing flash heaters, instantaneous heaters could be installed at each fixture that requires hot water. Used in Europe for years, this sort of heater now is manufactured in the United States (Fig. 5–21). As water flows across special coils it is warmed by an electric heating element. The element is automatically turned off when water flow stops. There is neither standby nor piping heat loss for these elements. A better solution for providing hot water to a distant, seldom-used lavatory could hardly be found.

These units are made with heaters rated from 2,000 to 9,000 watts. If incoming water is only 40°F (4.4°C), a condition possible during the winter when there is no sunshine, then a 9,000-watt unit will heat .6 gallons per minute (2.3 liters/min) to 140°F (60°C) for dishwasher use. This flow rate is too low for most dishwashers. It would require two 1,000-watt units connected either in series or parallel to supply the needs of a dishwasher under these conditions. In addition to the extra cost for two units, they would demand 18 kilowatts, even

though the time period might be short. Under many electric pricing formulas, this fact could increase the rate for the entire month. A better solution would be to install one instantaneous heater and set the thermostat on the storage tank to a minimum temperature in order to preheat the water.

A similar improvement can be made for the circuit shown in Figure 5–18. This circuit is the one usually recommended by most solar-design books and, in fact, was the one originally installed in my own home. Energy from the sun preheats the water as much as possible in the preheat tank. The water then flows into a conventional heater where any additional heat is added. Both tanks are subject to standby losses. A major shortcoming of this scheme is that many times water in the preheat tank will be at service temperature, but after it is transferred to the conventional heater it will cool with time. This condition energizes the heating element. We tried turning off the conventional heater at the breaker panel, but—depending on the rate of use—the water sometimes cooled too much and required reheating. A definite improvement of this situation is shown in Figure 5–22. The two gate valves allow one to completely bypass the conventional heater during periods of favorable energy harvest. A household schedule in which the dish-washer is used during afternoon or early evening hours, and bathing occurs later in the evening, has allowed us to completely eliminate any energy other than solar for water heating for several months of the year. (Not quite true. We used 17 kilowatt-hours for water heating from May through September.) Anyone desirous of more automated control could replace the gate valves with mo-torized valves and aquastats or other electronic controls.

One other possible system should be described. In this layout a single storage tank with a heating element is used. However, the heating element is controlled not only by its thermostat but also by a timer. In most cases, if the timer is set to energize the heater from 5:00 to 9:00 or 10:00 P.M., hot-water requirements for most families will be met.

SOLAR SIDE DESIGN OF A SPACE-HEATING SYSTEM

A first step in designing a solar system for space heating is to determine the building's heating needs by calculation. Even though this is a neces-sary step, more often than not the actual size of a collector array is determined by available roof or wall surface or economics. The rule-of-thumb col-lector area of 25 to 40 percent of the building floor area is usually a satisfactory estimate. Once the size has been determined, the system may pro-ceed as follows.

1. Lay out panels in an array. This array should be as simple as possible. If it must be split into two or more parts, attempt to make them equal in area and arrangement.
2. Decide how the panels are to be joined with each other. Although a number of arrangements are possible, some will require more materials and job labor than others (Fig. 5–23).
3. Sketch in the circuit piping from the array to the heat exchanger at the thermal storage and return. Strive for the most direct route with the fewest number of fittings. Make a tentative choice of tubing size.

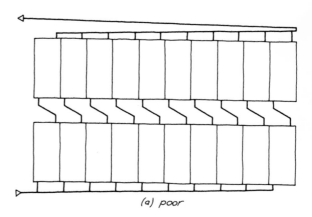

(a) poor

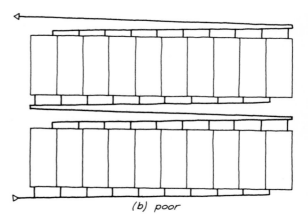

(b) poor

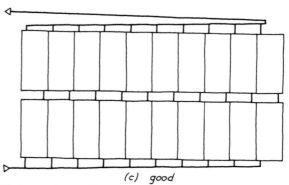

(c)　good

FIG. 5–23. Various methods of piping the array. Notice that some methods use more piping, fittings, and labor than others.

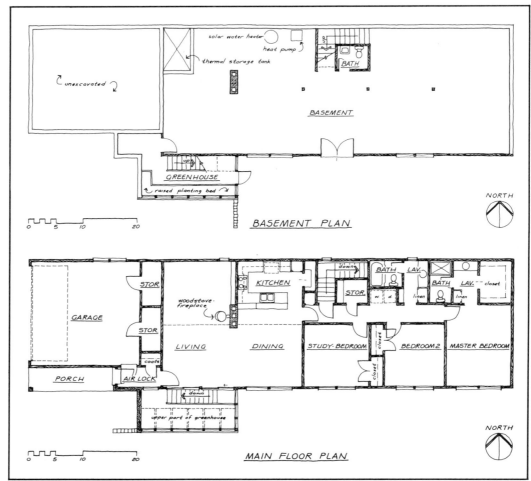

FIG. 5–24. Floor plans for walkout basement and main floor. Design by the author.

FIG. 5–25. Exterior view.

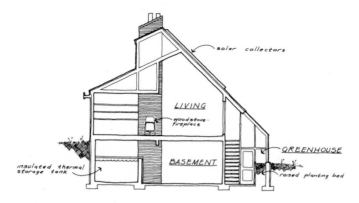

FIG. 5–26. Transverse section through main living area.

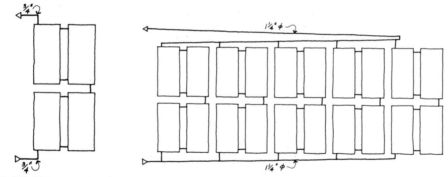

FIG. 5–27. Four-panel subarray.　　　FIG. 5–28. Total heating array.

4. Select heat exchanger.

5. Calculate the flow rate through the system and the pressure drop due to friction of water. Convert the values obtained to those for an antifreeze solution. These adjusted values will determine the pump size.

6. Choose pump. If the size is larger than wished, it may be possible to use a smaller pump by increasing the diameter of the circuit piping.

7. Check schematic drawings for inclusion and locations for valves, drains, expansion tank, and air vents.

A good way to illustrate the manner in which these steps proceed is by an example. This case is a house in Lawrence, Kansas, at the latitude of about 40° north and a winter design temperature of −5°F(−20.6°C). Floor plans and elevations are shown in Figures 5–24 and 5–25. A section through the house is shown in Figure 5–26. Notice the

semiburied greenhouse attached to the house that serves a dual function as a passive collector.

The building contains 1,600 square feet (148.6m²) on its main floor, the only level that is heated. Its south-facing roof was designed for twenty-four Sunworks collector panels having an area of 18.67 square feet (1.73m²) each. Four of the panels are double-glazed for domestic water heating, while twenty panels having an area of 373 square feet (34.7m²) are single-glazed for space heating in conjunction with a water-source heat pump. The justification for the single glazing and the apparently small collector area will become obvious later.

These twenty panels can conveniently be divided into five groups of four panels each. Each four-panel group may be connected as shown in Figure 5–27. Then each group is considered as one large panel as far as the circuit is concerned. The total array is shown in Figure 5–28.

A 1,500-gallon (5.68m³) thermal-storage tank is

located in the basement. It was poured at the same time as the basement walls, so that only two additional walls, plus a little extra steel reinforcement, were needed for its construction. Its interior received a .040-inch (1mm) liner of glass-fiber-reinforced resin. It is insulated on all sides with 2-inch (5.1cm) closed-cell insulation and has a removable lid of the same material. A 2-inch (5.1cm) drain with a bronze gate valve located beneath the floor outside the tank allows it to be drained to a low point on the site.

The tank has plan dimensions of 5×8 feet (1.52×2.44m) and a design depth of 5 feet (1.52m). When filled to this depth, it has a capacity of about 1,500 gallons (5.68m³). For most of the heating season this is too much capacity, so the water level is dropped to 3 or 4 feet (.91 or 1.22m). The full capacity is used during summer months to enhance the performance of the heat pump.

If one were to choose a commercial tube-in-shell heat exchanger for this system, it probably would be about 6×48 inches (15.2×121.9cm), six-pass, with a 2-inch (5.1cm) baffle, but this should be verified with the manufacturer. Flow rates would be about 15 gpm (56.8 liters/min) on the solar circuit and 13 gpm (49.2 liters/min) on the water side. Some 15 square feet (1.39m²) of heat-exchanger surface is needed. Pressure drops through both sides are modest.

Another choice for heat exchanger is the tank-immersed serpentine coil previously described. For economy's sake, we will use this configuration. About 40 square feet (3.72m²) of heat-transfer surface will be required. If Type M tubing is used, then 1-inch-diameter (2.54cm) tubing has an external surface area of .294 square feet per linear foot (896cm²/m), while 1¼-inch-diameter (3.18cm) tubing has an external surface area of .360 square feet per linear foot of tubing (1,097cm²/m). In order to provide the required 40 square feet (3.72m²) of heat-transfer surface, about 136 feet (41.45m) of 1-inch (2.34cm) tubing or 111 feet (33.8m) of 1¼-inch (3.18cm) tubing will be required. Friction losses are less in the larger tubing, while the cost per foot is less for the smaller size. Even for the 1¼-inch tubing, fluid velocity is in the range of 3.5 feet

per second (1.07m/sec). This velocity guarantees a Reynolds number sufficiently high to ensure turbulent flow and good heat transfer.

Actually, the 40 square feet (3.72m²) of heat-transfer area is necessary only when the solar-fluid and tank temperature are nearly equal, say at 20°F (11.1°C) apart. During most collection periods this difference will be greater, so that less heat-transfer area would be required. As a reasonable compromise, let us build our heat exchanger of 100 feet (30.48m) of 1¼-inch-diameter (3.18cm) Type M tubing. We will use five 20-foot (6.1m) lengths, each cut into 6 foot 8 inch (2.03m) sections. Consequently, fifteen 90° elbows and fifteen 90° street elbows will be needed for its fabrication in addition to end fittings.

Now that we have laid out the array and storage tank and chosen a heat exchanger, we can tentatively lay out the circuit piping. This is best done using both plans and sections. Strive for a simple route that requires the least number of fittings. For new construction it will not usually be necessary to make special provisions for the pipe runs, since they probably will fit into stud spaces or between joists. Space should be allowed for pipe insulation. When one of these systems is added to an existing building, stud spaces usually are not available. Utilizing a 4×6-inch (10.2×15.2cm) vertical space in the rear corner of a closet should provide adequate space.

Friction loss (or pressure drop) and flow rate throughout the circuit must be calculated before a pump can be selected. The calculations are made first for water as the liquid and then modified for the antifreeze solution.

For these collectors, the manufacturer recommends a flow of .55 gpm (2.08 liters/min) per collector. Consequently, the flow through each four-panel subarray will be 2.2 gpm (8.33 liters/min) and flow for the entire array and the circuit piping and heat exchanger will be 11 gpm (41.64 liters/min). Calculated pressure-drop data through the collector is supplied by the manufacturer. This will be minimal, about .2 psi (.014kg/cm²) through each four-panel group.

Pressure drop through the heat exchanger is

easily calculated. Actual tubing length is 100 feet (30.48m). From Figure 4–41 (page 69) we find that thirty 90° elbows (fifteen standard 90° elbows and fifteen street elbows) have the equivalent length of 2 feet (.61m) each. Consequently, the equivalent length of the heat exchanger is 160 feet (48.77m). From Figure 4-39, a flow rate of 11 gpm (41.64 liters/min) through 1¼-inch (3.18cm) Type M tubing is about 1.1 psi per 100 feet. The pressure drop through the heat exchanger is $160 \times \frac{1.1}{100} = 1.76$ psi.

Suppose that the heat exchanger has been fabricated of 1-inch (2.54cm) Type M tubing. Then 140 feet (42.67m) would have been required. For this case, forty-two elbows are needed, each with an equivalent length of 1.5 feet (45.7cm), so that the equivalent heat-exchanger length is 203 feet (61.87m). Referring to Figure 4-39, an 11-gpm (41.64-liter/min) flow through 1-inch (2.54cm) Type M tubing causes a pressure drop of 2.8 psi per 100 feet (.006kg/cm²-m), so that the total pressure drop through a 1-inch (2.54cm) heat exchanger is $203 \times \frac{2.8}{100} = 5.68$ psi (.399kg/cm²). The larger piping causes additional installed costs but requires a smaller pump and reduced operating costs. It probably is wise to choose the larger-diameter tubing.

Pressure drop through the circuit piping is calculated in the same manner. Actual tubing length is determined by scale measurement of the drawings. Friction loss through the fittings is determined by counting the fittings and noting their equivalent length in Figure 4-41. The total equivalent length may be summarized as follows:

190 feet actual tube length = 190 feet (5.79m)
4 gate valves at .4 feet = 1.6 feet (.49m)
16 90° elbows at 2 feet = 32 feet (9.75m)
2 side branch tees at 3 feet = 6 feet (1.83m)
4 couplings at .6 feet = 2.4 feet (.73m)
total equivalent length = 232 feet (70.71m)

Since the pressure drop per 100 feet through the 1¼-inch tube with a flow rate of 11 gpm is 1.1 psi (.077kg/cm²), the pressure drop through the circuit

piping is 2.55 psi (.179kg/cm²). Total pressure drop through the circuit will be the sum of this amount, pressure drop through a collector subarray, and pressure drop through the heat exchanger. Thus:

Total P.D. $= 2.55 + 0.2 + 1.76 = 451$ psi $= 10.4$ feet (3.17m)

Remember that the required flow rate of 11 gpm (41.64 liters/min) and this pressure drop of 10.4 feet (3.17m) are based on the use of water as the heat-transfer liquid. However, the system will be filled with a 50 percent glycol antifreeze solution.

In order to calculate the required flow rate and pressure drop for the glycol solution, it is necessary to determine the lowest fluid temperature at which the system will operate. This particular system is used in conjunction with a water-source heat pump. Consequently, fluid temperatures as low as 100°F (37.8°C) or less will supply usable energy. By reference to Figure 4-52, we find that the adjusted flow rate is $11 \times 1.16 = 12.76$ gpm (48.3 liters/min). Figure 4-53 gives the pressure-drop correction factor for the antifreeze solution. For a minimum operating temperature of 100°F (37.8°C), the corrected pressure drop is $10.4 \times 1.49 = 15.5$ feet (4.72m). Which means that a pump must be selected that will deliver 12.76 gpm (48.3 liters/min) against a 15.5-foot (4.72m) head.

These pumping requirements are modest enough so that an in-line pump may be used. Figure 5-29 illustrates the performance curve of the Bell and Gossett Series PR pump. This pump is driven by a ⅙-horsepower motor drawing 3.3 amps. Another choice might be to use two Grundfos UP26-64 ¹/₁₂-horsepower pumps (Figure 4-42), each drawing 1.65 amps. If two of these pumps are used in series, the 12.76 gpm (48.3 liters/min) can be delivered against a 24-foot (7.32m) head (2×12). If they are used in parallel, then $2 \times 6.5 = 13$ gpm (49.2 liters/min) can be delivered against a 15.5-foot (4.72m) head. For this application, the series arrangement will be preferable. The choice between the use of one larger pump or two smaller pumps will be influenced by cost, space, availability, and personal preference.

In order to calculate the fluid volume of the sys-

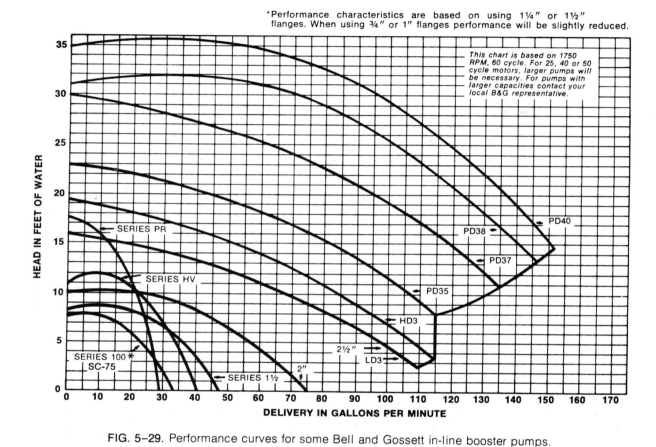

*Performance characteristics are based on using 1¼″ or 1½″ flanges. When using ¾″ or 1″ flanges performance will be slightly reduced.

FIG. 5–29. Performance curves for some Bell and Gossett in-line booster pumps.

tem, we first determine the total tubing length. Thus:

heat exchanger	100 feet (30.48m)
circuit piping	190 feet (57.91m)
fittings, etc., about	15 feet (4.57m)
Total	305 feet (92.96 m)

From Figure 4–2 (page 49), note that 1¼-inch (3.18cm) Type M tubing has a cross-sectional area of 1.31 square inches (8.45cm²). Therefore, one foot of this tube has a volume of $12 \times 1.31 = 15.72$ cubic inches. Total volume in piping is

$$305 \times 15.72 = 4{,}794.6 \text{ cubic inches} = \frac{4{,}794.6}{1{,}728 \text{ ft}^3}$$

$$= 2.775 \text{ cubic feet } (.0786\text{m}^3)$$

Since 1 cubic foot contains 7.48 gallons, the piping volume is 20.75 gallons. Manufacturers' literature states that the liquid capacity for each collector is .36 gallons. Twenty collectors will have a capacity of 7.2 gallons. If we allow for a small quantity of liquid in the expansion tank and pump, the system capacity may be taken as 30 gallons (113.6 liters), half of which will be glycol.

One may be tempted to use a smaller tubing size than the 1¼-inch-diameter (3.18cm) used for this circuit. After all, 1-inch-diameter (2.54cm) tubing is 40 to 50 percent less expensive. We have already designed a heat exchanger using this smaller size and calculated the pressure drop through it when using water as a heat-transfer fluid. Now let's examine the circuit piping as we did for the 1¼-inch (3.18cm) tubing:

Item	Equivalent Length (feet)
190-foot tube length	190
4 gate valves at .3 ft.	1.2
16 90° elbows at 1.5 ft.	24
2 side branch tees at 2.5 ft.	5
4 coupling at .45 ft.	1.8
Total equivalent length	222 (67.67m)

For our required flow rate of 11 gpm (41.64 liters/min), the pressure drop through 1-inch (2.54cm) Type M tubing is about 2.8 psi per 100 feet (Fig. 4-39), so that pressure drop through the circuit is $2.8 \times \frac{222}{100} = 6.16$ psi (.433kg/cm²). Total pressure drop through the system is:

heat exchanger	5.68 psi
circuit piping	6.16 psi
subarray	.2 psi
Total P.D.	12.04 psi = 27.7 feet (8.44m)

The adjusted flow rate for the glycol solution is the same as in the previous example. However, the adjusted pressure drop—at 100°F. (37.8°C) working fluid temperature—now is:

$$27.7 \times 1.49 = 41.3 \text{ feet (12.59m)}$$

The consequence of this action, if the Grundfos UP26-64 pump were still to be used, would be to require *four* such pumps installed in series. Not only would the savings in tube cost be more than offset by the additional pump cost, but operating costs would be twice as high for the life of the system. This condition suggests that piping be liberally sized. Of course with any system such as this, an optimum solution is likely to be found only by testing (analytically) two or more possible configurations.

Once the circuit piping and heat exchanger have been designed, other fittings may be selected and indicated on the drawings. Isolation valves should be installed at pump and heat exchanger. A boiler drain located at the low point of the system will facilitate draining. Between the pump and array a check valve should be installed to prevent reverse thermocirculation during nonsunny periods. Unless the pump is matched exactly to the flow and pressure-drop requirements, a flow-control valve may be necessary. Install an air vent at the high point of the system to facilitate filling, and an expansion tank sized to hold slightly more than the quantity of liquid in the collector array. A pressure-relief valve is required and may be intalled in the expansion tank. A drain line carried from this valve to a drain on the building exterior may, at some time, avoid the possibility of dripping ceilings. Thermometers, usually mounted in wells, are not essential for the operation of the system but may enhance the system's credibility to the building occupant.

CONTROLS

For a system of the sort that we are considering to operate efficiently, control must be exercised over the pump. If liquid temperature in the collectors is sufficiently greater than storage-tank temperature, then the pump should operate. Just as important, if liquid in the collectors is near to or below the temperature of storage, then the pump should not operate.

For most systems, temperatures are measured on the collector absorber or outlet manifold and in the storage tank or outlet of the heat exchanger by means of sensors (thermistors). These devices have resistances that are inversely proportional to their temperature. The temperature measurement is transmitted to a solar-controlled differential thermostat through low-voltage wiring where a decision is made as to whether the pump is to operate or not. Typically, these units activate the pump when the collector temperature is around 20°F (11.1°C) above storage temperature and stop it when the collector temperature is about 3°F (1.67°C) above storage temperature. Some controllers are capable of modulating the flow according to the temperature difference in order to enhance collector performance.

At the beginning of a collection period the collector temperature rises above the storage temperature, although liquid in the circuit between these two may be much lower. The pump is energized and cool liquid from the circuit rapidly cools the collector sensor. Without additional control, the pump could cycle unnecessarily. Likewise, at the end of a collection period when the pump is turned off, the collector temperature could rise, causing the pump to be reactivated. Some differential thermostats have circuits that prevent either of these occurrences.

There are a number of differential thermostats on the market (Fig. 4–54). Some of these have better user reports than others. Indeed, some do not seem to work at all. Since the cost of any of these devices is small, it might seem wise to purchase on the basis of its reputation rather than on initial cost.

Even the more modest of these devices may be equipped with an additional sensor to prevent overheating of a domestic-hot-water storage tank. It is unlikely that thermal storage for space heating could be overheated. Some sensors are capable of draining a system or restarting circulation when ambient temperatures approach freezing. However, a new generation of differential thermostats is appearing in which more functions may be controlled. The cost of such units frequently is far more than that for the more simple one-function controller. Furthermore, the availability of home minicomputers capable of controlling not only these functions but a variety of others may doom the more elaborate controllers.

There is a fundamental difference between solar heating systems and those systems using conven-

tional fuels. The conventional system normally does not contain a thermal-storage system. Hot-water or steam temperatures, or the temperature of a heat exchanger, are constant and known in advance. Consequently, the control of such a system is a simple matter. If the thermostat in a space calls for more heat, then the system is energized. When the space temperature reaches a certain point, the system shuts down.

For a solar heating system there are several other factors affecting its operation, including the temperature of thermal storage, a possible modulation of flow rates, and some means of activating the backup system whenever this is necessary. Control of one of these systems may be automated to almost any level. Most people in this country have grown to expect attention-free operation not only of heating systems but also of the multitude of other systems and devices that are used daily. However, when the same expectation is made of a solar heating system, the cost of controls may increase dramatically. I was recently involved in one such project. The cost of the control system exceeded the cost of the total collector array by about 25 percent. This cost would have been reduced substantially had the owner accepted the responsibility for the occasional flick of a switch.

Even when one has properly designed an array, when optimum storage capacity has been determined, when circuit piping and pumps are chosen for minimum energy input, and when an appropriate control system has been decided on, it still is impossible to estimate system efficiency or that portion of the heating needs that may be supplied by the solar assist. In order to arrive at reasonable values for these estimates, it is necessary to know how this solar heat will be supplied to the building. The following chapter discusses several systems.

CHAPTER SIX

USING SOLAR HEAT WITH CONVENTIONAL SYSTEMS

Even when a flat-plate collector array has been properly piped, the appropriate pump and controls have been provided, and a suitable thermal storage system is present, the efficiency of the system cannot yet be predicted. Efficiency is also a function of the collector design and construction, orientation and tilt angle of the array, availability of radiation, and the temperature difference between the collector fluid and ambient air.

For a well-designed system, the temperature of the collector fluid will be only a few degrees, say 10°F (5.6°C), warmer than the water in storage. Minimum usable temperature for the storage water will be determined by the type of building heating system to be employed. In new construction the heating system may be chosen to result in maximum solar efficiency. In a retrofit situation, certain compromises may be necessary.

It has previously been mentioned that sizing a solar system to provide all of a building's heating needs is not economically justified. Such a system would require a much larger array and storage system in order to meet the heating demand during a cloudy and cold January than for other months. The full capacity of the system would not be used during most of the heating season nor, of course, during any of the summer months. It is far more economically desirable to size the system to supply a significant portion during most of the winter and somewhat less during extreme weather. It appears that a system sized to supply 50 to 70 percent of the heating needs on a seasonal basis offers the best economic return.

The point to be made is that in order to assure continuous comfort, a solar system is always accompanied by a heating system that uses a conventional fuel. These systems may operate in conjunction with the solar energy system or may operate independently. Depending on system configuration, they are called supplementary, standby, or backup systems. Such a system might be as simple as a wood-burning stove similar to the one I use (Fig. 6–1). Obviously, if wood is used

FIG. 6–1. Wood-burning stove installed in the author's home. The stove is capable of maintaining the 1,900-square-foot residence at 70°F (21.1°C) with outside temperature as low as −10°F (−23.3°C).

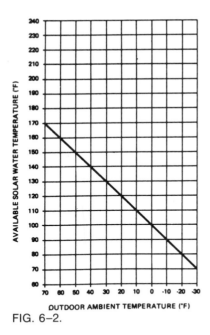

FIG. 6–2.

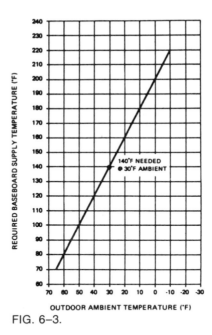

FIG. 6–3.

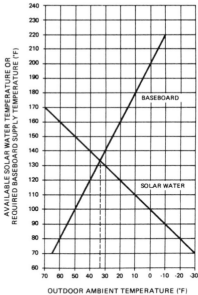

FIG. 6–4.

FIG. 6–2. Relationship between solar-heated water temperature and outdoor temperature for $\Delta T_c = 100°F$.

FIG. 6–3. Temperature need for conventional baseboard terminal (the average building can be maintained at 70°F without using heat if the average daily temperature is at least 65°F).

FIG. 6–4. Outdoor temperature at which water from solar storage can meet full load for conventional baseboard heating system (design ambient temperature = –10°F; design terminal temperature = 220°F; $\Delta T_c = 100°F$).

for backup heat, then a prime requirement for the wood burner is its safety and efficiency. For this reason, wood-burning stoves or wood-burning furnaces hold a definite advantage over fireplaces. Some wood stoves such as mine have a disappearing door so that the view of open flames rather than efficiency is possible when the occasion demands.

Before describing specific system types, it is necessary to have some idea of the range of storage temperatures attainable. In January during the best collection hours, between 10:00 A.M. and 2:00 P.M., the available insolation, q_i, will average about 250 Btu/ft²-hr (790w/m²). Suppose that the temperature difference between the liquid in the solar circuit and outside air, ΔT_c, is 100°F (37.8°C). Then the fluid parameter is $\frac{100}{250} = .40$ and, from Figure 2–13 (page 27), collector efficiency is about 40 percent. This is a reasonable efficiency. By lowering the liquid flow rate, higher temperatures can be obtained, but at lowered efficiency. Conversely, a lower temperature difference will result in higher efficiencies. For our first examples, let us

assume that the 100°F (37.8°C) difference will be used. Available solar-liquid temperature as a function of outdoor ambient temperature is shown in Figure 6–2.

A first impulse may be to use solar assist for a conventional hydronic baseboard heating system, especially for a retrofit application. Conventional baseboard systems are designed for a supply water temperature of between 200° and 220°F (93.3° and 104.4°C) and return water temperature about 10°F (5.6°C) less. Suppose that the system has been designed for an outdoor temperature of –10°F (–23.3°C). When the outside temperature is above –10°F (–23.3°C), then lower-temperature supply water will provide the building's needs. Thus, if the outside temperature is 20°F (–6.7°C), then a baseboard supply temperature of 160°F (71.1°C) will suffice. The relationship between outside temperature and required baseboard supply temperature is shown in Figure 6–3. When the relationship shown in this figure and Figure 6–2 are plotted on the same drawing, we find the minimum outside temperature at which the

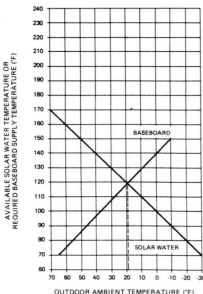

FIG. 6–5.

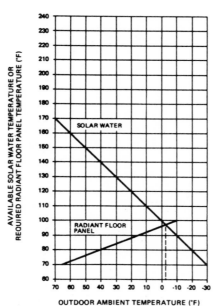

FIG. 6–6.

FIG. 6–5. Modified baseboard system.

FIG. 6–6. Outdoor temperatures at which radiant floor panels are usable ($\Delta T_c = 100°F$).

solar-heated water is usable (Fig. 6–4). For our assumed conditions, the solar system will operate whenever the outside temperature is above 34°F (1°C), but becomes inoperable when storage temperature is below about 120°F (48.9°C). This means that much of the stored heat will be unused.

One way to overcome this situation is to redesign the system to use water at a lower temperature, say 150°F (65.6°C). This modified system will be operable down to about 19°F (−7.2°C) ambient, at which point backup heat will be required (Fig. 6–5). New buildings can be designed with the increased radiation surface required by a lower water temperature. For existing buildings an increased length of baseboard will have to be added.

The problem is not as severe when radiant-panel heating is employed. Ceiling panels usually are designed for 120°F (48.9°C) supply water. Floor panels, depending on floor covering, generally require supply water at about 100°F (37.8°C). For this latter case, the solar system will operate with outside temperatures as low as −5°F (−20.6°C),

as shown in Figure 6–6. For new construction a perimeter loop of one or two copper tubes placed in the concrete floor slab near outside walls will supply a significant portion of the building's heating needs with this low-temperature water, even though a forced-air system is also to be installed.

Most houses built today employ forced-air heating systems. These systems are capable not only of heating a building, but also of providing the other functions of a true air-conditioning system—ventilation, filtration, and humidity control. In most dwellings, a forced-air furnace is employed. This furnace contains a blower and heat exchanger as well as connections for supply and return plenums and controls. In the case of an electric furnace, the heat exchanger is replaced by a resistance heater. The furnace may have its supply plenum on the top (upflow) or on the bottom (counterflow), or a supply plenum on one end and a return plenum on the other end or side (horizontal flow). When cooling is desired, a direct-expansion refrigerant coil is placed in the supply plenum. A humidifier for winter operation also may be located there. Provision for an air filter is made at some point in the re-turn-air plenum. In addition to electricity, furnaces may also use natural gas, LPG (propane or butane), or oil.

Another method of supplying space heat with a forced-air system is to use a fan-coil unit. Usually, but not always, this system is used for a building consisting of several zones. The fan-coil unit consists of a blower, a coil through which hot or chilled water flows, provision for an air filter, and associated controls. Sometimes two coils are employed—one for hot water and the other for chilled water. In either event, hot water flows through the coil when the space calls for heat, the blower is energized, and heat from this water is transferred to the supply air stream. An external source of hot water, such as a boiler, is necessary. Most hot-water coils are sized for entering water at about 150°F (65.6°C). Air off the coil is perhaps 20° to 30°F (−6.67° to −1.11°C) lower. These temperatures are comparable to those obtained from a forced-air furnace, although a bit lower.

Theoretically, if the temperature of supply air is above that of the conditioned space, then heating will be accomplished. Practically, two factors conspire to constrain severely this ideal situation. If the supply-air temperature is not much higher than room temperature, then a greater volume of this lower-temperature air is required. This greater volume requires either a larger blower or larger ducts or both. For buildings that are also summer cooled, it is possible that duct sizes are adequate for supply air in the 85° to 95°F (29.4° to 35°C) range. Otherwise, a larger blower is indicated.

Even though supply air transports enough energy to heat the space, if its terminal velocity at a grille, register, or diffuser is too high, then the air will be perceived by people as cool, and the space will be considered "drafty." This condition is caused by a "wiping" of skin areas by high-velocity air, a situation that encourages evaporative cooling. Consequently, when low-temperature air, down to about 85°F (29.4°C), is used for supply in forced-air systems, terminal velocity should be limited to about 400 fpm (2.03m/sec).

There are no technical obstacles to using stor-

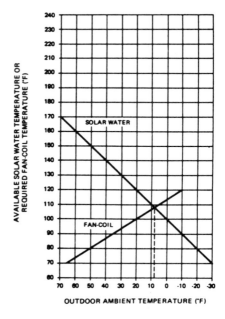

FIG. 6–7. Outdoor temperatures at which fan-coil system is usable ($\Delta T_c = 100$°F).

age temperatures of 120°F (48.9°C) or lower, provided that an adequate volume of air can be moved and that terminal velocities are limited. Figure 6–7 indicates the limits of operation for water at 120°F (48.9°C) in a fan-coil system.

Two possibilities exist for solar assist to a forced-air system. In the first of these, an auxiliary hot-water coil is added to the supply-air plenum of a system using either a forced-air furnace or a fan-coil unit (Fig. 6–8). In operation, water from storage of above about 120°F (48.9°C) is circulated through the auxiliary coil, and the furnace or coil in the fan-coil unit is inoperative. Below this value, solar-heated water ceases to circulate and heating is provided by the conventionally fired unit.

On the other hand, the auxiliary hot-water coil could be installed in the return-air plenum (Fig. 6–9). When solar temperatures are adequate, then the furnace or conventionally heated water coil is inoperative. As the solar-storage temperature decreases, circulation is maintained so that return air is preheated by solar-heated water as cool as

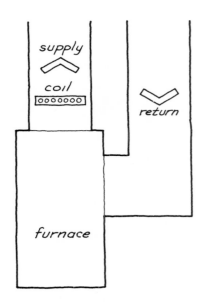

FIG. 6–8. Forced-air solar system with auxiliary standby heat unit.

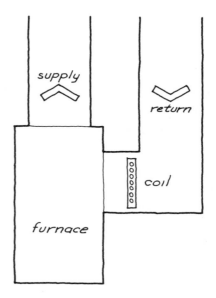

FIG. 6–9. Forced-air solar system with supplementary standby heat unit.

about 80°F (26.7°C). Below this temperature the solar assist would cease to circulate.

If pressed for an opinion, I would have to contend that the solar-assisted heat pump is the optimum system that can be installed. By any standard, it meets the specifications for appropriate technology, since it uses two well-developed technologies to a greater end. Both the flat-plate collectors and the heat pump operate more efficiently together than either would alone. Since the collectors may be single-glazed for most locations, economies in initial cost would be realized.[1]

For a better understanding of what a heat pump is and how it works, here is an example. When you touch a working stove, heat flows from its hot surface to your cool finger. If you touch an ice cube, heat flows from your warm finger to the cold ice. These two situations are examples of the second principle of thermodynamics, which states that heat always flows from a body that is at a higher temperature to a body at a lower one.

Although it does not violate the principle of the second law, an ingenious device is capable of extracting heat from a body at a lower temperature and supplying heat to a body at a higher temperature. This device is called a heat pump, since it pumps heat "uphill." However, as in pumping water from a well, energy is required to move this heat uphill.

Invented in Scotland in the middle of the last century, the heat pump enjoyed a brief popularity in this country during the 1950s, but it was plagued with cost and reliability problems. Both of these problems now have been overcome.

A heat pump works on the vapor-compression refrigeration cycle. Most residential units, including window as well as automobile air conditioners, also work on this cycle (see Figure 6–10).

In addition to the circuit piping, there are four elements in the system—an evaporator, a compressor, a condenser, and an expansion device. The latter is either a valve or a capillary tube, the tube

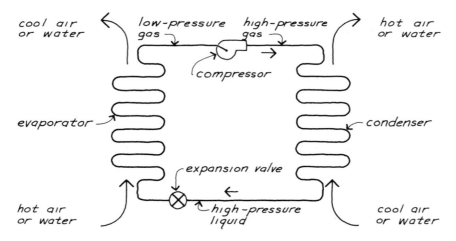

FIG. 6–10. The vapor-compression refrigeration cycle.

being somewhat like a long orifice. As the gas/liquid mixture leaves the small opening, it expands, turning to gas and absorbing heat as it does so.

The circuit is filled with a refrigerant, usually a fluorinated hydrocarbon (Freon is a trademark of the Du Pont Company), which has the appropriate boiling point.

In operation, the system works like this. Liquid refrigerant is allowed to boil in the evaporator, thereby absorbing heat from the surroundings. (Remember that water absorbs about 1,070 Btu/lb when it boils at atmospheric pressure, even though its temperature does not change.) In the case of the familiar room air conditioner, the evaporator is a finned-tube direct-expansion (DX) coil, and the surroundings are a moving stream of air. This is the portion of the system that cools. Refrigerant leaving the evaporator is a mixture of vapor and liquid.

The compressor not only maintains the proper pressure in the evaporator, it also compresses the vapor. When this high-pressure vapor leaves the compressor, it is at a temperature higher than that surrounding the condenser. As it passes through the condenser, it gives up heat to the surroundings and changes into a liquid.

These surroundings usually also are a fluid, either air or water, but also may be earth. For automobile or window air conditioners, the fluid surrounding both the evaporator and the condenser is air.

It isn't difficult to see that the fluid cooling the condenser is heated in this process. You can feel the heat if you put your hand in the downstream airflow from the condenser. This is a heat pump in summertime operation.

For wintertime, imagine that the condenser is moved indoors and air is blown across it for space heating. The evaporator is moved to the outdoors. Now we have a heat pump. However, not too many of us want to reverse the locations of these units physically from one season to another, so a piping and control scheme takes care of this change, as indicated in Figure 6–11. Notice that the coils now are called "inside" and "outside" coils, since each serves as both evaporator and condenser, depending on whether it's the heating or cooling season.

If the fluid surrounding both coils is air, then we speak of an air-to-air heat pump. If the fluid surrounding the outside coil (which may be located indoors, even in the same cabinet as the inside coil) is water, then we have a water-to-air heat pump. This is the sort of heat pump in my own house, but mostly this type is used in large build-

pens, the aquastat-controlled three-way valve directs circulation through the heat pump. The water can be used until its temperature is as low as 60°F (15.6°C), while still maintaining a COP of about 3. During the severe January of 1977, I actually rejected water from the heat pump at 40°F (4.4°C). Below this temperature, it is necessary to fire up the wood stove or resort to resistance heating.

Heat pumps are an excellent example of high technology applied to appropriate use. Solar-assisted heat pumps are an even better example. In my opinion, most all homes will use heat pumps someday, either with or without a solar assist.

Figure 6–14 indicates the outdoor temperature at which the solar-assisted heat pump may be used. Notice that for this system the solar-heated liquid needs to be only about 70°F (21.1°C) above the outdoor ambient temperature in order for the system to be operative. This lower operating temperature permits even single-glazed collectors to perform with an enhanced efficiency. If double glazing is employed with this lowered temperature difference, the efficiency is even better. In Figure 6–15 operating temperatures for several system types are combined in a single chart so that system comparisons may be made.

When a water-source heat pump is used for cooling, a source of condensing water is necessary. Since most of us do not have streams or ponds or wells with an unlimited source of water, cooling towers ordinarily are used (Fig. 6–16). Prior to the 1960s, practically all refrigeration systems used these towers, since they are inherently more efficient than air-cooled condensers. On the other hand, towers require periodic maintenance. This required maintenance was undoubtedly a major factor in the decline in the use of cooling towers. Nevertheless, with increasing energy costs, we should expect to witness a return to the use of these towers.

A natural-draft cooling tower should be located so that it is not shielded from summer breezes. Location of a forced-draft tower is less critical. Although a forced-draft tower requires energy for its fan motor, its pumping requirements are not as

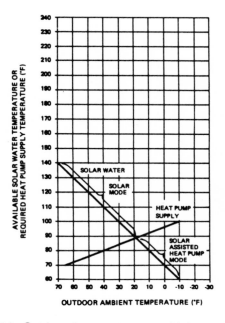

FIG. 6–14. Outdoor temperature at which a solar-assisted heat pump is operable. Note that the system will meet full load requirements with ΔTc = 70°F.

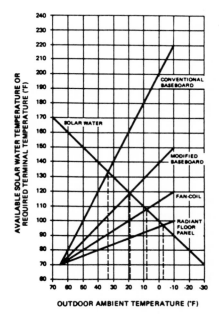

FIG. 6–15. Outdoor temperatures at which various heating systems are operable (ΔTc = 100°F).

FIG. 6–16. A forced-draft cooling tower. Courtesy Marley Cooling Tower Company.

great as are those found in a natural-draft tower.

These towers are rated according to their cooling capacity. The usual design conditions are 95°F (35°C) entering water, 85°F (29.4°C) leaving water, and a 78°F (25.6°C) wet-bulb ambient condition. This wet-bulb condition is equivalent to a 95°F (35°C) dry bulb and about 48 percent relative humidity, which might be the case for a hot summer afternoon. The towers were meant to be installed in a piping circuit that has no appreciable thermal-storage capacity.

The thermal-storage capacity of a solar system can be used to good advantage to reduce cooling costs. Even during the hottest part of the summer, the wet-bulb temperature at night will frequently be 70°F (21.1°C) or less. By controlling the cooling tower with a timer so as to operate only at night, the heat pump may be supplied with water as cool as about 70°F (21.1°C). A heat pump supplied with 75°F (23.9°C) water may have 10 percent more capacity and may draw 14 percent less electrical current than one served with 100°F (37.8°C) incoming water. Furthermore, energy consumed by the cool-

ing tower will be during off-peak hours of electrical demand.

While this arrangement offers definite advantages, its use requires two important design considerations. It may be necessary to increase the storage-tank size in order to provide a large enough heat sink to "coast" through a hot day. Alternatively, the timer may be programed to operate during two or more periods. Since the cooling of the water is due to evaporation, some water is constantly being lost from storage. Consequently, a float valve installed in the storage tank will enable it to maintain a constant volume.

Hundreds of thousands of air-to-air heat pumps are presently in use throughout the country. It appears desirable to combine a solar assist with this sort of heating system. Several federally funded projects have investigated the feasability of this combination by modifying the heat-pump components. I have a singular objection to this approach. Such modifications might be handily made by a highly skilled and technically qualified engineer. But what about the average air-conditioning serviceman? What about summertime changeover? Since it is the fluid temperature across the outside unit that we wish to elevate, why modify the equipment at all?

I have developed a scheme for solar assist for air-to-air heat pumps similar to the one described for water-source heat pumps, although it is not quite as simple. Yet it still allows for normal summer operation and requires no modification of the refrigeration equipment.

The system is installed as indicated in Figure 6–17. If water in storage is above 100°F, operation is in the purely solar mode. When the storage temperature drops below this value, a solar assist is provided by means of a finned-tube coil mounted in a shroud enclosing the outside unit.

Since the circuit serving the outside coil is exposed to outside temperatures, it will generally be necessary to use an antifreeze solution in it. If glycol or silicone is used for this purpose, it must be remembered that the viscosity of the solution increases rapidly with decreasing temperature so that increased pumping effort is required.[2]

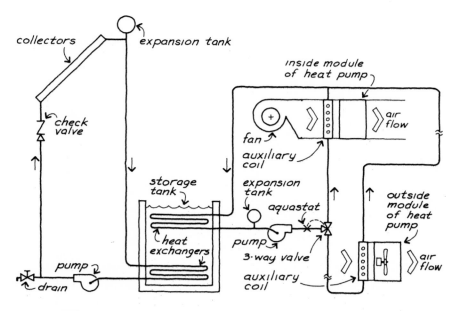

FIG. 6–17. Schematic of solar assist for air-to-air heat pump.

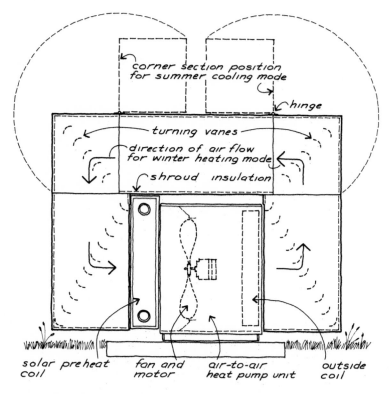

FIG. 6–18. Solar-assist shroud for air-to-air heat pump.

The shroud around the outside unit and supplementary coil is of utmost importance. Without the shroud some heat may be extracted from the solar supplement, but most of it is wasted to the surrounding air. The shroud minimizes this waste. Insulation on the inside of the shroud and thorough sealing of joints to prevent air leaks contribute to even higher efficiency. Since propeller fans can move large amounts of air but cannot overcome as much static pressure as blowers, turning vanes should be installed (Fig. 6–18).

The COP of a heat pump fitted in this manner may be improved with liquid temperatures as low as 40°F, regardless of outside ambient temperature. For a liquid temperature of 90°F, the COP can be increased to 5.[3] For new construction one might choose a solar-assisted water-source heat pump, but for the vast majority of air-to-air heat pumps already in use this scheme provides quite a valuable assist.

We can see that a solar supplement can be used in conjunction with a variety of conventional heating systems. The lowest storage temperature which could alone satisfy a building's needs is about 100°F. When a coil is installed in the return-air stream of a hot-air furnace, then a useful supplement is available with water temperature as low as 80°F. When heat pumps are used, then water temperatures as low as 60°F or lower can be used. On the other hand, conventional baseboard systems may require water temperatures far in excess of this value.

Operating at lower temperatures offers at least three advantages—the capacity of thermal storage is increased, collectors can operate at higher efficiencies, and initial cost may be reduced by using single rather than double glazing. Nevertheless, a final decision to use one heating system rather than another may involve considerations other than collector efficiency.

NOTES

1. T. S. Dean, "Solar Assisted Heat Pump Air Conditioning System," *Sharing the Sun,* Vol. 3, *Proceedings of International Solar Energy Society, Winnipeg* (Elmsford, N.Y.: Pergamon Press, 1976).
2. T. S. Dean and M. S. Drake, "Assist of an Air to Air Heat Pump Using Solar Heated Hot Water," Heat Pump Technology Conference, Oklahoma State University, 1979.
3. T. S. Dean and T. H. Roberts, "A Heat Regain System for Solar Assisted Air to Air Heat Pump," Heat Pump Technology Conference, Oklahoma State University, 1979.

CHAPTER SEVEN

SYSTEM PERFORMANCE

Most of us would like to know the magnitude of the energy supplement that might be expected from a proposed flat-plate array and its associated system. We would like to know the predicted energy harvest so that the design might be refined to supply larger or smaller portions of a building's heating needs. Such a knowledge is fundamental to deriving any sort of economic analysis. The values used in the analysis of one of these systems are not difficult to calculate, though it must be remembered that they are based on average, mean, or normal values. The difference between actual and predicted performance for any day, week, or month could be significant. Over a year's span, this difference should be less. Over the period of ten years, the gap between actual and predicted performance can be minimal.

Essential to any analysis is the "degree day" concept. Extensive testing has established that if the outside temperature averages 65°F (18.3°C) for a twenty-four hour period, then no fuel is required to maintain the building's interior at 70°F (21.1°C) or above. Obviously, this observation is a generalization, since buildings with large south-facing glass areas and considerable insulated thermal mass can be maintained at 70°F without fuel even though the outside temperature is below 65°F. In any event, a building's heating requirements for a day with an average temperature of 45°F (7.2°C) is about twice that required for a day whose average temperature is 55°F (12.8°C). A day with an average temperature of 55°F (12.8°C) would have a heating load of 10 degree days (65° minus 55°), while a day with an average temperature of 45°F would have 20 degree days (65° minus 45°). The total number of degree days during a season at a given location is a good indicator of the severity of the climate.

For any given month or year, the number of degree days experienced is available from the local U.S. Weather Bureau. A synopsis of this and other meteorological data for many locations throughout the country are available from:

U.S. Department of Commerce
National Oceanic and Atmospheric Administration
Environmental Data Service
National Climatic Center
Federal Building
Asheville, N.C. 28801

These informative four-page fact sheets report not only the number of heating degree days per month and year, but also minimums, maximums, and means for cooling degree days, precipitation, wind, sunshine, and humidity.

When designing a conventional heating system, the maximum heat loss under "design conditions" is calculated and the heating components are sized to meet this requirement. A usual indoor temperature under design conditions frequently is taken at 70° or 72°F (21.1° or 22.2°C), although some new guidelines limit this temperature to 68°F (20°C). The outdoor design temperature to be used is not the lowest recorded temperature, since such a temperature might be experienced for only a few hours and, obviously, not in every year. A reasonable estimate for the outdoor design temperature is to add 10° to 15° to the lowest recorded temperature.

Line	Description	Source	Units	Data
1	Indoor Design Temp.	Heat Loss Calc.	°F	
2	Outdoor Design Temp.	Heat Loss Calc.	°F	
3	Design Temp. Difference	(1) - (2)	°F	

Line	Description	Source	Units	Data
4	Bldg. Design Ht. Loss; BTU/hr	Ht. Loss / 1000	1000 BTU Per Hr.	
5	Daily Design Bldg. Heat Loss	(4) x 24	1000 BTU Per Day	
6	Bldg. Heat Loss BTU per Deg. Day	(5) / (3)	1000 BTU Per D.D.	

Line	Description	Source	Units	Data											
7	Month			J	F	M	A	M	J	J	A	S	O	N	D
8	Day/Mo.			31	28	31	30	31	30	31	31	30	31	30	31
9	Degree Day Per Month	Climatic Atlas	D.D./month												
10	Bldg. Heat Loss Per Month	(6) x (9) / 1000	Million BTU/Mo.												
11	Bldg. Heat Loss Per Day	(10)/(8) x 1000	1000 BTU/Day												

FIG. 7–1. Chart for estimating a building's daily, monthly, and annual heating needs.

Suppose that inside and outside design temperatures are taken to be 70°F (21.1°C) and −5°F (−20.6°C), respectively. Then the design temperature difference is 75°F (41.7°C). Moreover, suppose that a building's heat loss at this temperature difference is 40,000 Btu/hr (40 MBH). For a twenty-four-hour period under these conditions the heat loss would be

40,000 Btu/hr × 24 hr/day
= 960,000 Btu/day (281 kwh/DD)

and the heat loss per degree day is

$$\frac{960,000 \text{ Btu/day}}{75°} = 12,800 \text{ Btu/DD} (3.75 \text{ kwh/DD})$$

The NEMA (National Electrical Manufacturers Association) has modified the degree-day concept slightly. NEMA contends that houses built to its specifications for electric heat will have heating requirements of $\frac{18.5 \times 100}{24} = 77$ percent of that needed by houses heated by other methods. Their specifications include very good insulation, the use of a vapor barrier, and no chimney fuel-air-draft requirements. All in all, this is a sensible approach that can be used for new construction built to NEMA specifications, but is not likely to be appropriate for existing construction.

The building's monthly and daily space-heating needs are most simply calculated in tabular form, using a table such as that shown in Figure 7–1. As an example, let us use our earlier example located near Kansas City, Missouri. This climate is not nearly as favorable for a solar installation as Albuquerque, Phoenix, or Denver. Nevertheless, like most parts of the United States, it is still favorable for solar.

Completing this chart is hardly more than a mechanical process. Lines 1 through 6 are entered with the quantities that have just been discussed. Data for line 9 are available from the previously mentioned meteorological synopsis or the Climatic Atlas. Notice that the units for line 10 are *millions* of Btu/month, while the units for line 11 are *thousands* of Btu/day. From experience, you will know that the heat loads for both June and September are inconsequential. The mere presence of one person (whose metabolism produces around 400 to 600 Btu/hr) in the building will more than compensate for the average June heat loss. The annual heating budget for this building is 66 million Btu, far less than most buildings of 1,600 square feet in this climate. It must be remembered that the design was intentionally energy conserving and that a heat loss of twice this amount for a building of similar size would not be unusual. Even so, if this 66 million Btu were supplied by resistance heat costing 6¢/kwh, the annual heating budget would be $1,160, with the January, February, and December usages each above $200.

You may recall that the instantaneous efficiency of a collector was given by the equation in column two on page 25. For a given collector, orientation, and mass-flow rate, instantaneous efficiency becomes a function of the "fluid parameter,"

$$\frac{\overline{T} - T_a}{q_i}$$

where

$\overline{T}$ = average temperature of collector fluid, °F
T_a = outdoor ambient temperature, °F
q_i = insolation, Btu/ft²-hr

For convenience, let us define

$$\Delta T_c = \overline{T} - T_a$$

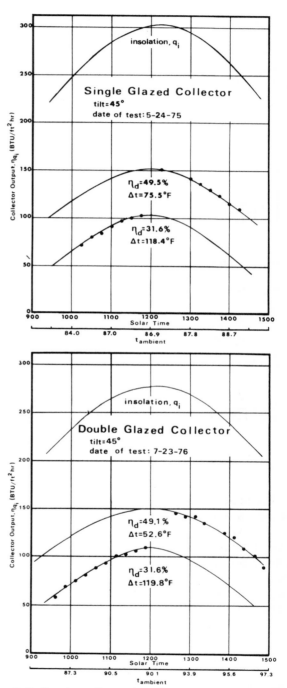

Fig. 7-2. Day-long thermal performance of a collector. Note that these tests were made during the latter part of May, and July. Efficiencies during January would be lower.

A collector's efficiency is directly affected by the magnitude of ΔT_c. *Increasing* ΔT_c will result in a *decrease* in collector efficiency. The significance of this situation may be seen in Figure 7–2, which indicates the results of actual testing. For this test, the mass-flow rate through the collector and inlet temperature were held constant. When ΔT_c was 75.5°F, then the day-long efficiency was 49.5 percent. Increasing ΔT_c to 118.4°F lowered the efficiency to 31.6 percent. Greatest system efficiency occurs when ΔT_c, and consequently $\bar{T}$, is maintained as small as possible consistent with terminal requirements. It should be noted that both $\bar{T}$ and T_a will ordinarily increase throughout the day. Of these two temperatures, the increase in $\bar{T}$ will usually be the greater, so that ΔT_c will also increase. This increase lowers system efficiency during afternoon hours. It is for this reason that some authorities recommend a slight bias, say 10°, west of south for the array in order to enhance available insolation during the afternoon hours of collection.

The magnitude of ΔT_c is determined by two factors. One of these is the outdoor temperature. This temperature fluctuates widely, but the values of daily maximums, minimums, and averages are available from Weather Bureau data. The vast middle part of this country, generally an area bounded by the Rocky Mountains on the west and the Mississippi River on the east, is categorized as a "modified continental" climate. Temperatures in this region may take sudden and violent plunges, although a springlike day in January is not unusual.

The other factor that affects the magnitude of ΔT_c is $\bar{T}$, the average temperature of fluid through the collector. This temperature is related to the temperature of the storage system, which, in turn, is related to the required terminal temperature. For example, a conventional baseboard system requires a significantly higher terminal temperature than does a radiant floor panel. Consequently, the baseboard system will necessitate a higher ΔT_c than will the radiant-panel system.

The system that we will use as an example utilizes a water-source heat pump with an auxiliary hot-water coil in the return-air plenum. This coil is

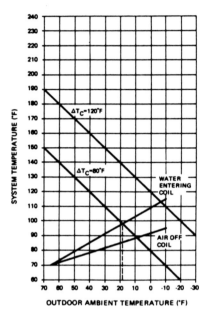

FIG. 7–3. System evaluation chart for example in text. Notice that $\Delta T_c = 120$°F is required for the full design load, while $\Delta T_c = 80$°F will satisfy full load down to about 18°F outside temperature.

sized to provide total building heating needs with supply water at 115°F (46.1°C) and air off the coil at 95°F (35°C). These values are shown on the system evaluation chart, Figure 7–3. When storage temperature is inadequate for this mode of operation, water is diverted to the heat pump by means of a three-way valve. In this manner, full house heating is maintained without resistance-heating backup through the full range of outside temperatures. Resistance heating will, however, be required during extended periods of cloudy weather.

A number of methods for estimating collector performance over a period of time are available. Each of these methods depends upon a simplified version of the second equation on page 25. In this simplified version, entering and leaving collector fluid temperatures are replaced by $\bar{T}$, the average fluid temperature.

Of the several methods available for estimating system performance, the "f-chart" method developed by Klein, Beckman, and Duffie at the University of Wisconsin[1] is probably in widest use. Not only does it conform in most respects to ASHRAE 93-77, but it has been adopted as the required estimating method by government agencies. The method is described in detail in Appendix A (122 pp), *Solar Heating and Domestic Hot Water Systems*, HUD Intermediate Minimum Property Standards Supplement, 1977 edition. The use of this method of estimating efficiency is mandatory for anyone anticipating federal funding for a solar system.

This method must be considered fairly accurate, at least. In comparison with actual performance data for MIT Solar House IV over a two-year period, the difference between actual performance and estimated performance using the f-chart method was about 8 percent.

Although the f-chart method is both accurate and in widespread use, it is by no means without limitations. Both this method and ASHRAE 93-77 are predicated on the use of an external heat exchanger of the shell-and-tube type and its associated additional pump. Furthermore, the number and complexity of the required calculations seem to me to be more amenable to computer solution than to simple hand calculation, although programs are available or can be written for several programable hand calculators.

Of the other methods available for estimating system performance, the one developed by the Fluid Handling Division of International Telephone and Telegraph Corporation (Bell and Gossett) seems the best to me. Such a method requires little knowledge of mathematics, it can be used with hand calculation or a simple pocket calculator, it may be checked step by step, it is easy to modify, and it is easy to check. When I have calculated the performance of a system by both this method and the f-chart method, results have differed by less than 5 percent, although I have no idea which of the methods is most accurate. It is a modification of the Bell and Gossett method that will be used in the following example.

The essence of this method is a simplified procedure for estimating the temperature difference, ΔT_c, as a function of storage and outdoor tempera-

Line	Description	Source	Units	heat pump	Data										heat pump				
				J	F	M	A	M	J	J	A	S	O	N	D				
1	Month			J	F	M	A	M	J	J	A	S	O	N	D				
2	Start Tank Temperature	System Evaluation Chart	°F	96	60	96	96	96	96			96	96	96	60				
3	Daily Heat Load	Line 11, Fig A-9	1000 BTU/Day	476	272	308	134	46	5	0	0	18	97	274	280				
4	Tank Temp. Rise	(3) / Tank Cap (gal) × 8.33	°F	48	27	31	13	5					10	27	28				
5	Final Tank Temp.	(2) + (4)	°F	144	87	127	109	101					106	123	88				
6	Mean Tank Temp.	(2) + (5) / 2	°F	120	74	112	103	99					101	110	74				
7	Mean Ambient Temp.	Climatic Atlas	°F	28	33	41	55	58	65			69	59	44	32				
8	Base ΔT_c	(6) - (7)	°F	92	41	71	48	41					42	66	42				
9	Low Ambient Temp.	Climatic Atlas	°F	19	22	32	45	65	74			59	48	35	24				
10	Start ΔT_c	(2) - (9)	°F	77	38	64	51	31					48	61	36				
11	High Ambient Temp.	Climatic Atlas	°F	36	42	51	65	74	83			79	69	53	40				
12	Final ΔT_c	(5) - (11)	°F	108	45	76	44	27					37	70	48				
13	ΔT_c to 10 AM	(10) + (8) / 2	°F	85	40	68	50	36					45	64	39				
14	ΔT_c 10AM-2PM	(8)	°F	92	41	71	48	41					42	66	42				
15	ΔT_c after 2PM	(12) + (8) / 2	°F	100	43	74	46	34					40	68	45				

FIG. 7–4. Chart for estimating ΔT_c. February and December values are calculated for heat-pump operation. All other months are based on pure solar operation using a finned-tube coil in the return-air plenum. This chart is reproduced as Appendix A-10.

tures. In the Bell and Gossett method, the system evaluation chart is used to aid in making a judgment selection for a basic ΔT_c, which is then adjusted for differing ambient and storage-tank temperatures throughout the day. Subsequent calculations assist in selecting storage-tank capacity.

The modified Bell and Gossett method that we will use assumes that a storage volume has been preselected. Starting tank temperature is found from the system evaluation chart. The building's daily heating needs and storage volume determine the daily tank temperature rise. The difference between tank temperature and outside temperature determines ΔT_c for different time intervals.

A convenient tabular method for estimating ΔT_c is shown in Figure 7–4. A line-by-line explanation of this table follows.

Line 1 identifies the month for which the calculation is made. When using solar assist for a water-source heat pump, two or more sets of calculations may be made for some months, especially for December, January, and February. Blank columns may be used for this purpose.

Line 2 specifies the starting tank temperature. In our example, the average low temperature for January is 19°F (− 7.2°C). This temperature will occur at the beginning of the collection day, and coincides in time with the start temperature. From the system evaluation chart it may be seen that 96°F (35.6°C) storage water will satisfy the heating requirements at this outdoor temperature, for solar heating alone. If the storage tank is used to assist the heat pump, then its temperature may drift as low as 60°F (15.6°C). Our example will illustrate the different efficiencies available by using the solar alone and as a heat-pump assist.

The storage tank for our example was chosen to have a 1,200-gallon capacity. Because water weighs 8.33 pounds per gallon and has a specific heat of 1.0 Btu/lb-°F, the thermal storage capacity of the tank is 1,200 gal × 8.33 lb/gal × 1 Btu/lb-°F = 10,000 Btu/°F (5.27 kwh/°C).

Line 3 specifies the building's daily heating requirements. Since the average daily temperature in January is 28°F (− 2.2°C), then the average January day has a heating load of 65 minus 28 = 37 degree days. For our example, the building has a heat loss of 12,800 Btu per degree day. Therefore, the average daily heat requirement will be 12,800 Btu/DD × 37DD = 473,600 Btu/day (138.8 kwh/day).

In all honesty, the heat load for this typical January day will be somewhat less than this amount, since a significant amount of direct solar gain can be achieved. One adult occupant of the building for a twenty-four-hour period will reduce the load by about 9,000 Btu. Cooking, clothes drying, and lighting will make additional contributions.

Line 4, the daily tank temperature rise, may be found by dividing the daily heating requirements by the tank's thermal-storage capacity per degree. Under our assumed conditions, this would result in a 47°F (8.3°C) rise in the purely solar mode, so that the final tank temperature, line 5, is 143°F (61.7°C). Line 6, the mean tank temperature, is the average of the start and final tank temperatures, while the mean ambient temperature is available from weather data. Base ΔT_c is the difference between the mean tank temprature and mean ambient temperature. When a heat exchanger is used, as is usually the case, this value will be modified. Lines

9 through 15 are self-explanatory. The values shown in lines 13, 14, and 15 allow us to calculate the energy harvest a bit more accurately.

For our example, the solar component can be used to assist a heat pump. Most water-source heat pumps will operate with 60°F (15.6°C) water and maintain a COP of about 3. Thus, the 473,600 Btu/day heating requirement would be met by purchasing about 160,000 Btu/day heat equivalent of electric energy and supplying the remaining 320,000 Btu/day by solar. For this case, the daily tank temperature rise will be 32°F (17.8°C). Calculations for this condition are shown in Figure 7–5.

Actual calculation of the collectable insolation is carried out in Figure 7–6. A first step is to correct the available insolation for local conditions. Line 1, clearness factor, may be found from the clearness map, Figure 2–2. The smog factor, line 2, may usually be taken as unity for rural locations, although some urban locations may suggest a lower value. Line 3 allows for some degradation of performance due to dirt. I have found that a value of .95 for this value is appropriate. Collector glazing tends to be dirtier during the summer or other periods of least rainfall. Usually, a rinsing with a garden hose will cleanse the glazing of excess dust or dirt.

Lines 5 through 15 are generally self-explanatory. In order to complete line 7, both latitude and tilt angle must be known. In our example, I have assumed a tilt angle of 45° and have averaged the given values for tilt angles of 40° and 50°. Appropriate insolation values are given in the insolation tables in the Appendix. Line 9 gives the values for ΔT_c which we have previously calculated. Lines 10 and 11 modify these values for use with a heat exchanger. Since collector area is relatively expensive, it is wise to employ an efficient heat exchanger in order to minimize the approach temperature ΔT_c. An approach temperature of 10°F (5.6°C) is reasonable. Line 12 lists the fluid parameters, which must be used with a performance curve for a specified collector in order to determine the hourly (actually, the instantaneous) efficiency. Finally, hourly and daily collectable insolation are recorded on lines 14 and 15.

It will be necessary to prepare one of these

FIG. 7-5.

Line	Description	Source	Units	Data												
				J	F	M	A	M	J	J	A	S	O	N	D	
1	Month															
2	Start Tank Temperature	System Evaluation Chart	°F	60												
3	Daily Heat Load	Line 11, Fig A-9	1000 BTU Day	317 (COP=3; ⅔ of load by solar, ⅓ of load by electric)												
4	Tank Temp. Rise	(3)/(Tank Cap (gal) x 8.33)	°F	32												
5	Final Tank Temp.	(2)+(4)	°F	92												
6	Mean Tank Temp.	(2)+(5)/2	°F	76												
7	Mean Ambient Temp.	Climatic Atlas	°F	28												
8	Base ΔT_C	(6)-(7)	°F	48												
9	Low Ambient Temp.	Climatic Atlas	°F	19												
10	Start ΔT_C	(2)-(9)	°F	41												
11	High Ambient Temp.	Climatic Atlas	°F	36												
12	Final ΔT_C	(5)-(11)	°F	56												
13	ΔT_C to 10 AM	(10)+(8)/2	°F	45												
14	ΔT_C 10AM-2PM	(8)	°F	48												
15	ΔT_C after 2PM	(12)+(8)/2	°F	52												

FIG. 7-5. Chart for estimating ΔT_c with heat pump, January.

Determine insolation correction factor.

Line	Description	Source	Data	Line	Description	Source	Data
1	Clearness Factor	Clearness Factor Chart	1.0	3	Dirt, Etc. Factor		.95
2	Smog Factor		1.0	4	Insolation Correc. Factor	(1) x (2) x (3)	.95

Determine Daily collector insolation for month of January (Fan Coil)

Line	Description	Source	Unit	6	7	8	9	10	11	12	1	2	3	4	5	6
5	Time		AM-PM					A.M.		Noon				P.M.		
6	Daily Time		Hour	6	7	8	9	10	11	12	1	2	3	4	5	6
7	Available Insolation	ASHRAE Insolation Table	BTU/Ft² Per Hr.			77	176	243	283	297	283	243	176	77		
8	Corrected Insolation	(4) x (7)	BTU/Ft² Per Hr.			73	167	231	269	282	269	231	167	73		
9	ΔT_C	Fig. A-10	°F			85	85	85	92	92	92	100	100	100		
10	Glycol to Water HX approach ΔT	Design of HX if Used	°F			←				10				→		
11	Corrected ΔT_C	(9)+(10)	°F			95	95	95	102	102	102	110	110	110		
12	Fluid Parameter	(11)/(8)	°F / BTU/Ft²Hr.			1.30	.57	.41	.38	.36	.38	.48	.66	1.51		
13	Panel Efficiency	Use (12) w/Panel Eff. Chart				0	.10	.31	.34	.37	.34	.23	0	0		
14	Collectable Hourly Insol.	(8) x (13)	BTU/Ft² Per Hr.			0	17	72	91	104	91	53	0	0		
15	Total Daily Collectable Insol.	Summation Line (14)	BTU/Ft² Per Day							428						

FIG. 7-6. Chart for estimating collectable insolation during January when operating in the pure solar mode.

Determine insolation correction factor.

Line	Description	Source	Data	Line	Description	Source	Data
1	Clearness Factor	Clearness Factor Chart	1.0	3	Dirt, Etc. Factor		.95
2	Smog Factor		1.0	4	Insolation Correc. Factor	(1) x (2) x (3)	.95

Determine Daily collector insolation for month of January (Heat Pump)

Line	Description	Source	Unit	6	7	8	9	10	11	12	1	2	3	4	5	6
5	Time		AM-PM					A.M.		Noon				P.M.		
6	Daily Time		Hour	6	7	8	9	10	11	12	1	2	3	4	5	6
7	Available Insolation	ASHRAE Insolation Table	BTU/Ft² Per Hr.			77	176	243	283	297	283	243	176	77		
8	Corrected Insolation	(4) x (7)	BTU/Ft² Per Hr.			73	167	231	269	282	269	231	167	73		
9	ΔT_C	Fig. A-10	°F			45	45	45	48	48	48	52	52	52		
10	Glycol to Water HX approach ΔT	Design of HX if Used	°F			←				10				→		
11	Corrected ΔT_C	(9)+(10)	°F			55	55	55	58	58	58	62	62	62		
12	Fluid Parameter	(11)/(8)	°F / BTU/Ft²Hr.			.75	.33	.24	.22	.21	.22	.27	.37	.85		
13	Panel Efficiency	Use (12) w/Panel Eff. Chart				0	.42	.51	.56	.57	.56	.46	.36	0		
14	Collectable Hourly Insol.	(8) x (13)	BTU/Ft² Per Hr.			0	70	118	151	161	151	106	60	0		
15	Total Daily Collectable Insol.	Summation Line (14)	BTU/Ft² Per Day							817						

FIG. 7-7. Chart showing possible collectable insolation during January when using solar energy to assist a heat pump. Compare with Fig. 7-6.

FIG. 7-8.

Line	Description	Source	Units	heat pump	J	F	M	A	M	J	J	A	S	O	N	D	heat pump J
1	Month				J	F	M	A	M	J	J	A	S	O	N	D	J
2	Day/Month				31	28	31	30	31	30	31	31	30	31	30	31	31
3	Collector Area	Assume	Ft²		396	396	396	396	396	396	396	396	396	396	396	396	396
4	Collected Daily Insolation	Fig. A-11	BTU/Ft² Per Day		428	1086	791	976	997					976	617	774	817
5	Possible Monthly Coll. Insolation	(2) x (3) x (4) / 1,000,000	Million BTU/Mo.		5.25	12.04	9.71	11.59	12.24					11.98	7.33	9.50	10.03
6	Sunshine Factor	Climatic Atlas			.55	.57	.59	.60	.64	.70	.76	.73	.70	.67	.59	.52	.55
7	Probable Monthly Collection	(5) x (6)	Million BTU/Mo.		2.89	6.86	5.73	6.96	7.83					8.03	4.32	4.94	5.52
8	Heat Load/Month	Fig. A-9	Million BTU/Mo.		14.76	11.43	9.54	4.02	1.42	.15	0	0	.54	3.01	8.22	12.98	14.76
9	Solar Heat Used/Month	Smaller of (7) or (8)	Million BTU/Mo.		2.89	6.86	5.73	4.02	1.42	.15	0	0	.54	3.01	4.32	4.94	5.52
10	Monthly % Solar	(9) x 100 / (8)	%		19.6	60.0	60.0	100	100	100	-	-	100	100	52.6	38.1	374
11	Solar Heat Used Per Year	Summary of (9)	Million BTU/Yr.							36.51							
12	Total Heat Load Per Year	Fig. A-9	Million BTU/Yr.							66.07							
13	% Solar Heat	(11) x 100 / (12)	%							55.3 %							

FIG. 7-8. Chart for calculating solar portion of heating load.

charts for each month of the heating season. In some cases, such as in our example, where either of two modes of operation is possible, it will be necessary to prepare two charts for a month in order to decide which mode is the more efficient. Two charts for January are shown in Figure 7–7. It can be seen that the collectors achieve almost twice the efficiency for the heat-pump mode as for straight solar space heating. This is to be expected, since single-glazed collectors would be a poor choice for the latter case in the example climate.

We now are in a position to calculate that portion of the monthly and annual heat requirements that may be met by the solar supplement. These calculations are made with the aid of the chart shown in Figure 7–8. Although the methods for performing these calculations are explained on the chart, a few comments may be helpful.

Line 3 requires that a collector area be assumed. A common rule of thumb suggests that 50 to 75 percent of a building's heating needs can be met with a collector array whose area is 25 to 40 percent of the building's floor area. Obviously, this is a gross generalization, but it serves as a starting point. I have found that when solar supplements a water-source heat pump, then about 25 percent of the floor area is adequate in many localities. In any event, the collector area is assumed and completion of the chart yields monthly and annual solar contribution. If this contribution is less than desired, then the collector area may be increased as necessary. Remember that the cost of the collectors usually is less than half the cost of the system, so that adding collector area will not increase the cost of the system proportionately.

The sunshine factor is tabulated in line 6. Of all the Weather Bureau data, the percentage sunshine is probably the least reliable for our uses. However, this lack of reliability should not be counted against the recording stations, but rather on the method of collection of the data. I remember a recent January that frequently had sunny early mornings and late afternoons, but solid cloud cover during the middle of most days. I counted four days during which a reasonable energy harvest might be possible. The local Weather Bureau recorded 53 percent possible sunshine.

Each of the tables shown in Figures 7–1, 7–4, 7–6, and 7–8 illustrate the set of calculations I have described. These tables are reproduced in the Appendix. I would suggest duplicating them before attempting actual computations.

Unfortunately, some persons will look to the results of these charts as predictions for day-to-day system performance. This attitude is inherent in our "figures do not lie" syndrome, to which most of us subscribe, at least in part.

In fact, the analysis that we have performed is probably not accurate for any given day or month. It is reasonable for a statistically long period. It is possible that a series of cloudy, cool days during October may force the system into a heat-pump mode. It is just as likely that a series of sunny days during January, especially if the weather is not too cold, will allow return to the purely solar mode for a day or two. Mild ambient temperatures will increase the start tank temperature. This situation will depress system efficiency, but it also will allow for higher final storage temperature.

The best thing to remember about a system performance analysis is that it is relatively accurate in the long run, although it may be in extreme error for any short time interval. This is a prime reason for requiring backup heat for any solar energy system.

Notes

1. W. A. Beckman, S. A. Klein, and J. A. Duffie, *Solar Heating Design by the F-Chart Method* (New York: John Wiley, 1977).

CHAPTER EIGHT

SYSTEM ECONOMICS

It is fashionable nowadays to speak of amortization periods, payback analysis, lifetime costs, and similar buzz words or expressions from the field of economics when discussing solar. In fact, none of these has much application to our homes or personal possessions. What is the payback on a second bathroom? Does a large (or expensive) automobile offer an increased economic advantage over a small car? Is "designer" clothing a better investment than apparel available through national mail-order catalogs? Of course not! Our purchasing and investment patterns are conditioned by a number of factors, only one of which is economic.

Nevertheless, many persons will opt for a solar heating system, or stand back at arm's length from it, on the basis of an economic analysis. Forget the possible unavailability of energy from conventional sources. Forget that even the most astute economic analyses are frequently in error.

Economics is an unusual science. It manipulates data from the past, as does sociology and the other "soft" sciences. It projects into the future, as do these other soft sciences. What gives economics a credibility not always enjoyed by the others is its use of mathematics—particularly statistics and probability—to justify its projections. A certain respectability has been achieved by the use of mathematics, even if the results are totally in error. For every accurate economic prediction, one can discover at least one inaccurate prediction.

My point is not to ridicule economic considerations or forecasts. Instead, I would like to suggest that even the best economic analysis can become grossly in error as a result of unforeseen events. Furthermore, such an analysis involves so many variables that the cost-effectiveness of each solar installation will differ.

A good deal of insight into a solar system's cost-effectiveness can be gained by discussing these variables. They include the cost of a system and its maintenance, local climatic factors, whether a system is used year-round or just during the heating season, the present cost of energy and its projected rate of escalation, and several tax-related items, including tax incentives, the possibility of increased property taxes, and one's own income-tax bracket. Let's examine some of these factors.

The cost of a solar heating system is subject to wide variation. As in other segments of the economy, free and open competition tends to reduce costs. If you live in an area where there are a number of completed solar systems, your cost probably will be lower than in a location where the contractor is entering on a new venture. What level of control do you require? I have several installations in which the cost of the controllers is hardly more than for a thermostat. I also have one installation—a banking facility—for which the controls cost 25 percent *more* than all the collectors. In my estimation, the minimally controlled installations will perform almost as well as the elaborately controlled one.

For a person who performs his own installation, the payback period will be relatively short—probably not more than five years for space heating. Constructing your own collectors will reduce this time, and tax incentives will reduce it even more. Of course, your own efforts have a monetary worth, but this is not a cash investment.

At the other extreme are some systems heavily subsidized by the federal government. Although these demonstration programs were a well-intentioned effort to erase much of the skepticism surrounding solar heating and cooling systems, they were also hamstrung by the multiplicity of requirements imposed by the bureaucracy. Some of these requirements are desirable, while others serve no useful purpose. The net result is that installations made as part of the demonstration programs cost as much as five times more than installations without government funding, but utilizing the same basic equipment.

Items such as glazing will affect both initial cost and performance. For example, low-iron-content glass with its greater transmission may allow as much as 10 percent more radiation to reach the absorber, as compared with ordinary glass. For panels heating domestic water, this increase may be of the order of 15,000 Btu/ft²-year (40,680kg-cal/m²-year). The prudent investor will compare the value of this enhanced collection with the increased cost of low-iron-content glass. As desirable as low-iron glass is, it is not always cost-effective.

A similar comparison may be made for single versus double glazing. Double glazing will certainly allow for a higher efficiency at large fluid parameters, say above .20, than will single glazing. Nevertheless, for small fluid parameters, single glazing actually is more efficient than double glazing.

One should not always choose the most efficient collector, since its economic return is a function not only of its efficiency but also of its cost. Five percent added efficiency is hardly justified if the cost is 20 percent greater. Pay particular attention to a collector's installation requirements. Attempt to minimize the number of field-installed connections. What are the recommended flashing details? The finished cost of a solar system depends on a number of these individual details which, taken together, can significantly alter the cost of a system.

Local climate also will have a strong influence on the amortization period for one of these systems. When compared with electric energy, solar-heated domestic water is a good choice in almost every location today, even without tax incentives. Space heating is another matter, and so is space cooling.

Long winters will extend the period during which

a system will be used. The amount of sunshine will affect the amount of energy harvested. Low ambient temperatures will seriously curtail the amount of energy collected unless a low-temperature terminal, such as a heat pump or radiant-floor-panel system, is employed.

Although I have not discussed the subject of solar cooling, this is possible using an absorption chiller. Currently, there is only one manufacturer making these units in sizes suited to most houses, and their cost is high. This unit employs lithium bromide as a refrigerant. In order to operate at full capacity it needs water in the 200°F (93.3°C) range, although it can deliver a lesser amount of cooling with water as cool as 160°F (71.1°C). A backup source of cooling generally is recommended with a solar assist.

Double glazing is indicated for a system such as this, and the cost of the overall solar-assisted heating and cooling system may be excessive. On the other hand, the collectors in this kind of system can be used in summer as well as winter so that their amortization is accelerated.

The present cost of energy is highly variable, depending on both the type of energy and the geographical location. Considering a single type of fuel, its cost may vary by a factor of five from one part of the country to another. The fact is, most persons are not aware of the unit price of the energy they buy. Mostly, they are dismayed by the ever-increasing size of their utility bills.

Most homes are heated by one of four fuels—electricity, natural gas, LPG (liquefied petroleum gas, usually propane or butane), or fuel oil. Since natural gas is usually priced per thousand cubic feet (MCF), LPG and fuel oil are priced per gallon, and electric energy is priced per kilowatt-hour, and since each of these units has a different heat content, direct comparison of energy costs is not immediately visible. One way to overcome this difficulty is to calculate the cost of usable energy from these sources on a common basis, say the cost per million (10^6) Btu, although other units also could be used.

One cubic foot of natural gas has a heat content of about 1,000 Btu. Consequently, a MCF of natural gas contains approximately 1 million Btu. Although most gas-fired furnaces and water heaters are rated at 70 percent efficiency, generally this high value is obtainable only with new, properly adjusted devices in a laboratory situation. A more reasonable estimate for the efficiency is 50 to 60 percent. If the gas is burned with an efficiency of 60 percent, then the cost to the user may be calculated by dividing the gas price per MCF by .6. For example, if gas costing $5.00 is burned with an efficiency of 60 percent, then cost/10^6 Btu = $\frac{5.00}{.6}$ = $8.33

LPG, or bottled gas, is priced by the gallon, each of which has a heat content of about 100,000 Btu. Therefore, 10 gallons will contain about 1 million Btu. This fuel is burned with about the same efficiency as natural gas, so that if LPG costs 70¢ per gallon, then cost/10^6 Btu = $\frac{.70 \times 10}{.6}$ = $11.67.

Fuel oil also is sold by the gallon. In a No. 2 grade it contains about 140,000 Btu/gallon, so that about 7 gallons contain 1 million Btu. If the No. 2 fuel oil costs $1.10 per gallon and burns with 60 percent efficiency, then cost/10^6 Btu = $\frac{7 \times 1.10}{.6}$ = $12.83

Electric energy is priced by the kilowatt-hour. Since 1 watt = 3.41 Btu/hour, then 1 kwh = 3,410 Btu, and therefore 10^6 Btu = $\frac{1,000,000}{3,410}$ = 293 kwh. Although the generation of electric power is not a 100 percent efficient operation, the direct use of this power—say to heat water or air—may be considered 100 percent efficient. Therefore, if electric energy costs 6¢ per kwh, then cost/10^6 Btu = 293 × .06 = $17.58. It should be remembered that if this energy is used for a heat pump whose COP is 2, then the cost is only half this amount.

These examples serve only to indicate how energy costs may be compared. They should not be taken as actual costs, since the variation of energy prices is extreme.

With the foregoing information, a rudimentary economic analysis for a solar system may be performed. The solar-system cost can be estimated or

bid. Methods for estimating the annual heat collection were presented in the last chapter. Consequently, it is possible to assign a monetary value to the collection which, in turn, is compared with system cost. As it happens, this is only part of the story.

In designing for the future, a critical element is the escalation of energy costs. I frequently state that the average cost of energy will quadruple in the next ten years. This number has been confirmed in private conversations with a number of utility executives, although to be honest, none of us can accurately predict ten years into the future. (One utility executive violently disagreed with me. He claimed that costs would escalate no more than 15 percent a year. This value is almost exactly a quadrupling in ten years.)

One key to energy costs is the price of newly discovered natural gas. This gas is controlled by the Natural Gas Policy Act of 1978, which is part of the National Energy Act, signed into law in November 1978. The price of this gas, as well as gas in several other categories, is subject to an "annual inflation adjustment factor." The price for a given month is arrived at by multiplying the price for the previous month by the monthly equivalent of the annual inflation factor. The price will escalate monthly, in addition to the inflation adjustment factor, by an annual rate of 3.5 percent until April 1981, after which the price will escalate by 4 percent. This is the law. Not only is the 15 percent annual escalation rate given credibility, but wishful estimates of a 6 percent annual escalation are permanently laid to rest.

Nor should the cost of building new or replacing worn-out steam-generating capacity be overlooked. Many of our old steam-generating plants (now almost ready to be replaced) cost $150 to $200 per installed kilowatt capacity. A recently completed coal-fired plant cost $400 per installed kilowatt. If construction of this plant were to begin today, its estimated cost would be $900 per installed kilowatt. Proposed nuclear plants have estimated costs of around $1,500 per installed kilowatt. All of these numbers affect the rate base for consumers of electricity.

What about the value of money? This certainly has a bearing on a solar system's payback. However, its impact depends on whether the money is borrowed or invested. It also depends on a person's income-tax bracket, although this dependency is not often acknowledged.

Suppose that money is borrowed to install one of these solar systems. Then we should expect that the loan interest and system-maintenance cost would be equal to, or less than, the value of the collected energy. Except for one minor, or not so minor, point. Under present tax laws, interest is a deductible expense, but utility costs for one's home are not. What might at first appear to be a marginally economic system can, in fact, offer greater value.

On the other hand, suppose that money is available for investment. Compared with a certificate of deposit or high-grade bonds, the same money will yield about *three times* the return when invested in solar domestic-water-heating systems. Furthermore, the income-tax advantage will still exist.

There are several tax situations to be considered. In some locations, the solar installation will increase the property valuation, and consequently the tax. Several states have enacted laws to prohibit this occurrence.

On the positive side, many states have passed legislation that encourages solar installations. These should be thoroughly investigated by anyone contemplating one of these systems. My own state of Kansas allows a 25 percent income-tax credit or $1,000, whichever is less, for a solar or wind system. A five-year carryover is available for those of us who do not pay $1,000 in state income taxes during a given year. Moreover, if the structure is 70 percent solar heated, then a 35 percent tax rebate on the *entire building* is awarded for a five-year period.

Available to almost everyone is the federal income-tax credit for a solar installation. I say almost everyone, since the National Energy Act excludes installations made before April 1977. My own home, as well as a handful of other houses built by experimenters, counterculturists, researchers, or, I like to think, prudent and responsible citizens, were built prior to that date. Nevertheless, this credit is substantial for those who qualify. It allows for a 30 percent credit for the first $2,000 in cost and a 20 percent credit for the next $8,000. Consequently, a $10,000 system will receive a $2,200 federal tax credit. This same act provides for fifteen-year loans of up to $8,000 at reduced interest rates for solar installations.

I hope that the points I have mentioned clearly indicate the possible variations in an economic analysis. Although such an analysis is not difficult to perform, in most cases it will be an individual matter. Although it may seem a broad statement, solar is almost a guaranteed investment for one who provides his own labor.

After discussing economic considerations, the following anecdote may seem incongruous. Yet I can think of no better way of ending.

Mr. Jones was president of the local small-town bank. An avid gardener, he had a well-equipped and well-insulated attached greenhouse (if it's like mine, it also is a very efficient and very inexpensive solar collector). One cold winter morning with lowering clouds and snowdrifts along every byway, he appeared in his office with a perfect tomato—tantalizing, beautiful, mouth-wateringly juicy, vine-ripened, just begging to be eaten. Mr. Jones was less than reticent in exhibiting this morsel to his friends and co-workers.

One of his audience, probably an accountant, remarked that the gem probably cost $2.

"Yep," Jones replied, "and worth every penny."

APPENDICES

A-1. Conversion factors

To Obtain	Multiply	By
cal/gram	Btu/lb	0.55556
cal/gram-°C	Btu/lb-°F	1.0
cal/sec-cm-°C	Btu/hr-ft-°F	0.0041336
cal/sec-sq cm	Btu/hr-sq ft	0.000075341
cal/sec-sq cm-°C	Btu/hr-sq ft-°F	0.0001355
centimeters	inches	2.540
cm/sec	ft/min	0.508
cm/sec	ft/sec	30.48
cu cm	cu ft	28.317
cu cm	cu in	16.387
cu cm	gal (U.S. liq)	3,785.43
cu cm/sec	cu ft/min	472.0
cu meters	cu ft	0.028317
cu meters	gal (U.S. liq)	0.0037854
cu meters/hr	gal/min	0.22712
cu meters/kg	cu ft/lb	0.062428
cu meters/min	cu ft/min	0.02832
cu meters/min	gal/sec	0.22712
cu meters/sec	gal/min	0.000063088
grams	lb	453.5924
grams/cm	lb/in	178.579
grams/cu cm	lb/cu ft	0.016018
grams/cu cm	lb/cu in	27.680
grams/cu cm	lb/gal	0.119826
joules	Btu	1,054.8
joules	ft lb	1.35582
kg	lb	0.45359
kg-cal	Btu	0.2520
kg-cal	ft lb	0.00032389
kg-cal	kw-hr	860.01
kg-cal/kg	Btu/lb	0.5556
kg-cal/kw-hr	Btu/kw-hr	0.2520

To Obtain	Multiply	By
kg/cal/min	ft lb/min	0.0003239
kg-cal/min	kw	14.33
kg-cal/sq meter	Btu/sq ft	2.712
kg/cu meter	lb/cu ft	16.018
kg/liter	lb/gal	0.11983
kg/meter	lb/ft	1.488
kg/sq cm	lb/sq in	0.0703
kg/sq meter	lb/sq ft	4.8824
kg/sq meter	lb/sq in	703.07
kw	Btu/min	0.01758
kw	ft lb/min	0.00002259
kw	ft lb/sec	0.00135582
kw-hr	Btu	0.000293
kw-hr	ft lb	0.0000003766
liters	cu ft	28.316
liters	cu in	0.01639
liters	gal (U.S. liq)	3.78533
liters/kg	cu ft/lb	62.42621
liters/min	cu ft/sec	1699.3
liters/min	gal (U.S. liq)/min	3.785
liters/sec	cu ft/min	0.47193
liters/sec	gal/min	0.063088
meters	feet	0.3048
meters	inches	0.0254
meters/min	ft/min	0.3048
meters/sec	ft/sec	0.3048
sq cm	sq ft	929.0
sq cm	sq in	6.4516
sq meters	sq ft	0.0929
watts	Btu/sec	1,054.8

FIG. A-2. Mean daily solar radiation by month for the United States *Reprinted by permission: United States Department of Commerce, National Oceanic and Atmospheric Administration, Environmental Data Service. The National Climatic Center considers the accuracy of this solar radiation information to be questionable. The best estimates of observed solar radiation may be obtained from their magnetic tapes in the SOLMET format.*

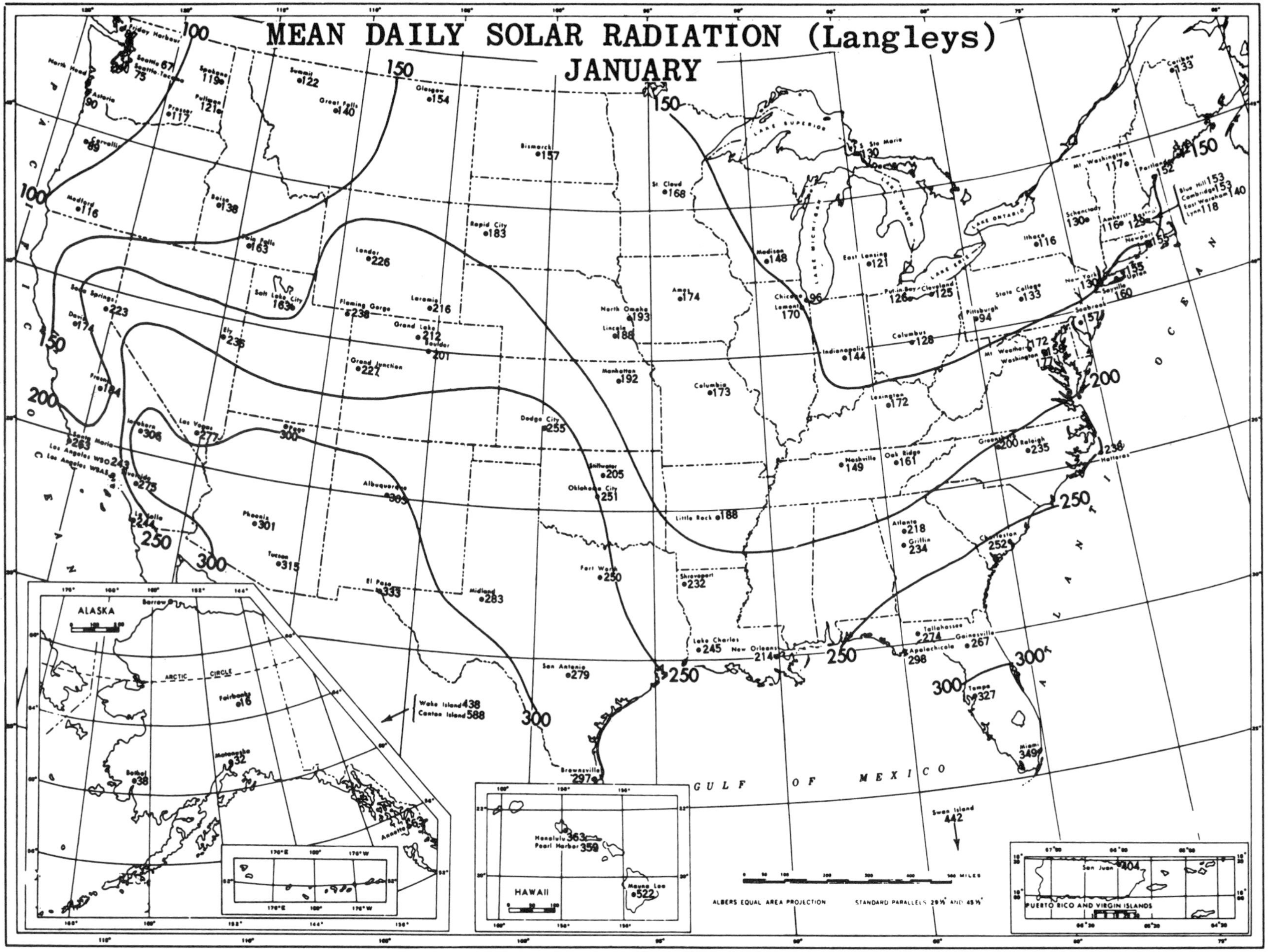

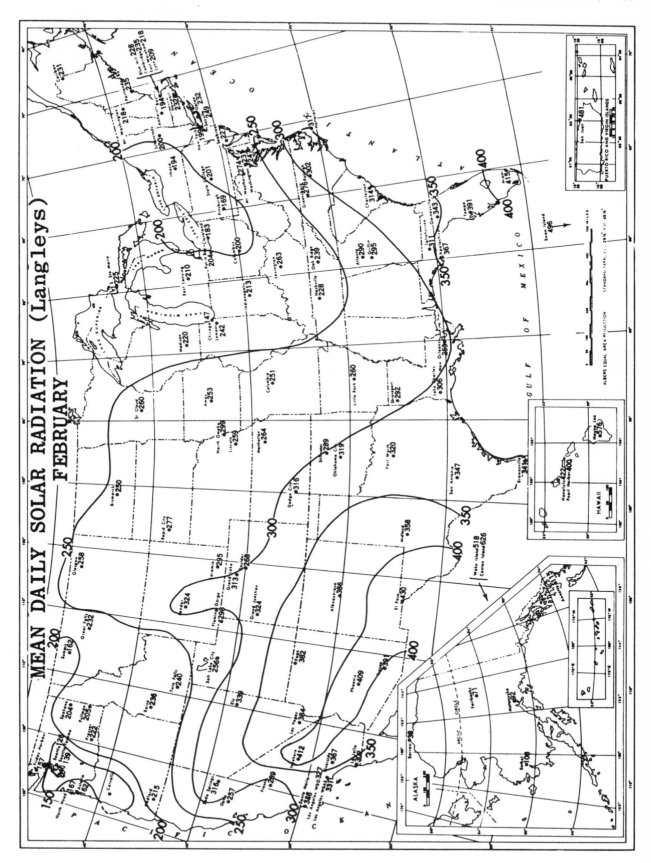

MEAN DAILY SOLAR RADIATION (Langleys)
FEBRUARY

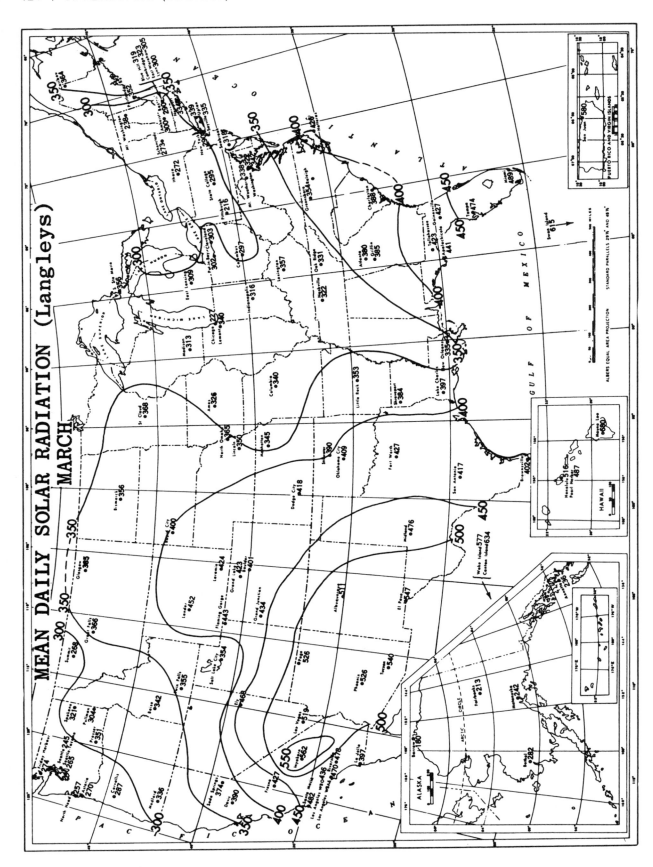

MEAN DAILY SOLAR RADIATION (Langleys)
MARCH

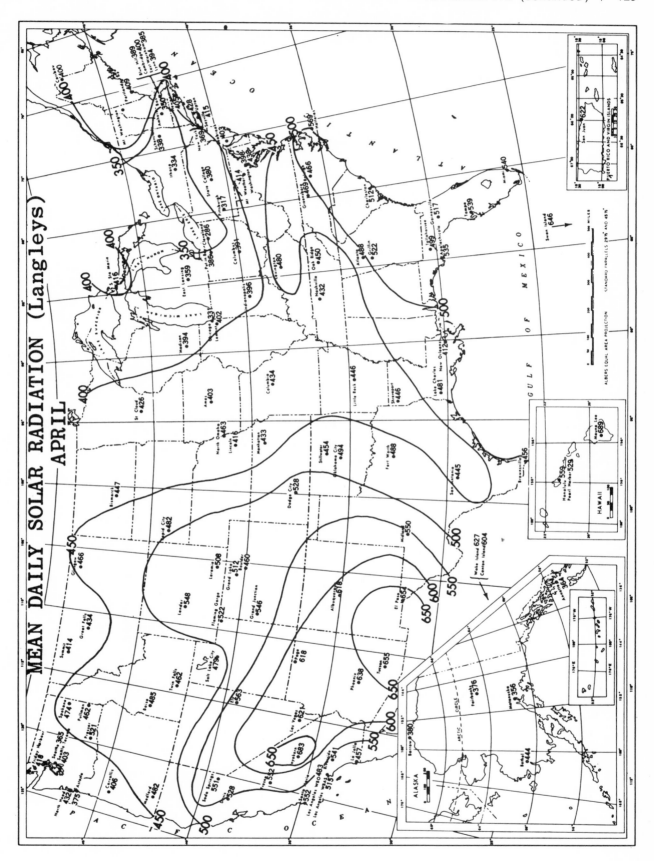

MEAN DAILY SOLAR RADIATION (Langleys)
APRIL

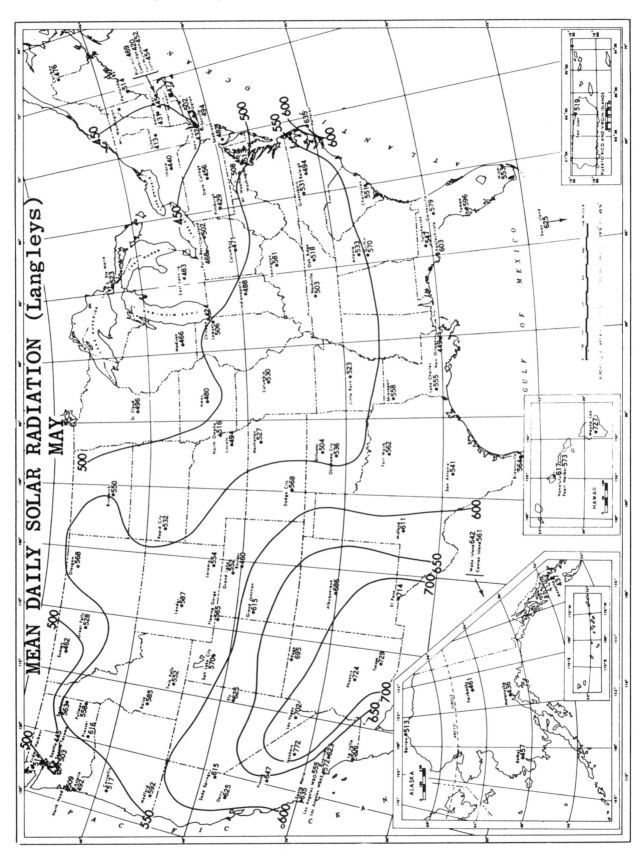

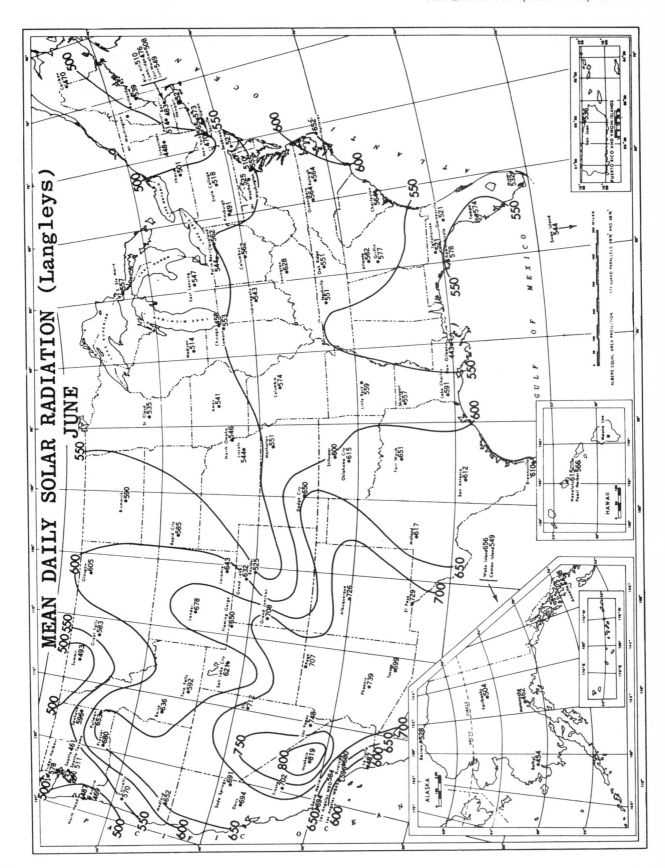

MEAN DAILY SOLAR RADIATION (Langleys)
JUNE

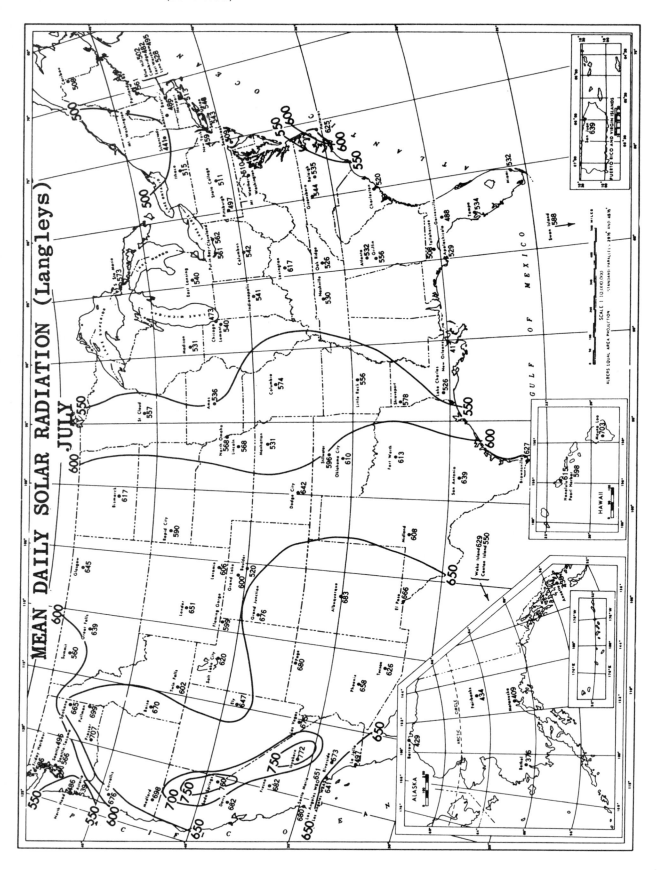

MEAN DAILY SOLAR RADIATION (Langleys)
JULY

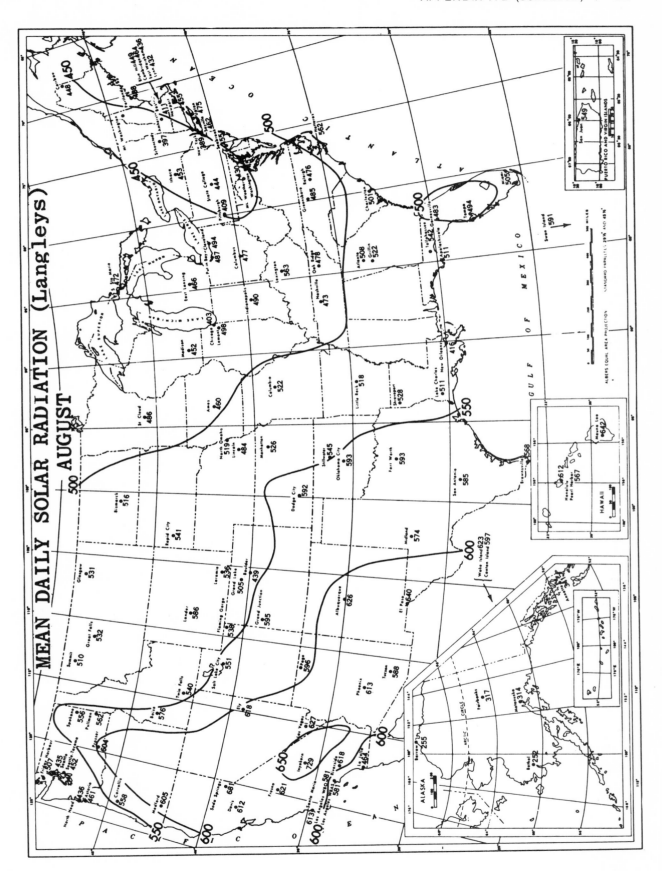

MEAN DAILY SOLAR RADIATION (Langleys)
AUGUST

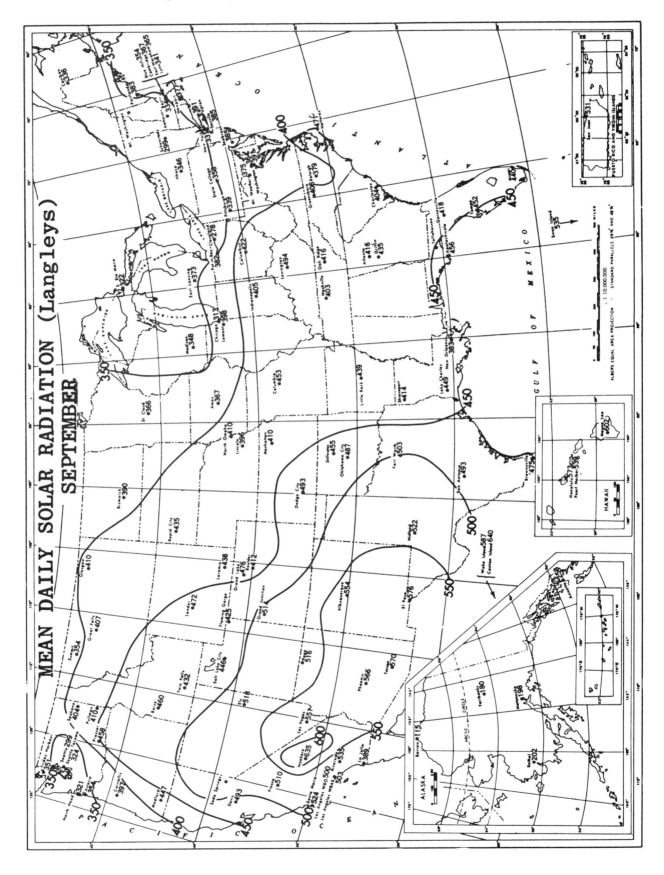

MEAN DAILY SOLAR RADIATION (Langleys)
SEPTEMBER

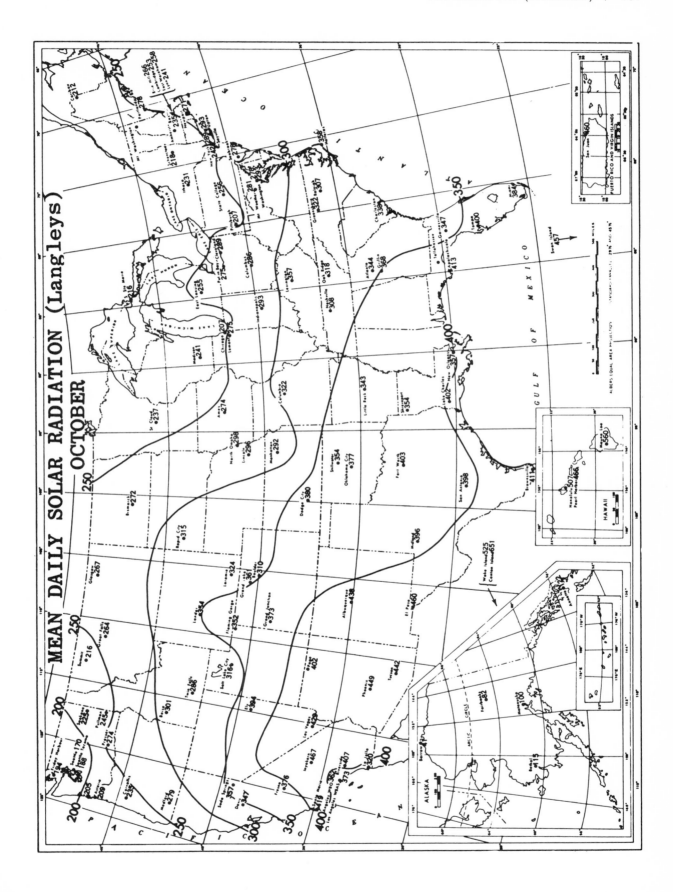

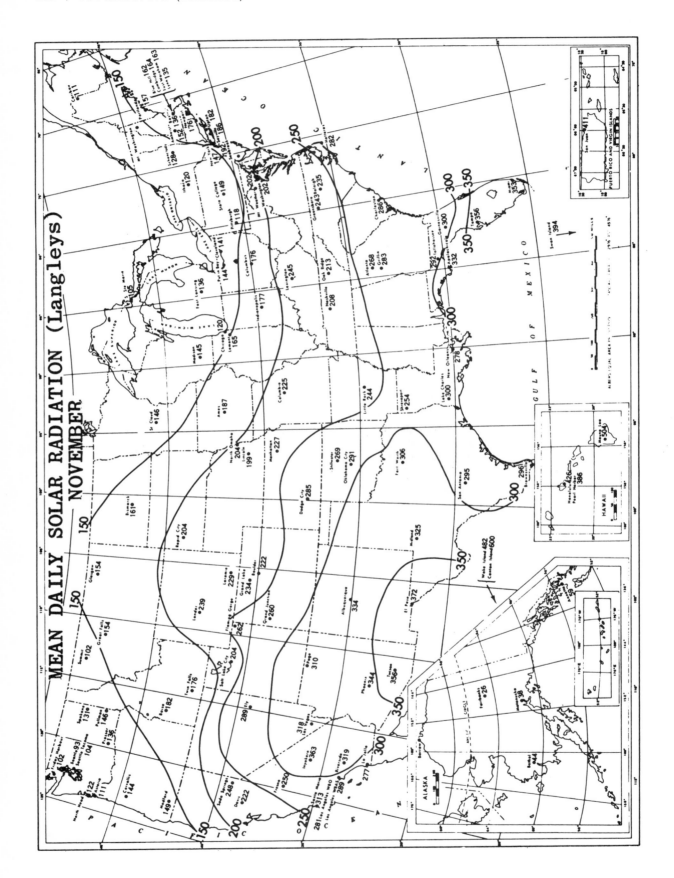

MEAN DAILY SOLAR RADIATION (Langleys)
NOVEMBER

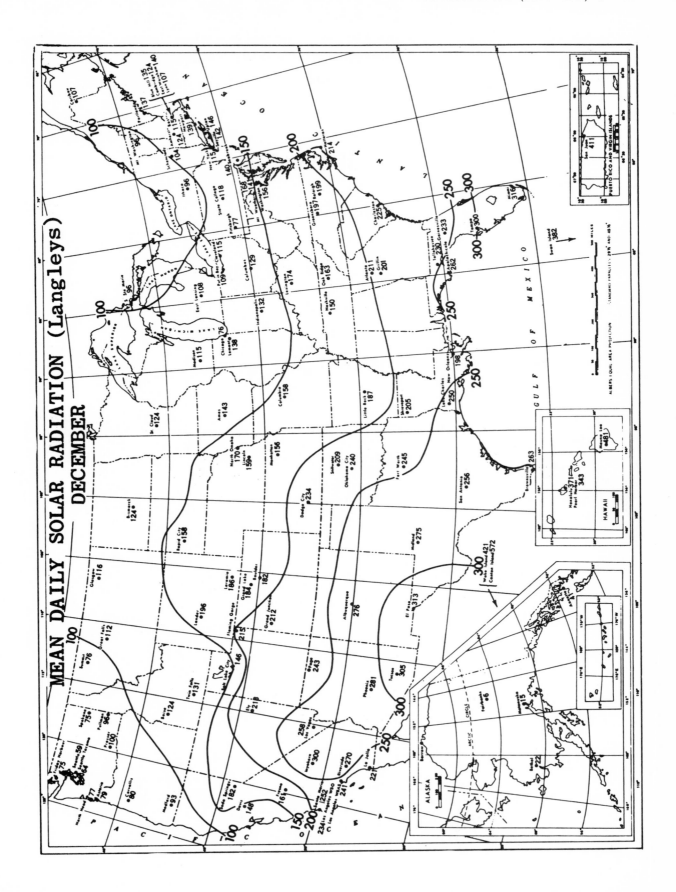

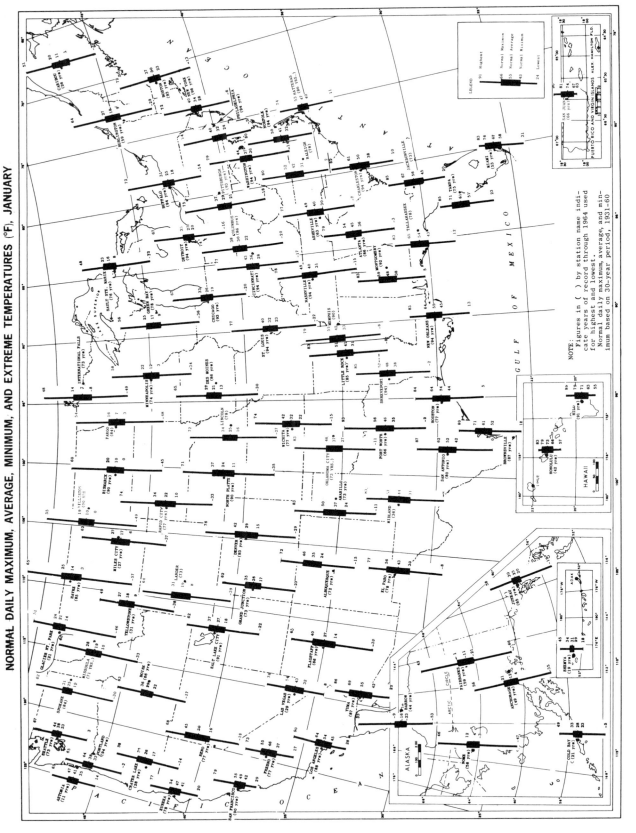

FIG. A-3. Normal daily maximum, average, minimum, and extreme temperatures (°F) by month for the United States. *Reprinted by permission: United States Department of Commerce, National Oceanic and Atmospheric Administration, Environmental Data Service.*

NORMAL DAILY MAXIMUM, AVERAGE, MINIMUM, AND EXTREME TEMPERATURES (°F), JANUARY

NOTE:
Figures in ( ) by station name indicate years of record through 1964 used for highest and lowest. Normal daily maximum, average, and minimum based on 30-year period, 1931–60.

134

NORMAL DAILY MAXIMUM, AVERAGE, MINIMUM, AND EXTREME TEMPERATURES (°F), FEBRUARY

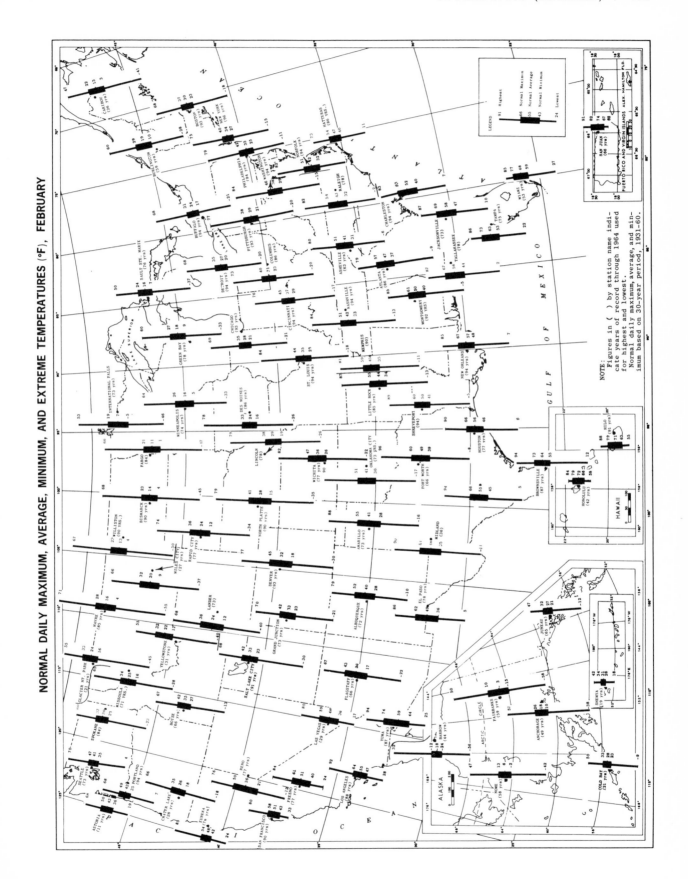

NOTE: Figures in ( ) by station name indicate years of record through 1964 used
for highest and lowest.
Normal daily maximum, average, and minimum based on 30-year period, 1931-60.

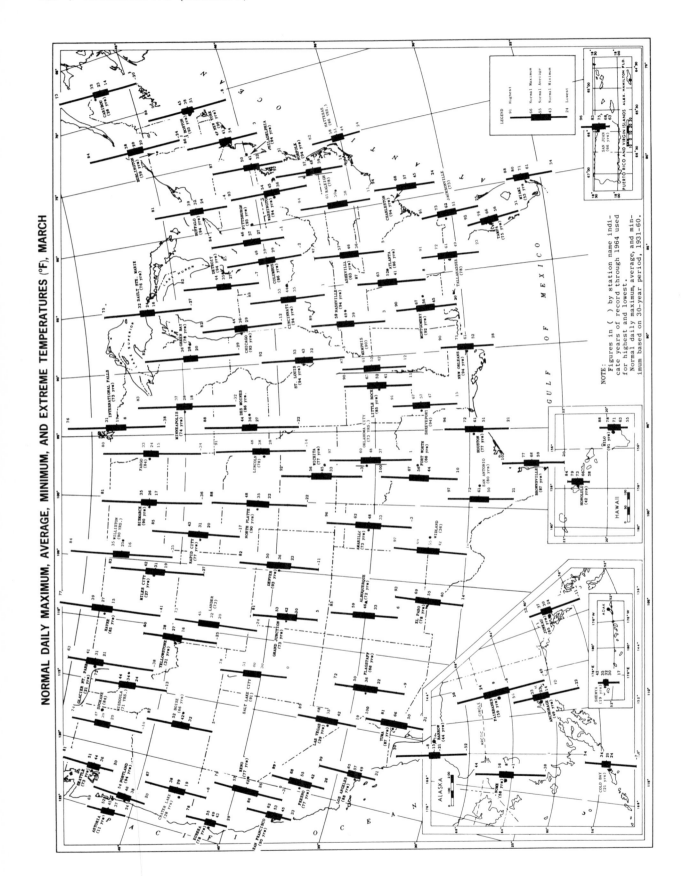

NORMAL DAILY MAXIMUM, AVERAGE, MINIMUM, AND EXTREME TEMPERATURES (°F), MARCH

NOTE:
Figures in ( ) by station name indicate years of record through 1964 used for highest and lowest. Normal daily maximum, average, and minimum based on 30-year period, 1931-60.

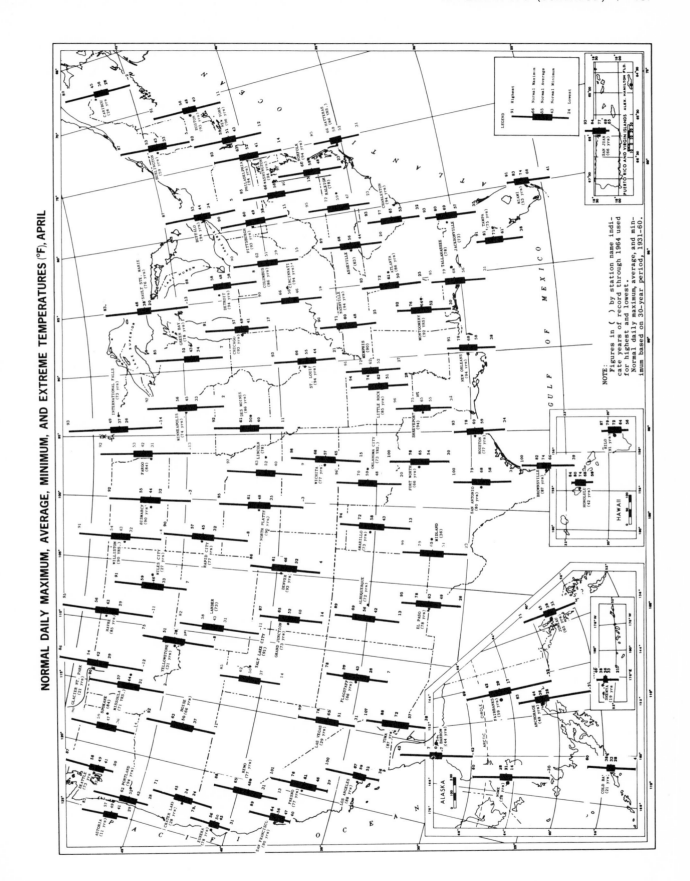

NORMAL DAILY MAXIMUM, AVERAGE, MINIMUM, AND EXTREME TEMPERATURES (°F), APRIL

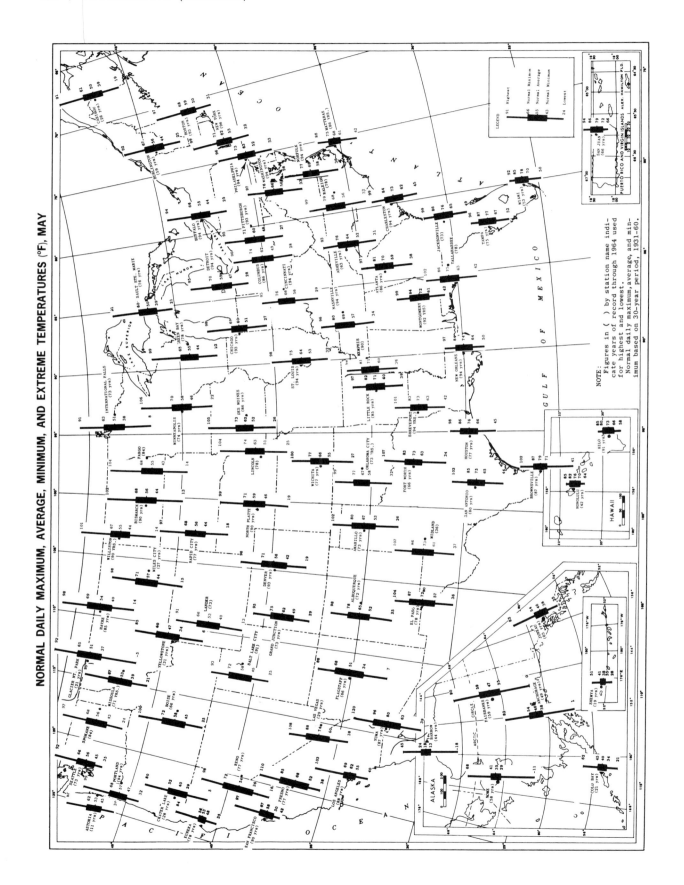

NORMAL DAILY MAXIMUM, AVERAGE, MINIMUM, AND EXTREME TEMPERATURES (°F), MAY

NORMAL DAILY MAXIMUM, AVERAGE, MINIMUM, AND EXTREME TEMPERATURES (°F), JUNE

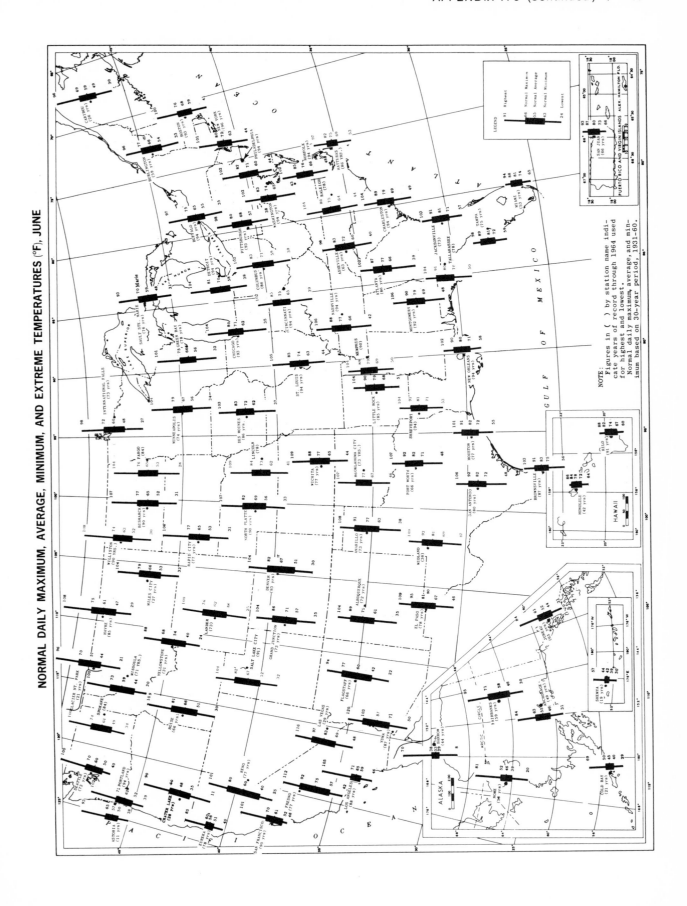

NOTE: Figures in ( ) by station name indicate years of record through 1964 used for highest and lowest. Normal daily maximum, average, and minimum based on 30-year period, 1931–60.

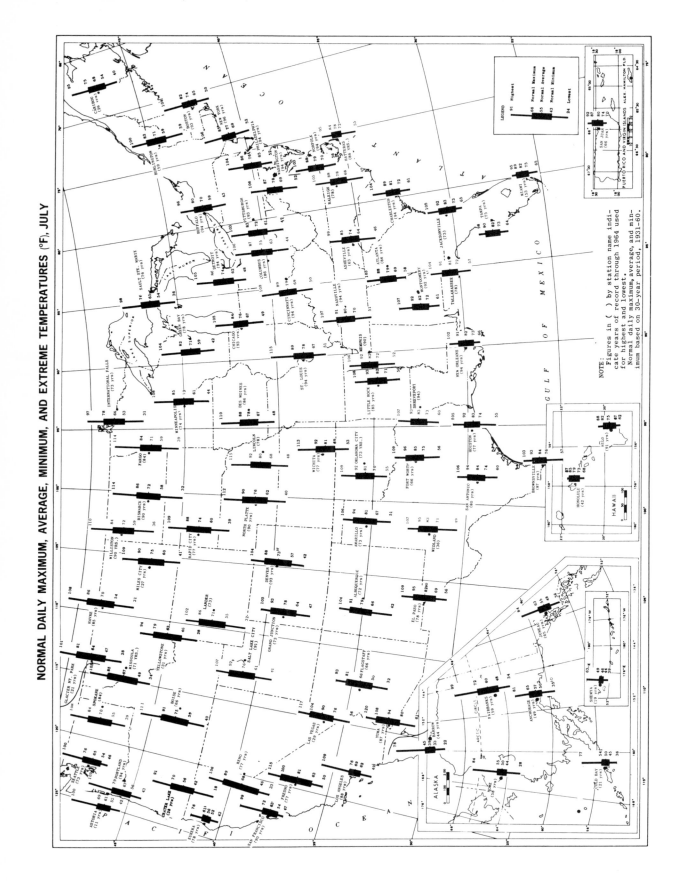

NORMAL DAILY MAXIMUM, AVERAGE, MINIMUM, AND EXTREME TEMPERATURES (°F), JULY

NOTE:
Figures in ( ) by station name indicate years of record through 1964 used for highest and lowest. Normal daily maximum, average, and minimum based on 30-year period, 1931-60.

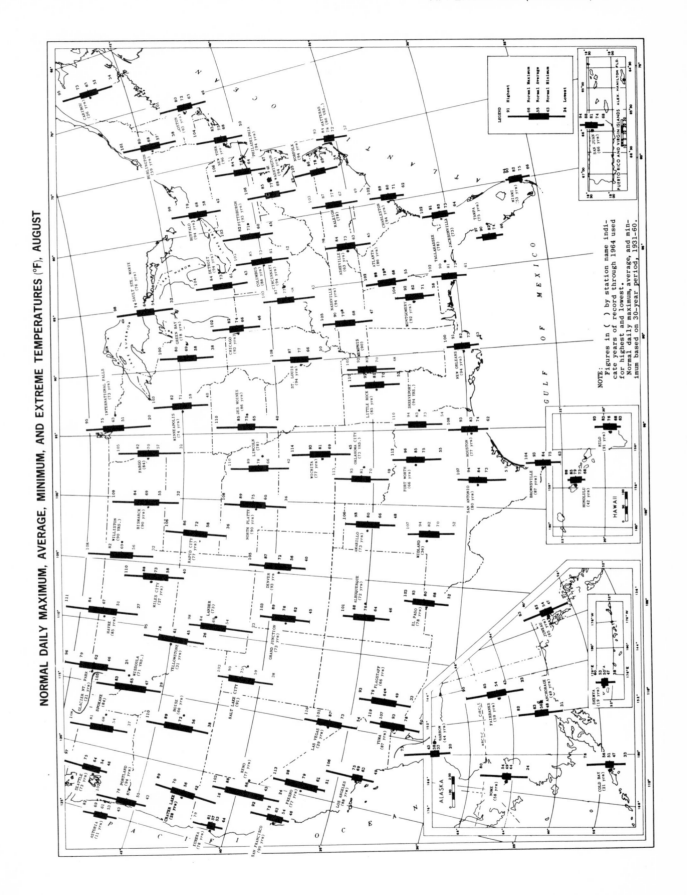

NORMAL DAILY MAXIMUM, AVERAGE, MINIMUM, AND EXTREME TEMPERATURES (°F), AUGUST

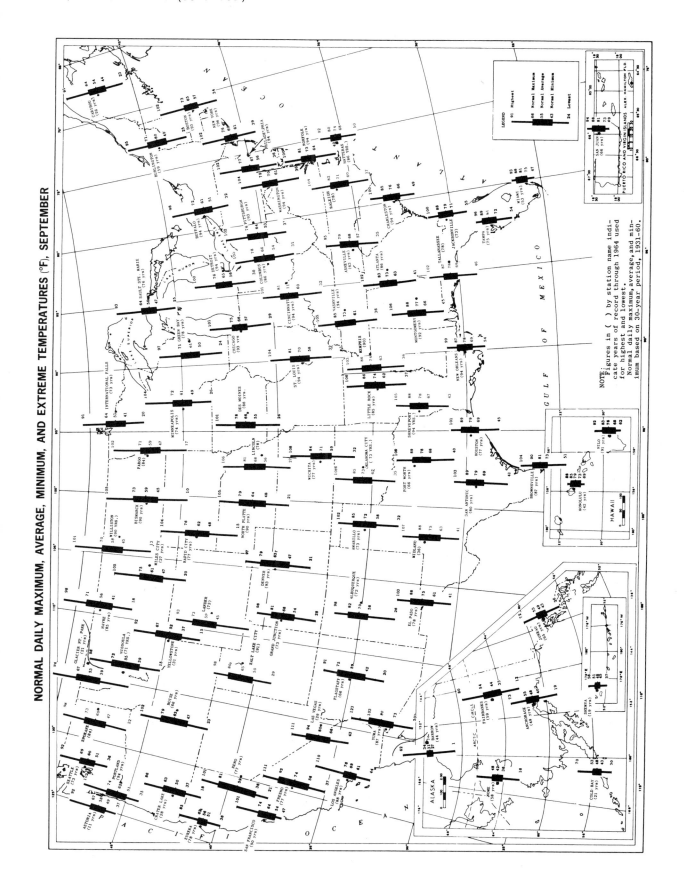

NORMAL DAILY MAXIMUM, AVERAGE, MINIMUM, AND EXTREME TEMPERATURES (°F), SEPTEMBER

NORMAL DAILY MAXIMUM, AVERAGE, MINIMUM, AND EXTREME TEMPERATURES (°F), OCTOBER

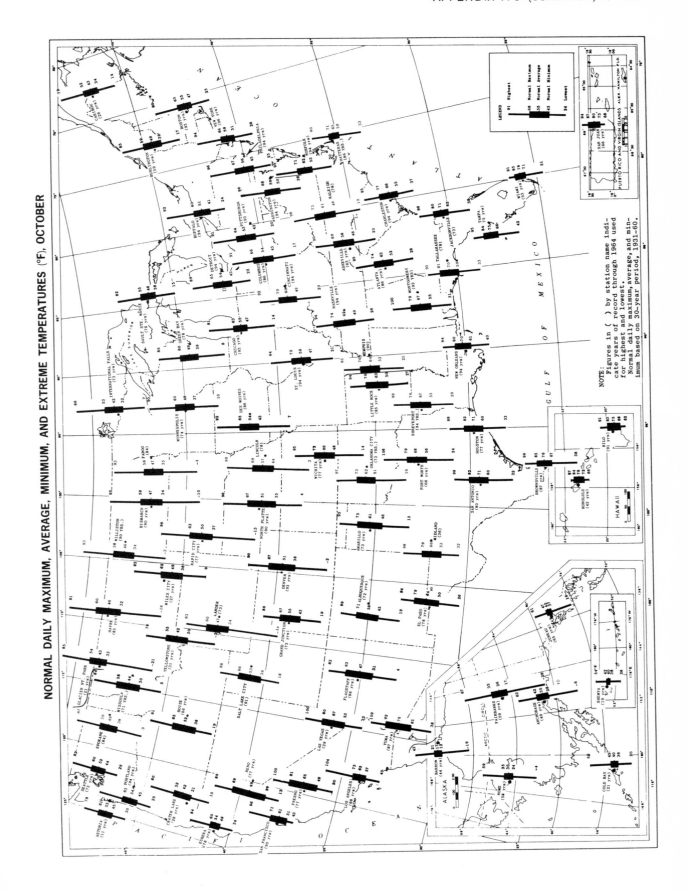

NOTE: Figures in ( ) by station name indicate years of record through 1964 used for highest and lowest. Normal daily maximum, average, and minimum based on 30-year period, 1931–60.

NORMAL DAILY MAXIMUM, AVERAGE, MINIMUM, AND EXTREME TEMPERATURES (°F), NOVEMBER

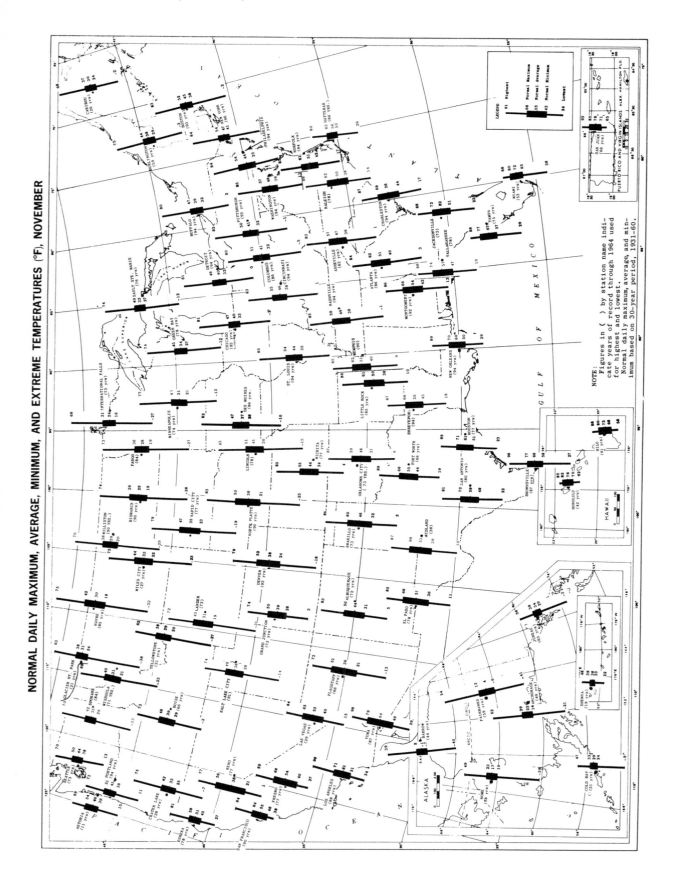

NOTE:
Figures in ( ) by station name indicate years of record through 1964 used for highest and lowest.
Normal daily maximum, average, and minimum based on 30-year period, 1931-60.

NORMAL DAILY MAXIMUM, AVERAGE, MINIMUM, AND EXTREME TEMPERATURES (°F), DECEMBER

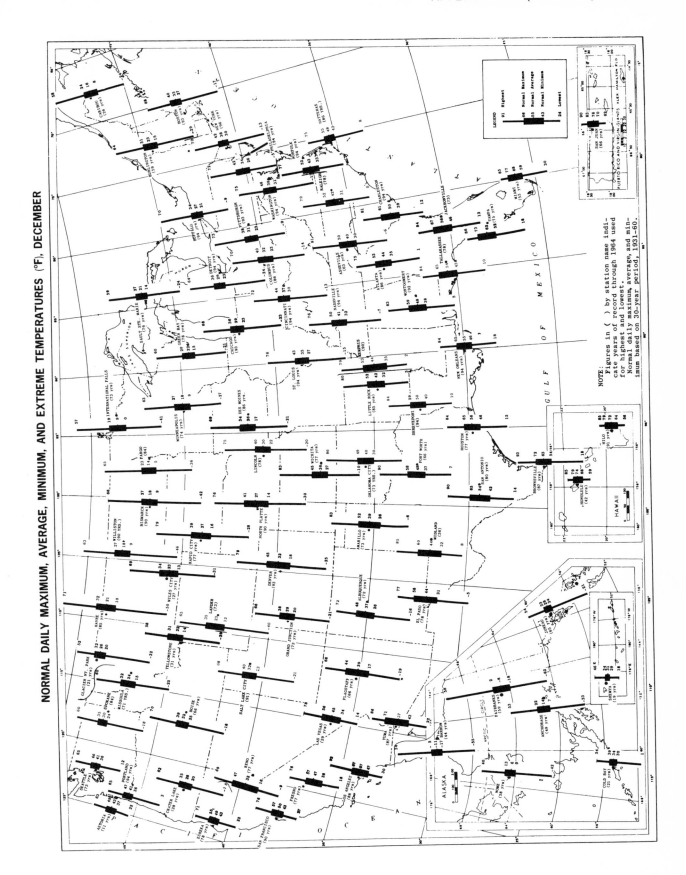

NORMAL TOTAL HEATING DEGREE DAYS
(Base 65°)

STATE AND STATION	JULY	AUG.	SEP.	OCT.	NOV.	DEC.	JAN.	FEB.	MAR.	APR.	MAY	JUNE	ANNUAL
ALA. BIRMINGHAM	0	0	6	93	363	555	592	462	363	108	9	0	2551
HUNTSVILLE	0	0	12	127	426	663	694	557	434	138	19	0	3070
MOBILE	0	0	0	22	213	357	415	300	211	42	0	0	1560
MONTGOMERY	0	0	0	68	330	527	543	417	316	90	0	0	2291
ALASKA ANCHORAGE	245	291	516	930	1284	1572	1631	1316	1293	879	592	315	10864
ANNETTE	242	208	327	567	738	899	949	837	843	648	490	321	7069
BARROW	803	840	1035	1500	1971	2362	2517	2332	2468	1944	1445	957	20174
BARTER IS.	735	775	987	1482	1944	2337	2536	2369	2477	1923	1373	924	19862
BETHEL	319	394	612	1042	1434	1866	1903	1590	1655	1173	806	402	13196
COLD BAY	474	425	525	772	918	1122	1153	1036	1122	951	791	591	9880
CORDOVA	366	391	522	781	1017	1221	1299	1086	1113	864	660	444	9764
FAIRBANKS	171	332	642	1203	1833	2254	2359	1901	1739	1068	555	222	14279
JUNEAU	301	338	483	725	921	1135	1237	1070	1073	810	601	381	9075
KING SALMON	313	322	513	908	1290	1606	1600	1333	1411	966	673	408	11343
KOTZEBUE	381	446	723	1249	1728	2127	2192	1932	2080	1554	1057	636	16105
MCGRATH	208	338	633	1184	1791	2232	2294	1817	1758	1122	648	258	14283
NOME	481	496	693	1094	1455	1820	1879	1666	1770	1314	930	573	14171
SAINT PAUL	605	539	612	862	963	1197	1228	1168	1265	1098	936	726	11199
SHEMYA	577	475	501	784	876	1042	1045	958	1011	885	837	696	9687
YAKUTAT	338	347	474	716	936	1144	1169	1019	1042	840	632	435	9092
ARIZ. FLAGSTAFF	46	68	201	558	867	1073	1169	991	911	651	437	180	7152
PHOENIX	0	0	0	22	234	415	474	328	217	75	0	0	1765
PRESCOTT	0	0	27	245	579	797	865	711	605	360	158	15	4362
TUCSON	0	0	0	25	231	406	471	344	242	75	6	0	1800
WINSLOW	0	0	6	245	711	1008	1054	770	601	291	96	0	4782
YUMA	0	0	0	0	148	319	363	228	130	29	0	0	1217
ARK. FORT SMITH	0	0	12	127	450	704	781	596	456	144	22	0	3292
LITTLE ROCK	0	0	9	127	465	716	756	577	434	126	9	0	3219
TEXARKANA	0	0	0	78	345	561	626	468	350	105	0	0	2533
CALIF. BAKERSFIELD	0	0	0	37	282	502	546	364	267	105	19	0	2122
BISHOP	0	0	42	248	576	797	874	666	539	306	143	36	4227
BLUE CANYON	34	50	120	347	579	766	865	781	791	582	397	195	5507
BURBANK	0	0	6	43	177	301	366	277	239	138	81	18	1646
EUREKA	270	257	258	329	414	499	546	470	505	438	372	285	4643
FRESNO	0	0	0	78	339	558	586	406	319	150	56	0	2492
LONG BEACH	0	0	12	40	156	288	375	297	267	168	90	18	1711
LOS ANGELES	28	22	42	78	180	291	372	302	288	219	158	81	2061
MT. SHASTA	25	34	123	406	696	902	983	784	738	525	347	159	5722
OAKLAND	53	50	45	127	309	481	527	400	353	255	180	90	2870
POINT ARGUELLO	202	186	162	205	291	400	474	392	403	339	298	243	3595
RED BLUFF	0	0	0	53	318	555	605	428	341	168	47	0	2515
SACRAMENTO	0	0	12	81	363	577	614	442	360	216	102	6	2773
SANDBERG	0	0	30	202	480	691	778	661	620	426	264	57	4209
SAN DIEGO	6	0	15	37	123	251	313	249	202	123	84	36	1439
SAN FRANCISCO	81	78	60	143	306	462	508	395	363	279	214	126	3015
SANTA CATALINA	16	0	9	50	165	279	353	308	326	249	192	105	2052
SANTA MARIA	99	93	96	146	270	391	459	370	363	282	233	165	2967

NORMAL TOTAL HEATING DEGREE DAYS
(Base 65°)

STATE AND STATION	JULY	AUG.	SEP.	OCT.	NOV.	DEC.	JAN.	FEB.	MAR.	APR.	MAY	JUNE	ANNUAL
COLO. ALAMOSA	65	99	279	639	1065	1420	1476	1162	1020	696	440	168	8529
COLORADO SPRINGS	9	25	132	456	825	1032	1128	938	893	582	319	84	6423
DENVER	6	9	117	428	819	1035	1132	938	887	558	288	66	6283
GRAND JUNCTION	0	0	30	313	786	1113	1209	907	729	387	146	21	5641
PUEBLO	0	0	54	326	750	986	1085	871	772	429	174	15	5462
CONN. BRIDGEPORT	0	0	66	307	615	986	1079	966	853	510	208	27	5617
HARDFORT	0	6	99	372	711	1119	1209	1061	899	495	177	24	6172
NEW HAVEN	0	12	87	347	648	1011	1097	991	871	543	245	45	5897
DEL. WILMINGTON	0	0	51	270	588	927	980	874	735	387	112	6	4930
FLA. APALACHICOLA	0	0	0	16	153	319	347	260	180	33	0	0	1308
DAYTONA BEACH	0	0	0	0	75	211	248	190	140	15	0	0	879
FORT MYERS	0	0	0	0	24	109	146	101	62	0	0	0	442
JACKSONVILLE	0	0	0	12	144	310	332	246	174	21	0	0	1239
KEY WEST	0	0	0	0	0	28	40	31	9	0	0	0	108
LAKELAND	0	0	0	0	57	164	195	146	99	0	0	0	661
MIAMI BEACH	0	0	0	0	0	40	56	36	9	0	0	0	141
ORLANDO	0	0	0	0	72	198	220	165	105	6	0	0	766
PENSACOLA	0	0	0	19	195	353	400	277	183	36	0	0	1463
TALLAHASSEE	0	0	0	28	198	360	375	286	202	36	0	0	1485
TAMPA	0	0	0	0	60	171	202	148	102	0	0	0	683
WEST PALM BEACH	0	0	0	0	6	65	87	64	31	0	0	0	253
GA. ATHENS	0	0	12	115	405	632	642	529	431	141	22	0	2929
ATLANTA	0	0	18	127	414	626	639	529	437	168	25	0	2983
AUGUSTA	0	0	0	78	333	552	549	445	350	90	0	0	2397
COLUMBUS	0	0	0	87	333	543	552	434	338	96	0	0	2383
MACON	0	0	0	71	297	502	505	403	295	63	0	0	2136
ROME	0	0	24	161	474	701	710	577	468	177	34	0	3326
SAVANNAH	0	0	0	47	246	437	437	353	254	45	0	0	1819
THOMASVILLE	0	0	0	25	198	366	394	305	208	33	0	0	1529
IDAHO BOISE	0	0	132	415	792	1017	1113	854	722	438	245	81	5809
IDAHO FALLS 46W	16	34	270	623	1056	1370	1538	1249	1085	651	391	192	8475
IDAHO FALLS 42NW	16	40	282	648	1107	1432	1600	1291	1107	657	388	192	8760
LEWISTON	0	0	123	403	756	933	1063	815	694	426	239	90	5542
POCATELLO	0	0	172	493	900	1166	1324	1058	905	555	319	141	7033
ILL. CAIRO	0	0	36	164	513	791	856	680	539	195	47	0	3821
CHICAGO	0	0	81	326	753	1113	1209	1044	890	480	211	48	6155
MOLINE	0	9	99	335	774	1181	1314	1100	918	450	189	39	6408
PEORIA	0	6	87	326	759	1113	1218	1025	849	426	183	33	6025
ROCKFORD	6	9	114	400	837	1221	1333	1137	961	516	236	60	6830
SPRINGFIELD	0	0	72	291	696	1023	1135	935	769	354	136	18	5429
IND. EVANSVILLE	0	0	66	220	606	896	955	767	620	237	68	0	4435
FORT WAYNE	0	9	105	378	783	1135	1178	1028	890	471	189	39	6205
INDIANAPOLIS	0	0	90	316	723	1051	1113	949	809	432	177	39	5699
SOUTH BEND	0	6	111	372	777	1125	1221	1070	933	525	239	60	6439
IOWA Burlington	0	0	93	322	768	1135	1259	1042	859	426	177	33	6114
DES MOINES	0	9	99	363	837	1231	1398	1165	967	489	211	39	6808
DUBUQUE	12	31	156	450	906	1287	1420	1204	1026	546	256	66	7376
SIOUX CITY	0	9	108	369	867	1240	1435	1198	989	483	214	39	6951
WATERLOO	12	19	138	428	909	1296	1460	1221	1023	531	229	54	7320

FIG. A–4. Normal total heating degree days (Base 65°) by month for the United States. One of the most practical of weather statistics is the "heating degree day." First devised some fifty years ago, the degree-day system has been in quite general use by the heating industry for more than thirty years.

Heating degree days are the number of degrees the daily average temperature is below 65°. Normally, heating is not required in a building when the outdoor average daily temperature is 65°. Heating degree days are determined by subtracting the average daily temperatures below 65° from the base 65°. A day with an average temperature of 50° has 15 heating degree days (65 – 50 = 15), while one with an average temperature of 65° or higher has none. Several characteristics make the degree day figures especially useful. They are cumulative so that the degree-day sum for a period of days represents the total heating load for that period. The rela-tionship between degree days and fuel consumption is linear; i.e., doubling the degree days usually doubles the fuel consumption. Comparing normal seasonal degree days in different locations gives a rough estimate of seasonal fuel consumption. For example, it would require roughly 4½ times as much fuel to heat a building in Chicago, where the mean annual total heating degree days are about 6,200, than to heat a similar building in New Orleans, where the annual total heating degree days are around 1,400. Using degree days has the advantage that the consumption ratios are fairly constant; i.e., the fuel consumed per 100 degree days is about the same whether the 100 degree days occur in only 3 or 4 days or are spread over 7 or 8 days.

Reprinted by permission: United States Department of Commerce, National Oceanic and Atmospheric Administration, Environmental Data Service.

NORMAL TOTAL HEATING DEGREE DAYS
(Base 65°)

STATE AND STATION	JULY	AUG.	SEP.	OCT.	NOV.	DEC.	JAN.	FEB.	MAR.	APR.	MAY	JUNE	ANNUAL
KANS. CONCORDIA	0	0	57	276	705	1023	1163	935	781	372	149	18	5479
DODGE CITY	0	0	33	251	666	939	1051	840	719	354	124	9	4986
GOODLAND	0	6	81	381	810	1073	1166	955	884	507	236	42	6141
TOPEKA	0	0	57	270	672	980	1122	893	722	330	124	12	5182
WICHITA	0	0	33	229	618	905	1023	804	645	270	87	6	4620
KY. COVINGTON	0	0	75	291	669	983	1035	893	756	390	149	24	5265
LEXINGTON	0	0	54	239	609	902	946	818	685	325	105	0	4683
LOUISVILLE	0	0	54	248	609	890	930	818	682	315	105	9	4660
LA. ALEXANDRIA	0	0	0	56	273	431	471	361	260	69	0	0	1921
BATON ROUGE	0	0	0	31	216	369	409	294	208	33	0	0	1560
BURRWOOD	0	0	0	0	96	214	298	218	171	27	0	0	1024
LAKE CHARLES	0	0	0	19	210	341	381	274	195	39	0	0	1459
NEW ORLEANS	0	0	0	19	192	322	363	258	192	39	0	0	1385
SHREVEPORT	0	0	0	47	297	477	552	426	304	81	0	0	2184
MAINE CARIBOU	78	115	336	682	1044	1535	1690	1470	1308	858	468	183	9767
PORTLAND	12	53	195	508	807	1215	1339	1182	1042	675	372	111	7511
MD. BALTIMORE	0	0	48	264	585	905	936	820	679	327	90	0	4654
FREDERICK	0	0	66	307	624	955	995	876	741	384	127	12	5087
MASS. BLUE HILL OBSY	0	22	108	381	690	1085	1178	1053	936	579	267	69	6368
BOSTON	0	9	60	316	603	983	1088	972	846	513	208	36	5634
NANTUCKET	12	22	93	332	573	896	992	941	896	621	384	129	5891
PITTSFIELD	25	59	219	524	831	1231	1339	1196	1063	660	326	105	7578
WORCESTER	6	34	147	450	774	1172	1271	1123	998	612	304	78	6969
MICH. ALPENA	68	105	273	580	912	1268	1404	1299	1218	777	446	156	8506
DETROIT (CITY)	0	0	87	360	738	1088	1181	1058	936	522	220	42	6232
ESCANABA	59	87	243	539	924	1293	1445	1296	1203	777	456	159	8481
FLINT	16	40	159	465	843	1212	1330	1198	1066	639	319	90	7377
GRAND RAPIDS	9	28	135	434	804	1147	1259	1134	1011	579	279	75	6894
LANSING	6	22	138	431	813	1163	1262	1142	1011	579	273	69	6909
MARQUETTE	59	81	240	527	936	1268	1411	1268	1187	771	468	177	8393
MUSKEGON	12	28	120	400	762	1088	1209	1100	995	594	310	78	6696
SAULT STE. MARIE	96	105	279	580	951	1367	1525	1380	1277	810	477	201	9048
MINN. DULUTH	71	109	330	632	1131	1581	1745	1518	1355	840	490	198	10000
INTERNATIONAL FALLS	71	112	363	701	1236	1724	1919	1621	1414	828	443	174	10606
MINNEAPOLIS	22	31	189	505	1014	1454	1631	1380	1166	621	288	81	8382
ROCHESTER	25	34	186	474	1005	1438	1593	1366	1150	630	301	93	8295
SAINT CLOUD	28	47	225	549	1065	1500	1702	1445	1221	666	326	105	8879
MISS. JACKSON	0	0	0	65	315	502	546	414	310	87	0	0	2239
MERIDIAN	0	0	0	81	339	518	543	417	310	81	0	0	2289
VICKSBURG	0	0	0	53	279	462	512	384	282	69	0	0	2041
MO. COLUMBIA	0	0	54	251	651	967	1076	874	716	324	121	12	5046
KANSAS	0	0	39	220	612	905	1032	818	682	294	109	0	4711
ST. JOSEPH	0	6	60	285	708	1039	1172	949	769	348	133	15	5484
ST. LOUIS	0	0	60	251	627	936	1026	848	704	312	121	15	4900
SPRINGFIELD	0	0	45	223	600	877	973	781	660	291	105	6	4561
MONT. BILLINGS	6	15	186	487	897	1135	1296	1100	970	570	285	102	7049
GLASGOW	31	47	270	608	1104	1466	1711	1439	1187	648	335	150	8996
GREAT FALLS	28	53	258	543	921	1169	1349	1154	1063	642	384	186	7750
HAVRE	28	53	306	595	1065	1367	1584	1364	1181	657	338	162	8700
HELENA	31	59	294	601	1002	1265	1438	1170	1042	651	381	195	8129
KALISPELL	50	99	321	654	1020	1240	1401	1134	1029	639	397	207	8191
MILES CITY	6	6	174	502	972	1296	1504	1252	1057	579	276	99	7723
MISSOULA	34	74	303	651	1035	1287	1420	1120	970	621	391	219	8125
NEBR. GRAND ISLAND	0	6	108	381	834	1172	1314	1089	908	462	211	45	6530
LINCOLN	0	6	75	301	726	1066	1237	1016	834	402	171	30	5864
NORFOLK	9	0	111	397	873	1234	1414	1179	983	498	233	48	6979
NORTH PLATTE	0	6	123	440	885	1166	1271	1039	930	519	248	57	6684
OMAHA	0	12	105	357	828	1175	1355	1126	939	465	208	42	6612
SCOTTSBLUFF	0	0	138	459	876	1128	1231	1008	921	552	285	75	6673
VALENTINE	9	12	165	493	942	1237	1395	1176	1045	579	288	84	7425
NEV. ELKO	9	34	225	561	924	1197	1314	1036	911	621	409	192	7433
ELY	28	43	234	592	939	1184	1308	1075	977	672	456	225	7733
LAS VEGAS	0	0	0	78	387	617	688	487	335	111	6	0	2709
RENO	43	87	204	490	801	1026	1073	823	729	510	357	189	6332
WINNEMUCCA	0	34	210	536	876	1091	1172	916	837	573	363	153	6761
N. H. CONCORD	6	50	177	505	822	1240	1358	1184	1032	636	298	75	7383
MT. WASH. OBSY.	493	536	720	1057	1341	1742	1820	1663	1652	1260	930	603	13817
N. J. ATLANTIC CITY	0	0	39	251	549	880	936	848	741	420	133	15	4812
NEWARK	0	0	30	248	573	921	983	876	729	381	118	0	4859
TRENTON	0	0	57	264	576	924	989	885	753	399	121	12	4980
N. MEX. ALBUQUERQUE	0	0	12	229	642	868	930	703	595	288	81	0	4348
CLAYTON	0	6	66	310	699	899	986	812	747	429	183	21	5158
RATON	9	28	126	431	825	1048	1116	904	834	543	301	63	6228
ROSWELL	0	0	18	202	573	806	840	641	481	201	31	0	3793
SILVER CITY	0	0	6	183	525	729	791	605	518	261	87	0	3705
N. Y. ALBANY	0	19	138	440	777	1194	1311	1156	992	564	239	45	6875
BINGHAMTON (AP)	22	65	201	471	810	1184	1277	1154	1045	645	313	99	7286
BINGHAMTON (PO)	0	28	141	406	732	1107	1190	1081	949	543	229	45	6451
BUFFALO	19	37	141	440	777	1156	1256	1145	1039	645	329	78	7062
CENTRAL PARK	0	0	30	233	540	902	986	885	760	408	118	9	4871
J. F. KENNEDY INTL.	0	0	36	248	564	933	1029	935	815	480	167	12	5219
LAGUARDIA	0	0	27	223	528	887	973	879	750	414	124	6	4811
ROCHESTER	9	31	126	415	747	1125	1234	1123	1014	597	279	48	6748
SCHENECTADY	0	22	123	422	756	1159	1283	1131	970	543	211	30	6650
SYRACUSE	6	28	132	415	744	1153	1271	1140	1004	570	248	45	6756
N.C. ASHEVILLE	0	0	48	245	555	775	784	683	592	273	87	0	4042
CAPE HATTERAS	0	0	0	78	273	521	580	518	440	177	25	0	2612
CHARLOTTE	0	0	6	124	438	691	691	582	481	156	22	0	3191
GREENSBORO	0	0	33	192	513	778	784	672	552	234	47	0	3805
RALEIGH	0	0	21	164	450	716	725	616	487	180	34	0	3393
WILMINGTON	0	0	0	74	291	521	546	462	357	96	0	0	2347
WINSTON SALEM	0	0	21	171	483	747	753	652	524	207	37	0	3595
N. DAK. BISMARCK	34	28	222	577	1083	1463	1708	1442	1203	645	329	117	8851
DEVILS LAKE	40	53	273	642	1191	1634	1872	1579	1345	753	381	138	9901
FARGO	28	37	219	574	1107	1569	1789	1520	1262	690	332	99	9226
WILLISTON	31	43	261	601	1122	1513	1758	1473	1262	681	357	141	9243

NORMAL TOTAL HEATING DEGREE DAYS
(Base 65°)

STATE AND STATION	JULY	AUG.	SEP.	OCT.	NOV.	DEC.	JAN.	FEB.	MAR.	APR.	MAY	JUNE	ANNUAL
OHIO AKRON	0	9	96	381	726	1070	1138	1016	871	489	202	39	6037
CINCINNATI	0	0	54	248	612	921	970	837	701	336	118	9	4806
CLEVELAND	9	25	105	384	738	1088	1159	1047	918	552	260	66	6351
COLUMBUS	0	6	84	347	714	1039	1088	949	809	426	171	27	5660
DAYTON	0	6	78	310	696	1045	1097	955	809	429	167	30	5622
MANSFIELD	9	22	114	397	768	1110	1169	1042	924	543	245	60	6403
SANDUSKY	0	6	66	313	684	1032	1107	991	868	495	198	36	5796
TOLEDO	0	16	117	406	792	1138	1200	1056	924	543	242	60	6494
YOUNGSTOWN	6	19	120	412	771	1104	1169	1047	921	540	248	60	6417
OKLA. OKLAHOMA CITY	0	0	15	164	498	766	868	664	527	189	34	0	3725
TULSA	0	0	18	158	522	787	893	683	539	213	47	0	3860
OREG. ASTORIA	146	130	210	375	561	679	753	622	636	480	363	231	5186
BURNS	12	37	210	515	867	1113	1246	988	856	570	366	177	6957
EUGENE	34	34	129	366	585	719	803	627	589	426	279	135	4726
MEACHAM	84	124	288	580	918	1091	1209	1005	983	726	527	339	7874
MEDFORD	0	0	78	372	678	871	918	697	642	432	242	78	5008
PENDLETON	0	0	111	350	711	884	1017	773	617	396	205	63	5127
PORTLAND	25	28	114	335	597	735	825	644	586	396	245	105	4635
ROSEBURG	22	16	105	329	567	713	766	608	570	405	267	123	4491
SALEM	37	31	111	338	594	729	822	647	611	417	273	144	4754
SEXTON SUMMIT	81	81	171	443	666	874	958	809	818	609	465	279	6254
PA. ALLENTOWN	0	0	90	353	693	1045	1116	1002	849	471	167	24	5810
ERIE	0	25	102	391	714	1063	1169	1081	973	585	288	60	6451
HARRISBURG	0	0	63	298	648	992	1045	907	766	396	124	12	5251
PHILADELPHIA	0	0	60	291	621	964	1014	890	744	390	115	12	5101
PITTSBURGH	0	9	105	375	726	1063	1119	1002	874	480	195	39	5987
READING	0	0	54	257	597	939	1001	885	735	372	105	0	4945
SCRANTON	0	19	132	434	762	1104	1156	1028	893	498	195	33	6254
WILLIAMSPORT	0	9	111	375	717	1073	1122	1002	856	468	177	24	5934
R. I. BLOCK IS.	0	16	78	307	594	902	1020	955	877	612	344	99	5804
PROVIDENCE	0	16	96	372	660	1023	1110	988	868	534	236	51	5954
S. C. CHARLESTON	0	0	0	59	282	471	487	389	291	54	0	0	2033
COLUMBIA	0	0	0	84	345	577	570	470	357	81	0	0	2484
FLORENCE	0	0	0	78	315	552	552	459	347	84	0	0	2387
GREENVILLE	0	0	0	112	387	636	648	535	434	120	12	0	2884
SPARTANBURG	0	0	15	130	417	667	663	560	453	144	25	0	3074
S. DAK. HURON	9	12	165	508	1014	1432	1628	1355	1125	600	288	87	8223
RAPID CITY	22	12	165	481	897	1172	1333	1145	1051	615	326	126	7345
SIOUX FALLS	19	25	168	462	972	1361	1544	1285	1082	573	270	78	7839
TENN. BRISTOL	0	0	51	236	573	828	828	700	598	261	68	0	4143
CHATTANOOGA	0	0	18	143	468	698	722	577	453	150	25	0	3254
KNOXVILLE	0	0	30	171	489	725	732	613	493	198	43	0	3494
MEMPHIS	0	0	18	130	447	698	729	585	456	147	22	0	3232
NASHVILLE	0	0	30	158	495	732	778	644	512	189	40	0	3578
OAK RIDGE (CO)	0	0	39	192	531	772	778	669	552	228	56	0	3817
TEX. ABILENE	0	0	0	99	366	586	642	470	347	114	0	0	2624
AMARILLO	0	0	18	205	570	797	877	664	546	252	56	0	3985
AUSTIN	0	0	0	31	225	388	468	325	223	51	0	0	1711
BROWNSVILLE	0	0	0	0	66	149	205	106	74	0	0	0	600
CORPUS CHRISTI	0	0	0	0	120	220	291	174	109	0	0	0	914
DALLAS	0	0	0	62	321	524	601	440	319	90	6	0	2363
EL PASO	0	0	0	84	414	648	685	445	319	105	0	0	2700
FORT WORTH	0	0	0	65	324	536	614	448	319	99	0	0	2405
GALVESTON	0	0	0	0	138	270	350	258	189	30	0	0	1235
HOUSTON	0	0	0	6	183	307	384	288	192	36	0	0	1396
LAREDO	0	0	0	0	105	217	267	134	74	0	0	0	797
LUBBOCK	0	0	18	174	513	744	800	613	484	201	31	0	3578
MIDLAND	0	0	0	87	381	592	651	468	322	90	0	0	2591
PORT ARTHUR	0	0	0	22	207	329	384	274	192	39	0	0	1447
SAN ANGELO	0	0	0	68	318	536	567	412	288	66	0	0	2255
SAN ANTONIO	0	0	0	31	207	363	428	286	195	39	0	0	1549
VICTORIA	0	0	0	6	150	270	344	230	152	21	0	0	1173
WACO	0	0	0	43	270	456	536	389	270	66	0	0	2030
WICHITA FALLS	0	0	0	99	381	632	698	518	378	120	6	0	2832
UTAH MILFORD	0	0	99	443	867	1141	1252	988	822	519	279	87	6497
SALT LAKE CITY	0	0	81	419	849	1082	1172	910	763	459	233	84	6052
WENDOVER	0	0	48	372	822	1091	1178	902	729	408	177	51	5778
VT. BURLINGTON	28	65	207	539	891	1349	1513	1333	1187	714	353	90	8269
VA. CAPE HENRY	0	0	0	112	360	645	694	633	536	246	53	0	3279
LYNCHBURG	0	0	51	223	540	822	849	731	605	267	78	0	4166
NORFOLK	0	0	0	136	408	698	738	655	533	216	37	0	3421
RICHMOND	0	0	36	214	495	784	815	703	546	219	53	0	3865
ROANOKE	0	0	51	229	549	825	834	722	614	261	65	0	4150
WASH. NAT'L. AP.	0	0	33	217	519	834	871	762	626	288	74	0	4224
WASH. OLYMPIA	68	71	198	422	636	753	834	675	645	450	307	177	5236
SEATTLE	50	47	129	329	543	657	738	599	577	396	242	117	4424
SEATTLE BOEING	34	40	147	384	624	763	831	655	608	411	242	99	4838
SEATTLE TACOMA	56	62	162	391	633	750	828	678	657	474	295	159	5145
SPOKANE	9	25	168	493	879	1082	1231	980	834	531	288	135	6655
STAMPEDE PASS	273	291	393	701	1008	1178	1287	1075	1085	855	654	483	9283
TATOOSH IS.	295	279	306	406	534	639	713	613	645	525	431	333	5719
WALLA WALLA	0	0	87	310	681	843	986	745	589	342	177	45	4805
YAKIMA	0	12	144	450	828	1039	1163	868	713	435	220	69	5941
W. VA. CHARLESTON	0	0	63	254	591	865	880	770	648	300	96	9	4476
ELKINS	9	25	135	400	729	992	1008	896	791	444	198	48	5675
HUNTINGTON	0	0	63	257	585	856	880	764	636	294	99	12	4446
PARKERSBURG	0	0	60	264	606	905	942	826	691	339	115	6	4754
WIS. GREEN BAY	28	50	174	484	924	1333	1494	1313	1141	654	335	99	8029
LA CROSSE	12	19	153	437	924	1339	1504	1277	1070	540	245	69	7589
MADISON	25	40	174	474	930	1330	1473	1274	1113	618	310	102	7863
MILWAUKEE	43	47	174	471	876	1252	1376	1193	1054	642	372	135	7635
WYO. CASPER	6	16	192	524	942	1169	1290	1084	1020	657	381	129	7410
CHEYENNE	19	31	210	543	924	1101	1228	1056	1011	672	381	102	7278
LANDER	6	19	204	555	1020	1299	1417	1145	1017	654	381	153	7870
SHERIAN	25	31	219	539	948	1200	1355	1154	1054	642	366	150	7683

FIG. A–5. Outdoor design conditions—Summer and Winter *Reprinted by permission: J. F. Kreider and F. Kreith,* Solar Heating and Cooling, *revised 1st edition, Hemisphere Publishing Corporation, 1977.*

Location	Latitude, deg[b]	Elevation, ft	Degree-days heating[c]	Winter[d] 99%	Winter[d] 97.5%	Summer[e] 1% DB	Summer[e] 2½%DB	Summer[e] 5% DB	Summer[e] 5% WB
USA									
Alabama, Birmingham	33	610	2,551	19	22	97	94	93	77
Alaska, Anchorage	61	90	10,864	−25	−20	73	70	67	59
Alaska, Juneau	58	17	9,075	−7	−4	75	71	68	62
Arizona, Phoenix	34	1,117	1,765	31	34	108	106	104	75
Arkansas, Little Rock	35	257	3,219	19	23	99	96	94	78
California, Los Angeles	34	312	2,061	42	44	94	90	87	69
California, Sacramento	39	17	2,502	30	32	100	97	94	69
California, San Francisco	38	52	3,015	42	44	80	77	73	61
Colorado, Denver	40	5,283	6,283	−2	3	92	90	89	63
Connecticut, Hartford	42	15	6,235	1	5	90	88	85	74
Delaware, Wilmington	40	78	4,930	12	15	93	90	87	76
District of Columbia	39	14	4,224	16	19	94	92	90	76
Florida, Jacksonville	31	24	1,239	29	32	96	94	92	79
Florida, Miami	26	7	214	44	47	92	90	89	79
Florida, Tampa	28	19	683	36	39	92	91	90	79
Georgia, Atlanta	34	1,005	2,961	18	23	95	92	90	76
Hawaii, Honolulu	21	7	0	60	62	87	85	84	73
Idaho, Boise	44	2,842	5,809	4	10	96	93	91	65
Illinois, Chicago	42	594	6,639	−3	1	94	91	88	75
Indiana, Indianapolis	40	793	5,699	0	4	93	91	88	76
Iowa, Des Moines	42	948	6,588	−7	−3	95	92	89	76
Kansas, Topeka	39	877	5,182	3	6	99	96	94	77
Kentucky, Louisville	38	474	4,660	8	12	96	93	91	77
Louisiana, New Orleans	30	3	1,385	32	35	93	91	90	79
Maine, Portland	44	61	7,511	−5	0	88	85	81	71
Maryland, Baltimore	39	146	4,654	12	15	94	91	89	77
Massachusetts, Boston	42	15	5,634	6	10	91	88	85	73
Michigan, Detroit, (Met.)	42	633	6,232	4	8	92	88	85	74
Michigan, Sault Ste. Marie	47	721	9,048	−12	−8	83	81	78	69
Minnesota, Duluth	47	1,426	10,000	−19	−15	85	82	79	69
Minnesota, Minneapolis/ St. Paul	45	822	8,382	−14	−10	92	89	86	74
Mississippi, Jackson	32	330	2,239	21	24	98	96	94	78
Missouri, Kansas City	39	742	4,711	4	8	100	97	94	76
Missouri, St. Louis	39	465	4,900	7	11	96	94	92	77
Montana, Billings	46	3,567	7,049	−10	−6	94	91	88	65
Montana, Butte	46	5,526	—	−24	−16	86	83	80	57
Nebraska, Omaha	41	978	6,612	−5	−1	97	94	91	76
Nevada, Las Vegas	36	2,162	2,709	23	26	108	106	104	70
New Hampshire, Manchester	43	253	—	−5	1	92	89	86	73
New Jersey, Atlantic City	40	11	4,812	14	18	91	88	85	76
New Mexico, Albuquerque	35	5,310	4,348	14	17	96	94	92	64
New York, Albany	43	277	6,875	−5	0	91	88	85	73
New York, Buffalo	43	705	7,062	3	6	88	86	83	72
New York, NYC-LaGuardia	41	19	4,811	12	16	93	90	87	75
North Carolina, Durham	36	406	—	15	19	94	92	89	76
North Dakota, Bismarck	47	1,647	8,851	−24	−19	95	91	88	70
Ohio, Cincinnati	39	761	4,410	8	12	94	92	90	76
Ohio, Cleveland	41	777	6,351	2	7	91	89	86	74
Oklahoma, Tulsa	36	650	3,860	12	16	102	99	96	77
Oregon, Portland	46	57	4,635	26	29	91	88	84	67
Pennsylvania, Philadelphia	40	7	5,144	11	15	93	90	87	76
Pennsylvania, Pittsburgh	41	749	5,987	7	11	90	88	85	73

Location	Latitude, deg	Elevation, ft	Degree-days heating	Winter 99%	Winter 97.5%	Summer 1% DB	Summer 2½% DB	Summer 5% DB	Summer 5% WB
USA *(cont.)*									
Rhode Island, Providence	42	55	5,954	6	10	89	86	83	74
South Carolina, Columbia	34	217	2,484	20	23	98	96	94	78
South Dakota, Sioux Falls	44	1,420	7,839	−14	−10	95	92	89	74
Tennessee, Memphis	35	263	3,232	17	21	98	96	94	78
Tennessee, Nashville	36	577	3,578	12	16	97	95	92	77
Texas, Dallas	33	481	2,363	19	24	101	99	97	78
Texas, Houston	30	158	1,396	29	33	96	94	92	79
Texas, San Antonio	30	792	1,546	25	30	99	97	96	76
Utah, Salt Lake City	41	4,220	6,052	5	9	97	94	92	65
Vermont, Burlington	45	331	8,269	−12	−7	88	85	83	71
Virginia, Richmond	38	162	3,865	14	18	96	93	91	77
Washington, Seattle	48	14	4,424	28	32	81	79	76	64
Washington, Spokane	48	2,357	6,655	−2	4	93	90	87	63
West Virginia, Charleston	38	939	4,476	9	14	92	90	88	74
Wisconsin, LaCrosse	44	652	7,589	−12	−8	90	88	85	75
Wisconsin, Milwaukee	43	672	7,635	−6	−2	90	87	84	73
Wyoming, Cheyenne	41	6,126	7,381	−6	−2	89	86	83	61
CANADA									
Alberta, Edmonton	54	2,219	10,268	−29	−26	86	83	80	65
Br. Columbia, Vancouver	49	16	5,515	15	19	80	78	76	65
Manitoba, Winnipeg	50	786	10,679	−28	−25	90	87	84	72
Ontario, Ottawa	45	339	8,735	−17	−13	90	87	84	73
Ontario, Toronto	44	578	6,827	−3	1	90	87	85	73
Quebec, Montreal	46	98	8,203	−16	−10	88	86	84	73
Quebec, Quebec	47	245	9,372	−19	−13	86	82	79	71
OTHER COUNTRIES									
Argentina, Buenos Aires	35	89	—	32	34	91	89	86	75
Australia, Sydney	34	138	—	40	42	89	84	80	72
Brazil, Sao Paulo	24	2,608	—	42	46	86	84	82	74
France, Paris	49	164	—	22	25	89	86	83	67
Germany, Berlin	52	187	—	7	12	84	81	78	66
Hong Kong, Hong Kong	22	109	—	48	50	92	91	90	80
India, Calcutta	23	21	—	52	54	98	97	96	82
Italy, Rome	42	377	—	30	33	94	92	89	72
Japan, Tokyo	36	19	—	26	28	91	89	87	79
Mexico, Mexico City	19	7,575	—	37	39	83	81	79	59
Netherlands, Amsterdam	52	5	—	20	23	79	76	73	63
Soviet Union, Moscow	56	505	—	−11	−6	84	81	78	65
Spain, Madrid	40	2,188	—	25	28	93	91	89	67
Sweden, Stockholm	59	146	—	5	8	78	74	72	60
United Kingdom, London	51	149	—	24	26	82	79	76	65

[a]Condensed from ASHRAE "Handbook of Fundamentals" and "Guide and Data Book," American Society of Heating, Refrigerating, and Air-Conditioning Engineers, 1972 and 1968, respectively. Extended data for over 1000 locations are given in these sources.

[b]Latitudes are given to the nearest degree.

[c]Degree-days are the yearly totals, 65°F base, i.e., for all days when the mean temperature was below 65°F. For monthly and yearly degree-days see Table A6.3.

[d]Winter temperatures are the temperatures equaled or exceeded 99 percent (and 97.5 percent) of the time during the coldest months. For average monthly temperatures see Table A6.4.

[e]Summer temperatures represent the highest 1 percent (or 2.5 or 5 percent) hourly dry-bulb (DB) or wet-bulb (WB) temperatures during the warmest months. In a normal season there would be about 30 hr above the 1 percent design temperature and 150 hr above the 5 percent dry-bulb design temperature. In most locations the 1 percent design wet-bulb temperature is about 2° above the 5 percent dry-bulb value.

FIG. A–6. Mean percentage of possible sunshine for selected locations *Reprinted by permission: The American Society of Heating, Refrigerating, and Air-Conditioning Engineers, Inc.*

MEAN PERCENTAGE OF POSSIBLE SUNSHINE FOR SELECTED LOCATIONS

STATE AND STATION	YEARS	JAN.	FEB.	MAR.	APR.	MAY	JUNE	JULY	AUG.	SEPT.	OCT.	NOV.	DEC.	ANNUAL
ALA. BIRMINGHAM	56	43	49	56	63	66	67	62	65	66	67	58	44	59
MONTGOMERY	49	51	53	61	69	73	72	66	69	69	71	64	48	64
ALASKA. ANCHORAGE	19	39	46	56	58	50	51	45	39	35	32	33	29	45
FAIRBANKS	20	34	50	61	68	55	53	45	35	31	28	38	29	44
JUNEAU	14	30	32	39	37	34	35	28	30	25	18	21	18	30
NOME	29	44	48	48	53	51	48	32	26	34	35	38	30	41
ARIZ. PHOENIX	64	76	79	83	88	93	94	84	84	89	88	84	77	85
YUMA	52	83	87	91	94	97	98	92	91	93	93	90	83	91
ARK. LITTLE ROCK	66	44	53	57	62	67	72	71	73	71	74	58	47	62
CALIF. EUREKA	49	40	44	50	53	54	56	51	46	52	48	42	39	49
FRESNO	55	46	63	72	83	89	94	97	97	93	87	73	47	78
LOS ANGELES	63	70	69	70	67	68	69	80	81	80	76	79	72	73
RED BLUFF	39	50	60	65	75	79	86	95	94	89	77	64	50	75
SACRAMENTO	48	44	57	67	76	82	90	96	95	92	82	65	44	77
SAN DIEGO	68	68	67	68	66	60	60	67	70	70	76	71	68	67
SAN FRANCISCO	64	53	57	63	69	70	75	68	63	70	70	62	54	66
COLO. DENVER	64	67	67	65	63	61	69	68	71	71	67	65	67	
GRAND JUNCTION	57	58	62	64	67	71	79	76	72	77	74	67	58	69
CONN. HARTFORD	48	46	55	56	54	57	60	62	60	57	55	46	46	56
D.C. WASHINGTON	66	46	53	56	57	61	64	64	62	62	61	54	47	58
FLA. APALACHICOLA	26	59	62	62	71	77	70	64	63	62	74	66	53	65
JACKSONVILLE	60	58	59	66	71	71	63	62	63	58	58	61	53	62
KEY WEST	45	68	75	78	78	76	70	69	71	65	65	69	66	71
MIAMI BEACH	48	66	72	73	73	68	62	65	67	62	62	65	65	67
TAMPA	63	63	67	71	74	75	66	61	64	64	67	67	61	68
GA. ATLANTA	48	48	53	57	65	68	68	62	63	65	67	60	47	62
HAWAII. HILO	9	48	42	41	34	31	41	44	38	42	41	34	36	39
HONOLULU	53	62	64	60	62	64	66	67	70	68	63	60	60	65
LIHUE	9	48	48	48	46	51	60	58	59	67	58	51	49	54
IDAHO. BOISE	20	40	48	59	67	68	75	89	86	81	66	46	37	66
POCATELLO	21	37	47	58	64	66	72	82	81	78	66	48	36	64
ILL. CAIRO	30	53	59	65	71	77	82	79	75	73	56	46	65	
CHICAGO	66	44	49	53	56	63	69	73	70	65	61	47	41	59
SPRINGFIELD	59	47	51	54	58	64	69	76	72	73	64	53	45	60
IND. EVANSVILLE	48	42	49	55	61	67	73	78	76	73	67	52	42	64
FT. WAYNE	48	38	44	51	55	62	69	74	69	64	58	41	38	57
INDIANAPOLIS	63	41	47	49	55	62	68	74	70	68	64	48	39	57
IOWA. DES MOINES	66	56	56	56	59	62	66	75	70	64	64	53	48	62
DUBUQUE	54	48	52	52	58	60	63	67	61	55	44	40	57	
SIOUX CITY	52	55	58	58	59	63	67	75	72	67	65	53	50	63
KANS. CONCORDIA	52	60	60	62	63	65	73	79	76	72	70	64	58	67
DODGE CITY	70	67	66	68	68	68	74	78	78	76	75	70	67	71
WICHITA	46	61	63	64	64	66	73	80	77	73	69	67	59	69
KY. LOUISVILLE	59	41	47	52	57	64	68	72	69	68	64	51	39	59
LA. NEW ORLEANS	69	49	50	57	63	66	64	58	60	64	70	60	46	59
SHREVEPORT	18	48	54	58	60	69	78	79	80	79	77	65	60	69
MAINE. EASTPORT	58	45	51	52	52	51	53	55	57	54	50	37	40	50
MASS. BOSTON	67	47	56	57	56	59	62	64	63	61	58	48	48	57
MICH. ALPENA	45	29	43	52	54	58	62	64	52	44	24	22	51	
DETROIT	69	34	42	48	52	58	65	69	66	61	54	35	29	53
GRAND RAPIDS	56	26	37	48	54	60	66	72	67	58	50	31	22	49
MARQUETTE	55	31	40	47	52	53	56	63	57	47	38	24	24	47
S. STE. MARIE	60	28	44	50	54	54	59	63	58	45	36	21	22	47
MINN. DULUTH	49	47	55	60	58	58	60	68	63	53	47	36	40	55
MINNEAPOLIS	45	49	54	55	57	60	64	72	69	60	54	40	40	56
MISS. VICKSBURG	66	46	50	57	64	69	73	69	72	74	71	60	45	64
MO. KANSAS CITY	69	55	57	59	60	64	70	76	73	70	67	59	52	65
ST. LOUIS	68	48	49	56	59	64	68	72	68	67	65	54	44	59
SPRINGFIELD	45	48	54	57	60	63	69	77	72	71	65	58	48	63
MONT. HAVRE	55	49	58	61	63	65	78	75	64	57	48	46	62	
HELENA	65	46	55	58	60	59	63	77	74	63	57	48	43	60
KALISPELL	50	28	40	49	57	58	60	77	73	61	50	28	20	53
NEBR. LINCOLN	55	57	59	60	60	63	69	76	71	67	66	59	55	64
NORTH PLATTE	53	63	63	64	62	64	72	78	74	72	70	62	58	68
NEV. ELY	21	61	64	68	65	67	79	79	81	81	73	67	62	72
LAS VEGAS	19	74	77	78	81	85	91	84	86	92	84	83	75	82
RENO	51	59	64	69	75	77	82	90	89	86	76	68	56	76
WINNEMUCCA	53	52	60	64	70	76	83	90	90	86	75	62	53	74
N.H. CONCORD	44	48	53	55	53	51	56	57	58	55	50	43	43	52
N.J. ATLANTIC CITY	62	51	57	58	59	62	65	67	66	65	54	58	52	60
N. MEX. ALBUQUERQUE	28	70	72	72	76	79	84	76	75	81	80	79	70	78
ROSWELL	47	69	72	75	77	76	80	76	75	74	74	74	69	74
N.Y. ALBANY	63	43	51	53	53	57	62	63	61	58	54	39	38	53
BINGHAMTON	63	31	39	41	44	50	56	54	51	47	43	29	26	44
BUFFALO	49	32	41	49	51	59	67	70	67	60	51	31	28	53
CANTON	43	37	47	50	48	54	61	63	61	54	45	30	31	49
NEW YORK	83	49	56	57	59	62	65	66	64	64	61	53	50	59
SYRACUSE	49	31	38	45	50	58	64	67	63	56	47	29	26	50
N.C. ASHEVILLE	57	48	53	56	61	64	63	59	59	62	64	59	48	58
RALEIGH	61	50	56	59	64	67	65	62	62	63	64	62	52	61
N. DAK. BISMARCK	65	52	58	56	57	58	61	73	69	62	59	49	48	59
DEVILS LAKE	55	53	60	59	60	59	62	71	67	59	56	44	45	58
FARGO	39	47	55	56	58	62	63	73	70	65	60	44	45	58
WILLISTON	43	51	59	60	63	66	66	78	75	65	60	48	46	63
OHIO. CINCINNATI	44	41	46	52	56	62	69	72	68	66	60	46	39	57
CLEVELAND	65	29	36	45	52	61	67	71	68	62	54	32	25	50
COLUMBUS	65	36	44	49	54	63	68	71	68	66	60	44	35	54
OKLA. OKLAHOMA CITY	62	57	60	63	64	65	74	78	78	74	68	64	57	68
OREG. BAKER	46	41	49	56	61	63	67	83	81	74	62	46	37	60
PORTLAND	69	27	34	41	49	52	55	70	65	55	42	28	23	48
ROSEBURG	29	24	32	40	51	57	59	79	77	68	47	28	18	51
PA. HARRISBURG	60	43	52	55	57	61	65	68	63	62	58	47	43	57
PHILADELPHIA	66	45	56	57	58	61	62	64	61	62	61	53	49	57
PITTSBURGH	63	32	39	45	50	57	62	64	61	62	61	39	30	49
R.I. BLOCK ISLAND	48	45	54	47	56	58	60	62	62	60	59	50	44	56
S.C. CHARLESTON	61	58	60	65	72	73	70	66	67	68	68	57	66	
COLUMBIA	55	53	57	62	68	69	68	63	65	64	68	64	51	63
S. DAK. HURON	62	55	62	60	62	65	68	76	72	66	61	52	49	63
RAPID CITY	53	58	62	63	62	61	66	73	73	69	66	58	54	64
TENN. KNOXVILLE	62	42	49	53	59	64	66	64	59	64	64	53	41	57
MEMPHIS	55	44	51	57	64	68	74	73	74	70	69	58	45	64
NASHVILLE	63	42	47	54	60	65	69	69	68	69	65	55	42	59
TEX. ABILENE	14	64	68	73	66	73	86	83	85	73	71	72	66	73
AMARILLO	54	71	71	75	75	75	82	81	81	79	76	76	70	76
AUSTIN	33	46	50	57	52	56	72	76	79	70	70	57	49	63
BROWNSVILLE	37	44	49	51	57	65	73	78	78	67	70	54	44	61
DEL RIO	36	53	55	61	56	60	66	75	80	69	66	58	52	63
EL PASO	53	74	77	81	85	87	87	78	78	80	82	80	73	80
FT. WORTH	33	56	57	61	75	78	78	74	70	63	58	68		
GALVESTON	66	50	50	55	61	69	78	72	71	70	74	62	49	63
SAN ANTONIO	57	48	51	56	58	60	69	74	75	69	67	55	49	62
UTAH. SALT LAKE CITY	22	48	53	61	68	73	78	82	82	84	73	56	49	68
VT. BURLINGTON	54	34	43	48	47	53	59	62	59	51	43	25	24	46
VA. NORFOLK	60	50	57	60	63	67	66	66	63	64	60	51	52	61
RICHMOND	56	49	55	59	63	67	66	65	62	63	64	58	50	61
WASH. NORTH HEAD	44	28	37	42	48	50	46	48	48	41	31	27	41	
SEATTLE	26	27	34	42	48	53	48	62	56	53	36	28	24	45
SPOKANE	62	26	41	53	63	64	68	82	79	68	53	28	22	58
TATOOSH ISLAND	49	26	36	39	45	47	46	48	44	47	38	26	23	40
WALLA WALLA	44	24	35	51	63	67	72	86	84	72	59	33	20	60
YAKIMA	18	34	49	62	70	72	74	86	81	76	61	38	29	65
W. VA. ELKINS	55	33	37	42	47	55	55	56	53	55	51	41	33	48
PARKERSBURG	62	30	36	42	49	58	62	66	60	53	37	29	48	
WIS. GREEN BAY	57	44	51	55	56	58	64	70	65	58	52	40	40	55
MADISON	59	44	49	52	53	58	64	70	66	60	56	41	38	56
MILWAUKEE	59	44	48	53	56	60	65	73	67	62	56	44	39	57
WYO. CHEYENNE	63	65	66	61	59	68	70	68	69	69	65	63	66	
LANDER	57	66	70	71	66	65	74	76	76	72	68	66	61	69
SHERIDAN	52	56	61	62	61	61	67	76	74	67	60	53	52	64
YELLOWSTONE PARK	35	39	51	55	52	56	63	73	71	65	57	45	38	56
P.R. SAN JUAN	57	64	69	71	66	59	62	65	67	61	63	63	65	65

Based on period of record through December 1959, except in a few instances.

FIG. A–7a. Solar position and insolation values for 24 degrees north latitude. *Reprinted by permission: J. F. Kreider and F. Kreith, Solar Heating and Cooling, revised 1st edition, Hemisphere Publishing Corporation, 1977.*

Date	Solar time AM	PM	Solar position Alt	Azm	Normal	Horiz.	14	24	34	44	90
Jul 21	6	6	8.2	109.0	81	23	16	11	10	9	6
	7	5	21.4	103.8	195	98	85	73	59	44	13
	8	4	34.8	99.2	239	169	157	143	125	104	16
	9	3	48.4	94.5	261	231	221	207	187	161	18
	10	2	62.1	89.0	272	278	270	256	235	206	21
	11	1	75.7	79.2	278	307	302	287	265	235	32
	12		86.6	0.0	280	317	312	298	275	245	36
	Surface daily totals				2932	2526	2412	2250	2036	1766	246
Aug 21	6	6	5.0	101.3	35	7	5	4	4	4	2
	7	5	18.5	95.6	186	82	76	69	60	50	11
	8	4	32.2	89.7	241	158	154	146	134	118	16
	9	3	45.9	82.9	265	223	222	214	200	181	39
	10	2	59.3	73.0	278	273	275	268	252	230	58
	11	1	71.6	53.2	284	304	309	301	285	261	71
	12		78.3	0.0	286	315	320	313	296	272	75
	Surface daily totals				2864	2408	2402	2316	2168	1958	470
Sep 21	7	5	13.7	83.8	173	57	60	60	59	56	26
	8	4	27.2	76.8	248	136	144	146	143	136	62
	9	3	40.2	67.9	278	205	218	221	217	206	93
	10	2	52.3	54.8	292	258	275	278	273	261	116
	11	1	61.9	33.4	299	291	311	315	309	295	131
	12		66.0	0.0	301	302	323	327	321	306	136
	Surface daily totals				2878	2194	2342	2366	2322	2212	992
Oct 21	7	5	9.1	74.1	138	32	40	45	48	50	42
	8	4	22.0	66.7	247	111	129	139	144	145	99
	9	3	34.1	57.1	284	180	206	217	223	221	138
	10	2	44.7	43.8	301	234	265	277	282	279	165
	11	1	52.5	24.7	309	268	301	315	319	314	182
	12		55.5	0.0	311	279	314	328	332	327	188
	Surface daily totals				2868	1928	2198	2314	2364	2346	1442
Nov 21	7	5	4.9	65.8	67	10	16	20	24	27	29
	8	4	17.0	58.4	232	82	108	123	135	142	124
	9	3	28.0	48.9	282	150	186	205	217	224	172
	10	2	37.3	36.3	303	203	244	265	278	283	204
	11	1	43.8	19.7	312	236	280	302	316	320	222
	12		46.2	0.0	315	247	293	315	328	332	228
	Surface daily totals				2706	1610	1962	2146	2268	2324	1730
Dec 21	7	5	3.2	62.6	30	3	7	9	11	12	14
	8	4	14.9	55.3	225	71	99	116	129	139	130
	9	3	25.5	46.0	281	137	176	198	214	223	184
	10	2	34.3	33.7	304	189	234	258	275	283	217
	11	1	40.4	18.2	314	221	270	295	312	320	236
	12		42.6	0.0	317	232	282	308	325	332	243
	Surface daily totals				2624	1474	1852	2058	2204	2286	1808

BTUH/sq. ft. total insolation on surfaces[b] — South facing surface angle with horiz.

Date	Solar time AM	PM	Solar position Alt	Azm	Normal	Horiz.	14	24	34	44	90
Jan 21	7	5	4.8	65.6	71	10	17	21	25	28	31
	8	4	16.9	58.3	239	83	110	126	137	145	127
	9	3	27.9	48.8	288	151	188	207	221	228	176
	10	2	37.2	36.1	308	204	246	268	282	287	207
	11	1	43.6	19.6	317	237	283	306	319	324	226
	12		46.0	0.0	320	249	296	319	332	336	232
	Surface daily totals				2766	1622	1984	2174	2300	2360	1766
Feb 21	7	5	9.3	74.6	158	35	44	49	53	56	46
	8	4	22.3	67.2	263	116	135	145	150	151	102
	9	3	34.4	57.6	298	187	213	225	230	228	141
	10	2	45.1	44.2	314	241	273	286	291	287	168
	11	1	53.0	25.0	321	276	310	324	328	323	185
	12		56.0	0.0	324	288	323	337	341	335	191
	Surface daily totals				3036	1998	2276	2396	2436	2424	1476
Mar 21	7	5	13.7	83.3	194	60	63	64	62	59	27
	8	4	27.2	76.8	267	141	150	152	149	142	64
	9	3	40.2	67.9	295	212	226	229	225	214	95
	10	2	52.3	54.8	309	266	285	288	283	270	120
	11	1	61.9	33.4	315	300	322	326	320	305	135
	12		66.0	0.0	317	312	334	339	333	317	140
	Surface daily totals				3078	2270	2428	2456	2412	2298	1022
Apr 21	6	6	4.7	100.6	40	7	5	4	4	3	2
	7	5	18.3	94.9	203	83	77	70	62	51	10
	8	4	32.0	89.0	256	160	157	149	137	122	16
	9	3	45.6	81.9	280	227	227	220	206	186	46
	10	2	59.0	71.8	292	278	282	275	259	237	61
	11	1	71.1	51.6	298	310	316	309	293	269	74
	12		77.6	0.0	299	321	328	321	305	280	79
	Surface daily totals				3036	2454	2458	2374	2228	2016	488
May 21	6	6	8.0	108.4	86	22	15	10	9	9	5
	7	5	21.2	103.2	203	98	85	73	59	44	12
	8	4	34.6	98.5	248	171	159	145	127	106	15
	9	3	48.3	93.6	269	233	224	210	190	165	16
	10	2	62.0	87.7	280	281	275	261	239	211	22
	11	1	75.5	76.9	286	311	307	293	270	240	34
	12		86.0	0.0	288	322	317	304	281	250	37
	Surface daily totals				3032	2556	2447	2286	2072	1800	246
Jun 21	6	6	9.3	111.6	97	29	20	12	12	11	7
	7	5	22.3	106.8	201	103	87	73	58	41	13
	8	4	35.5	102.6	242	173	158	142	122	99	16
	9	3	49.0	98.7	263	234	221	204	182	155	18
	10	2	62.6	95.0	274	280	269	253	229	199	18
	11	1	76.3	90.8	279	309	300	283	259	227	19
	12		89.4	0.0	281	319	310	294	269	236	22
	Surface daily totals				2994	2574	2422	2230	1992	1700	204

FIG. A-7b. Solar position and insolation values for 32 degrees north latitude.

Date	Solar time AM	Solar time PM	Alt	Azm	Normal	Horiz.	22	32	42	52	90
Jan 21	7	5	1.4	65.2	1	0	0	0	0	1	1
	8	4	12.5	56.5	203	56	93	106	116	123	115
	9	3	22.5	46.0	269	118	175	193	206	212	181
	10	2	30.6	33.1	295	167	235	256	269	274	221
	11	1	36.1	17.5	306	198	273	295	308	312	245
	12		38.0	0.0	310	209	285	308	321	324	253
	Surface daily totals				2458	1288	1839	2008	2118	2166	1779
Feb 21	7	5	7.1	73.5	121	22	34	37	40	42	38
	8	4	19.0	64.4	247	95	127	136	140	141	108
	9	3	29.9	53.4	288	161	206	217	222	220	158
	10	2	39.1	39.4	306	212	266	278	283	279	193
	11	1	45.6	21.4	315	244	304	317	321	315	214
	12		48.0	0.0	317	255	316	330	334	328	222
	Surface daily totals				2872	1724	2188	2300	2345	2322	1644
Mar 21	7	5	12.7	81.9	185	54	60	60	59	56	32
	8	4	25.1	73.0	260	129	146	147	144	137	78
	9	3	36.8	62.1	290	194	222	224	220	209	119
	10	2	47.3	47.5	304	245	280	283	278	265	150
	11	1	55.0	26.8	311	277	317	321	315	300	170
	12		58.0	0.0	313	287	329	333	327	312	177
	Surface daily totals				3012	2084	2378	2403	2358	2246	1276
Apr 21	6	6	6.1	99.9	66	14	9	6	6	5	3
	7	5	18.8	92.2	206	86	78	71	62	51	10
	8	4	31.5	84.0	255	158	156	148	136	120	35
	9	3	43.9	74.2	278	220	225	217	203	183	68
	10	2	55.7	60.3	290	267	279	272	256	234	95
	11	1	65.4	37.5	295	297	313	306	290	265	112
	12		69.6	0.0	297	307	325	318	301	276	118
	Surface daily totals				3076	2390	2444	2356	2206	1994	764
May 21	6	6	10.4	107.2	119	36	21	13	13	12	7
	7	5	22.8	100.1	211	107	88	75	60	44	13
	8	4	35.4	92.9	250	175	159	145	127	105	15
	9	3	48.1	84.7	269	233	223	209	188	163	33
	10	2	60.6	73.3	280	277	273	259	237	208	56
	11	1	72.0	51.9	285	305	305	290	268	237	72
	12		78.0	0.0	286	315	315	301	278	247	77
	Surface daily totals				3112	2582	2454	2284	2064	1788	469
Jun 21	6	6	12.2	110.2	131	45	26	16	15	14	9
	7	5	24.3	103.4	210	115	91	76	59	41	14
	8	4	36.9	96.8	245	180	159	143	122	99	16
	9	3	49.6	89.4	264	236	221	204	181	153	19
	10	2	62.2	79.7	274	279	268	251	227	197	41
	11	1	74.2	60.9	279	306	299	282	257	224	56
	12		81.5	0.0	280	315	309	292	267	234	60
	Surface daily totals				3084	2634	2436	2234	1990	1690	370

Date	Solar time AM	Solar time PM	Alt	Azm	Normal	Horiz.	22	32	42	52	90
Jul 21	6	6	10.7	107.7	113	37	22	14	13	12	8
	7	5	23.1	100.6	203	107	87	75	60	44	14
	8	4	35.7	93.6	241	174	158	143	125	104	16
	9	3	48.4	85.5	261	231	220	205	185	159	31
	10	2	60.9	74.3	271	274	269	254	232	204	54
	11	1	72.4	53.3	277	302	300	285	262	232	69
	12		78.6	0.0	279	311	310	296	273	242	74
	Surface daily totals				3012	2558	2422	2250	2030	1754	458
Aug 21	6	6	6.5	100.5	59	14	9	7	6	6	4
	7	5	19.1	92.8	190	85	77	69	60	50	12
	8	4	31.8	84.7	240	156	152	144	132	116	33
	9	3	44.3	75.0	263	216	220	212	197	178	65
	10	2	56.1	61.3	276	262	272	264	249	226	91
	11	1	66.0	38.4	282	292	305	298	281	257	107
	12		70.3	0.0	284	302	317	309	292	268	113
	Surface daily totals				2902	2352	2388	2296	2144	1934	736
Sep 21	7	5	12.7	81.9	163	51	56	56	55	52	30
	8	4	25.1	73.0	240	124	140	141	138	131	75
	9	3	36.8	62.1	272	188	213	215	211	201	114
	10	2	47.3	47.5	287	237	270	273	268	255	145
	11	1	55.0	26.8	294	268	306	309	303	289	164
	12		58.0	0.0	296	278	318	321	315	300	171
	Surface daily totals				2808	2014	2288	2308	2264	2154	1226
Oct 21	7	5	6.8	73.1	99	19	29	32	34	36	32
	8	4	18.7	64.0	229	90	120	128	133	134	104
	9	3	29.5	53.0	273	155	198	208	213	212	153
	10	2	38.7	39.1	289	204	257	269	273	270	188
	11	1	45.1	21.1	301	236	294	307	311	306	209
	12		47.5	0.0	304	247	306	320	324	318	217
	Surface daily totals				2696	1654	2100	2208	2252	2232	1588
Nov 21	7	5	1.5	65.4	2	0	0	0	0	1	1
	8	4	12.7	56.6	196	55	91	104	113	119	111
	9	3	22.6	46.1	263	118	173	190	202	208	176
	10	2	30.8	33.2	289	166	233	252	265	270	217
	11	1	36.2	17.6	301	197	270	291	303	307	241
	12		38.2	0.0	304	207	282	304	316	320	249
	Surface daily totals				2406	1280	1816	1980	2084	2130	1742
Dec 21	8	4	10.3	53.8	176	41	77	90	101	108	107
	9	3	19.8	43.6	257	102	161	180	195	204	183
	10	2	27.6	31.2	288	150	221	244	259	267	226
	11	1	32.7	16.4	301	180	258	282	298	305	251
	12		34.6	0.0	304	190	271	295	311	318	259
	Surface daily totals				2348	1136	1704	1888	2016	2086	1794

Note: Columns 22, 32, 42, 52, 90 = South facing surface angle with horiz.[b]

FIG. A-7c. Solar position and insolation values for 40 degrees north latitude.

Date	Solar time AM	Solar time PM	Alt	Azm	Normal	Horiz.	30	40	50	60	90
Jan 21	8	4	8.1	55.3	142	28	65	74	81	85	84
	9	3	16.8	44.0	239	83	155	171	182	187	171
	10	2	23.8	30.9	274	127	218	237	249	254	223
	11	1	28.4	16.0	289	154	257	277	290	293	253
	12		30.0	0.0	294	164	270	291	303	306	263
	Surface daily totals				2182	948	1660	1810	1906	1944	1726
Feb 21	7	5	4.8	72.7	69	10	19	21	23	24	22
	8	4	15.4	62.2	224	73	114	122	126	127	107
	9	3	25.0	50.2	274	132	195	205	209	208	167
	10	2	32.8	35.9	295	178	256	267	271	267	210
	11	1	38.1	18.9	305	206	293	306	310	304	236
	12		40.0	0.0	308	216	306	319	323	317	245
	Surface daily totals				2640	1414	2060	2162	2202	2176	1730
Mar 21	7	5	11.4	80.2	171	46	55	55	54	51	35
	8	4	22.5	69.6	250	114	140	141	138	131	89
	9	3	32.8	57.3	282	173	215	217	213	202	138
	10	2	41.6	41.9	297	218	273	276	271	258	176
	11	1	47.7	22.6	305	247	310	313	307	293	200
	12		50.0	0.0	307	257	322	326	320	305	208
	Surface daily totals				2916	1852	2308	2330	2284	2174	1484
Apr 21	6	6	7.4	98.9	89	20	11	8	7	7	4
	7	5	18.9	89.5	206	87	77	70	61	50	12
	8	4	30.3	79.3	252	152	153	145	133	117	53
	9	3	41.3	67.2	274	207	221	213	199	179	93
	10	2	51.2	51.4	286	250	275	267	252	229	126
	11	1	58.7	29.2	292	277	308	301	285	260	147
	12		61.6	0.0	293	287	320	313	296	271	154
	Surface daily totals				3092	2274	2412	2320	2168	1956	1022
May 21	5	7	1.9	114.7	1	0	0	0	0	0	0
	6	6	12.7	105.6	144	49	25	15	14	13	9
	7	5	24.0	96.6	216	114	89	76	60	44	13
	8	4	35.4	87.2	250	175	158	144	125	104	25
	9	3	46.8	76.0	267	227	221	206	186	160	60
	10	2	57.5	60.9	277	267	270	255	233	205	89
	11	1	66.2	37.1	283	293	301	287	264	234	108
	12		70.0	0.0	284	301	312	297	274	243	114
	Surface daily totals				3160	2552	2442	2264	2040	1760	724
Jun 21	5	7	4.2	117.3	22	4	3	3	2	2	1
	6	6	14.8	108.4	155	60	30	18	17	16	10
	7	5	26.0	99.7	216	123	92	77	59	41	14
	8	4	37.4	90.7	246	182	159	142	121	97	16
	9	3	48.8	80.2	263	233	219	202	179	151	47
	10	2	59.8	65.8	272	272	266	248	224	194	74
	11	1	69.2	41.9	277	296	296	278	253	221	92
	12		73.5	0.0	279	304	306	289	263	230	98
	Surface daily totals				3180	2648	2434	2224	1974	1670	610

BTUH/sq. ft. total insolation on surfaces[b] — South facing surface angle with horiz. (columns 30, 40, 50, 60, 90)

Date	Solar time AM	Solar time PM	Alt	Azm	Normal	Horiz.	30	40	50	60	90
Jul 21	5	7	2.3	115.2	2	0	0	0	0	0	0
	6	6	13.1	106.1	138	50	26	17	15	14	9
	7	5	24.3	97.2	208	114	89	75	60	44	14
	8	4	35.8	87.8	241	174	157	142	124	102	24
	9	3	47.2	76.7	259	225	218	203	182	157	58
	10	2	57.9	61.7	269	265	266	251	229	200	86
	11	1	66.7	37.9	275	290	296	281	258	228	104
	12		70.6	0.0	276	298	307	292	269	238	111
	Surface daily totals				3062	2534	2409	2230	2006	1728	702
Aug 21	6	6	7.9	99.5	81	21	12	9	8	7	5
	7	5	19.3	90.9	191	87	76	69	60	49	12
	8	4	30.7	79.9	237	150	150	141	129	113	50
	9	3	41.8	67.9	260	205	216	207	193	173	89
	10	2	51.7	52.1	272	246	267	259	244	221	120
	11	1	59.3	29.7	278	273	300	292	276	252	140
	12		62.3	0.0	280	282	311	303	287	262	147
	Surface daily totals				2916	2244	2354	2258	2104	1894	978
Sep 21	7	5	11.4	80.2	149	43	51	51	49	47	32
	8	4	22.5	69.6	230	109	133	134	131	124	84
	9	3	32.8	57.3	263	167	206	208	203	193	132
	10	2	41.6	41.9	280	211	262	265	260	247	168
	11	1	47.7	22.6	287	239	298	301	295	281	192
	12		50.0	0.0	290	249	310	313	307	292	200
	Surface daily totals				2708	1788	2210	2228	2182	2074	1416
Oct 21	7	5	4.5	72.3	48	7	14	15	17	17	16
	8	4	15.0	61.9	204	68	106	113	117	118	100
	9	3	24.5	49.8	257	126	185	195	200	198	160
	10	2	32.4	35.6	280	170	245	257	261	257	203
	11	1	37.6	18.7	291	199	283	295	299	294	229
	12		39.5	0.0	294	208	295	308	312	306	238
	Surface daily totals				2454	1348	1962	2060	2098	2074	1654
Nov 21	8	4	8.2	55.4	136	28	63	72	78	82	81
	9	3	17.0	44.1	232	82	152	167	178	183	167
	10	2	24.0	31.0	268	126	215	233	245	249	219
	11	1	28.6	16.1	283	153	254	273	285	288	248
	12		30.2	0.0	288	163	267	287	298	301	258
	Surface daily totals				2128	942	1636	1778	1870	1908	1686
Dec 21	8	4	5.5	53.0	89	14	39	45	50	54	56
	9	3	14.0	41.9	217	65	135	152	164	171	163
	10	2	20..	29.4	261	107	200	221	235	242	221
	11	1	25.0	15.2	280	134	239	262	276	283	252
	12		26.6	0.0	285	143	253	275	290	296	263
	Surface daily totals				1978	782	1480	1634	1740	1796	1646

FIG. A-7d. Solar position and insolation values for 48 degrees north latitude.

Date	Solar time AM	PM	Solar position Alt	Azm	Normal	Horiz.	38	48	58	68	90
Jan 21	8	4	3.5	54.6	37	4	17	19	21	22	22
	9	3	11.0	42.6	185	46	120	132	140	145	139
	10	2	16.9	29.4	239	83	190	206	216	220	206
	11	1	20.7	15.1	261	107	231	249	260	263	243
	12		22.0	0.0	267	115	245	264	275	278	255
	Surface daily totals				1710	596	1360	1478	1550	1578	1478
Feb 21	7	5	2.4	72.2	12	1	3	4	4	4	4
	8	4	11.6	60.5	188	49	95	102	105	106	96
	9	3	19.7	47.7	251	100	178	187	191	190	167
	10	2	26.2	33.3	278	139	240	251	255	251	217
	11	1	30.5	17.2	290	165	278	290	294	288	247
	12		32.0	0.0	293	173	291	304	307	301	258
	Surface daily totals				2330	1080	1880	1972	2024	1978	1720
Mar 21	7	5	10.0	78.7	153	37	49	49	47	45	35
	8	4	19.5	66.8	236	96	131	137	129	122	96
	9	3	28.2	53.4	270	147	205	207	203	193	152
	10	2	35.4	37.8	287	187	263	266	261	248	195
	11	1	40.3	19.8	295	212	300	303	297	283	223
	12		42.0	0.0	298	220	312	315	309	294	232
	Surface daily totals				2780	1578	2208	2228	2182	2074	1632
Apr 21	6	6	8.6	97.8	108	27	13	9	8	7	5
	7	5	18.6	86.7	205	85	76	69	59	48	21
	8	4	28.5	74.9	247	142	149	141	129	113	69
	9	3	37.8	61.2	268	191	216	208	194	174	115
	10	2	45.8	44.6	280	228	268	260	245	223	152
	11	1	51.5	24.0	286	252	301	294	278	254	177
	12		53.6	0.0	288	260	313	305	289	264	185
	Surface daily totals				3076	2106	2358	2266	2114	1902	1262
May 21	5	7	5.2	114.3	41	9	4	4	4	3	2
	6	6	14.7	103.7	162	61	27	16	15	13	10
	7	5	24.6	93.0	219	118	89	75	60	43	13
	8	4	34.7	81.6	248	171	156	142	123	101	45
	9	3	44.3	68.3	264	217	217	202	182	156	86
	10	2	53.0	51.3	274	252	265	251	229	200	120
	11	1	59.5	28.6	279	274	296	281	258	228	141
	12		62.0	0.0	280	281	306	292	269	238	149
	Surface daily totals				3254	2482	2418	2234	2010	1728	982
Jun 21	5	7	7.9	116.5	77	21	9	8	7	7	5
	6	6	17.2	106.2	172	74	33	19	18	16	12
	7	5	27.0	95.8	220	129	93	77	59	39	15
	8	4	37.1	84.6	246	181	157	140	119	95	35
	9	3	46.9	71.6	261	225	216	198	175	147	74
	10	2	55.8	54.8	269	259	262	244	220	189	105
	11	1	62.7	31.2	274	280	291	273	248	216	126
	12		65.5	0.0	275	287	301	283	258	225	133
	Surface daily totals				3312	2626	2420	2204	1950	1644	874

BTUH/sq. ft. total insolation on surfaces[b]. South facing surface angle with horiz.

Date	Solar time AM	PM	Solar position Alt	Azm	Normal	Horiz.	38	48	58	68	90
Jul 21	5	7	5.7	114.7	43	10	5	5	4	4	3
	6	6	15.2	104.1	156	62	28	18	16	15	11
	7	5	25.1	93.5	211	118	89	75	59	42	14
	8	4	35.1	82.1	240	171	154	140	121	99	43
	9	3	44.8	68.8	256	215	214	199	178	153	83
	10	2	53.5	51.9	266	250	261	246	224	195	116
	11	1	60.1	29.0	271	272	291	276	253	223	137
	12		62.6	0.0	272	279	301	286	263	232	144
	Surface daily totals				3158	2474	2386	2200	1974	1694	956
Aug 21	6	6	9.1	98.3	99	28	14	10	9	8	6
	7	5	19.1	87.2	190	85	75	67	58	47	20
	8	4	29.0	75.4	232	141	145	137	125	109	65
	9	3	38.4	61.8	254	189	210	201	187	168	110
	10	2	46.4	45.1	266	225	260	252	237	214	146
	11	1	52.2	24.3	272	248	293	285	268	244	169
	12		54.3	0.0	274	256	304	296	279	255	177
	Surface daily totals				2898	2086	2300	2200	2046	1836	1208
Sep 21	7	5	10.0	78.7	131	35	44	44	43	40	31
	8	4	19.5	66.8	215	92	124	124	121	115	90
	9	3	28.2	53.4	251	142	196	197	193	183	143
	10	2	35.4	37.8	269	181	251	254	248	236	185
	11	1	40.3	19.8	278	205	287	289	284	269	212
	12		42.0	0.0	280	213	299	302	296	281	221
	Surface daily totals				2568	1522	2102	2118	2070	1966	1546
Oct 21	7	5	2.0	71.9	4	0	1	1	1	1	1
	8	4	11.2	60.2	165	44	86	91	95	95	87
	9	3	19.3	47.4	233	94	167	176	180	178	157
	10	2	25.7	33.1	262	133	228	239	242	239	207
	11	1	30.0	17.1	274	157	266	277	281	276	237
	12		31.5	0.0	278	166	279	291	294	288	247
	Surface daily totals				2154	1022	1774	1860	1890	1866	1626
Nov 21	8	4	3.6	54.7	36	5	17	19	21	22	22
	9	3	11.2	42.7	179	46	117	129	137	141	135
	10	2	17.1	29.5	233	83	186	202	212	215	201
	11	1	20.9	15.1	255	107	227	245	255	258	238
	12		22.2	0.0	261	115	241	259	270	272	250
	Surface daily totals				1668	596	1336	1448	1518	1544	1442
Dec 21	9	3	8.0	40.9	140	27	87	98	105	110	109
	10	2	13.6	28.2	214	63	164	180	192	197	190
	11	1	17.3	14.4	242	86	207	226	239	244	231
	12		18.6	0.0	250	94	222	241	254	260	244
	Surface daily totals				1444	446	1136	1250	1326	1364	1304

Date	Solar time		Solar position		BTUH/sq. ft. total insolation on surfaces[b]						
	AM	PM	Alt	Azm	Normal	Horiz.	South facing surface angle with horiz.				
							46	56	66	76	90
Jan 21	9	3	5.0	41.8	78	11	50	55	59	60	60
	10	2	9.9	28.5	170	39	135	146	154	156	153
	11	1	12.9	14.5	207	58	183	197	206	208	201
	12		14.0	0.0	217	65	198	214	222	225	217
	Surface daily totals				1126	282	934	1010	1058	1074	1044
Feb 21	8	4	7.6	59.4	129	25	65	69	72	72	69
	9	3	14.2	45.9	214	65	151	159	162	161	151
	10	2	19.4	31.5	250	98	215	225	228	224	208
	11	1	22.8	16.1	266	119	254	265	268	263	243
	12		24.0	0.0	270	126	268	279	282	276	255
	Surface daily totals				1986	740	1640	1716	1742	1716	1598
Mar 21	7	5	8.3	77.5	128	28	40	40	39	37	32
	8	4	16.2	64.4	215	75	119	120	117	111	97
	9	3	23.3	50.3	253	118	192	193	189	180	154
	10	2	29.0	34.9	272	151	249	251	246	234	205
	11	1	32.7	17.9	282	172	285	288	282	268	236
	12		34.0	0.0	284	179	297	300	294	280	246
	Surface daily totals				2586	1268	2066	2084	2040	1938	1700
Apr 21	5	7	1.4	108.8	0	0					0
	6	6	9.6	96.5	122	32	14	9	8	7	6
	7	5	18.0	84.1	201	81	74	66	57	46	29
	8	4	26.1	70.9	239	129	143	135	123	108	82
	9	3	33.6	56.3	260	169	208	200	186	167	133
	10	2	39.9	39.7	272	201	259	251	236	214	174
	11	1	44.1	20.7	278	220	292	284	268	245	200
	12		45.6	0.0	280	227	303	295	279	255	209
	Surface daily totals				3024	1892	2282	2186	2038	1830	1458
May 21	4	8	1.2	125.5	0	0	0	0	0	0	0
	5	7	8.5	113.4	93	25	10	9	8	7	6
	6	6	16.5	101.5	175	71	28	17	15	13	11
	7	5	24.8	89.3	219	119	88	74	58	41	16
	8	4	33.1	76.3	244	163	153	138	119	98	63
	9	3	40.9	61.6	259	201	212	197	176	151	109
	10	2	47.6	44.2	268	231	259	244	222	194	146
	11	1	52.3	23.4	273	249	288	274	251	222	170
	12		54.0	0.0	275	255	299	284	261	231	178
	Surface daily totals				3340	2374	2374	2188	1962	1682	1218
Jun 21	4	8	4.2	127.2	21	4	2	2	2	2	1
	5	7	11.4	115.3	122	40	14	13	11	10	8
	6	6	19.3	103.6	185	86	34	19	17	15	12
	7	5	27.6	91.7	222	132	92	76	57	38	15
	8	4	35.9	78.8	243	175	154	137	116	92	55
	9	3	43.8	64.1	257	212	211	193	170	143	98
	10	2	50.7	46.4	265	240	255	238	214	184	133
	11	1	55.6	24.9	269	258	284	267	242	210	156
	12		57.5	0.0	271	264	294	276	251	219	164
	Surface daily totals				3438	2526	2388	2166	1910	1606	1120

Date	Solar time		Solar position		BTUH/sq. ft. total insolation on surfaces[b]						
	AM	PM	Alt	Azm	Normal	Horiz.	South facing surface angle with horiz.				
							46	56	66	76	90
Jul 21	4	8	1.7	125.8	0	0	0	0	0	0	0
	5	7	9.0	113.7	91	27	11	10	9	8	6
	6	6	17.0	101.9	169	72	30	18	16	14	12
	7	5	25.3	89.7	212	119	88	74	58	41	15
	8	4	33.6	76.7	237	163	151	136	117	96	61
	9	3	41.4	62.0	252	201	208	193	173	147	106
	10	2	48.2	44.6	261	230	254	239	217	189	142
	11	1	52.9	23.7	265	248	283	268	245	216	165
	12		54.6	0.0	267	254	293	278	255	225	173
	Surface daily totals				3240	2372	2342	2152	1926	1646	1186
Aug 21	5	7	2.0	109.2	1	0	0	0	0	0	0
	6	6	10.2	97.0	112	34	16	11	10	9	7
	7	5	18.5	84.5	187	82	73	65	56	45	28
	8	4	26.7	71.3	225	128	140	131	119	104	78
	9	3	34.3	56.7	246	168	202	193	179	160	126
	10	2	40.5	40.0	258	199	251	242	227	206	166
	11	1	44.8	20.9	264	218	282	274	258	235	191
	12		46.3	0.0	266	225	293	285	269	245	200
	Surface daily totals				2850	1884	2218	2118	1966	1760	1392
Sep 21	7	5	8.3	77.5	107	25	36	36	34	32	28
	8	4	16.2	64.4	194	72	111	111	108	102	89
	9	3	23.3	50.3	233	114	181	182	178	168	147
	10	2	29.0	34.9	253	146	236	237	232	221	193
	11	1	32.7	17.9	263	166	271	273	267	254	223
	12		34.0	0.0	266	173	283	285	279	265	233
	Surface daily totals				2368	1220	1950	1962	1918	1820	1594
Oct 21	8	4	7.1	59.1	104	20	53	57	59	59	57
	9	3	13.8	45.7	193	60	138	145	148	147	138
	10	2	19.0	31.3	231	92	201	210	213	210	195
	11	1	22.3	16.0	248	112	240	250	253	248	230
	12		23.5	0.0	253	119	253	263	266	261	241
	Surface daily totals				1804	688	1516	1586	1612	1588	1480
Nov 21	9	3	5.2	41.9	76	12	49	54	57	59	58
	10	2	10.0	28.5	165	39	132	143	149	152	148
	11	1	13.1	14.5	201	58	179	193	201	203	196
	12		14.2	0.0	211	65	194	209	217	219	211
	Surface daily totals				1094	284	914	986	1032	1046	1016
Dec 21	9	3	1.9	40.5	5	0	3	4	4	4	4
	10	2	6.6	27.5	113	19	86	95	101	104	103
	11	1	9.5	13.9	166	37	141	154	163	167	164
	12		10.6	0.0	180	43	159	173	182	186	182
	Surface daily totals				748	156	620	678	716	734	722

FIG. A-7f. Solar position and insolation values for 64 degrees north latitude.

Table 1 (Jan–Jun)

Date	Solar time AM	PM	Solar position Alt	Azm	BTUH/sq. ft. total insolation on surfaces[b] Normal	Horiz.	South facing surface angle with horiz. 54	64	74	84	90
Jan 21	10	2	2.8	28.1	22	2	17	19	20	20	20
	11	1	5.2	14.1	81	12	72	77	80	81	81
		12	6.0	0.0	100	16	91	98	102	103	103
	Surface daily totals				306	45	268	290	302	306	304
Feb 21	8	4	3.4	58.7	35	4	17	19	19	19	19
	9	3	8.6	44.8	147	31	103	108	111	110	107
	10	2	12.6	30.3	199	55	170	178	181	178	173
	11	1	15.1	15.3	222	71	212	220	223	219	213
		12	16.0	0.0	228	77	225	235	237	232	226
	Surface daily totals				1432	400	1230	1286	1302	1282	1252
Mar 21	7	5	6.5	76.5	95	18	30	29	29	27	25
	8	4	12.7	62.6	185	54	101	102	99	94	89
	9	3	18.1	48.1	227	87	171	172	169	160	153
	10	2	22.3	32.7	249	112	227	229	224	213	203
	11	1	25.1	16.6	260	129	262	265	259	246	235
		12	26.0	0.0	263	134	274	277	271	258	246
	Surface daily totals				2296	932	1856	1870	1830	1736	1656
Apr 21	5	7	4.0	108.5	27	5	2	2	2	1	1
	6	6	10.4	95.1	133	37	15	9	8	7	6
	7	5	17.0	81.6	194	76	70	63	54	43	37
	8	4	23.3	67.5	228	112	136	128	116	102	91
	9	3	29.0	52.3	248	144	197	189	176	158	145
	10	2	33.5	36.0	260	169	246	239	224	203	188
	11	1	36.5	18.4	266	184	278	270	255	233	216
		12	37.6	0.0	268	190	289	281	266	243	225
	Surface daily totals				2982	1644	2176	2082	1936	1736	1594
May 21	4	8	5.8	125.1	51	11	5	4	4	3	3
	5	7	11.6	112.1	132	42	13	11	10	9	8
	6	6	17.9	99.1	185	79	29	16	14	12	11
	7	5	24.5	85.7	218	117	86	72	56	39	28
	8	4	30.9	71.5	239	152	148	133	115	94	80
	9	3	36.8	56.1	252	182	204	190	170	145	128
	10	2	41.6	38.9	261	205	249	235	213	186	167
	11	1	44.9	20.1	265	219	278	264	242	213	193
		12	46.0	0.0	267	224	288	274	251	222	201
	Surface daily totals				3470	2236	2312	2124	1898	1624	1436
Jun 21	3	9	4.2	139.4	21	4	2	2	2	2	1
	4	8	9.0	126.4	93	27	10	9	8	7	6
	5	7	14.7	113.6	154	60	16	15	13	11	10
	6	6	21.0	100.8	194	96	34	19	17	14	13
	7	5	27.5	87.5	221	132	91	74	55	36	23
	8	4	34.0	73.3	239	166	150	133	112	88	73
	9	3	39.9	57.8	251	195	204	187	164	137	119
	10	2	44.9	40.4	258	217	247	230	206	177	157
	11	1	48.3	20.9	262	231	275	258	233	202	181
		12	49.5	0.0	263	235	284	267	242	211	189
	Surface daily totals				3658	2488	2342	2118	1862	1558	1356

Table 2 (Jul–Dec)

Date	Solar time AM	PM	Solar position Alt	Azm	BTUH/sq. ft. total insolation on surfaces[b] Normal	Horiz.	South facing surface angle with horiz. 54	64	74	84	90
Jul 21	4	8	6.4	125.3	53	13	6	5	5	4	4
	5	7	12.1	112.4	128	44	14	13	11	10	9
	6	6	18.4	99.4	179	81	30	17	16	13	12
	7	5	25.0	86.0	211	118	86	72	56	38	28
	8	4	31.4	71.8	231	152	146	131	113	91	77
	9	3	37.3	56.3	245	182	201	186	166	141	124
	10	2	42.2	39.2	253	204	245	230	208	181	162
	11	1	45.4	20.2	257	218	273	258	236	207	187
		12	46.6	0.0	259	223	282	267	245	216	195
	Surface daily totals				3372	2248	2280	2090	1864	1588	1400
Aug 21	5	7	4.6	108.8	29	6	3	3	2	2	2
	6	6	11.0	95.5	123	39	16	11	10	8	7
	7	5	17.6	81.9	181	77	69	61	52	42	35
	8	4	23.9	67.8	214	113	132	123	112	97	87
	9	3	29.6	52.6	234	144	190	182	169	150	138
	10	2	34.2	36.2	246	168	237	229	215	194	179
	11	1	37.2	18.5	252	183	268	260	244	222	205
		12	38.3	0.0	254	188	278	270	255	232	215
	Surface daily totals				2808	1646	2108	2008	1862	1662	1522
Sep 21	7	5	6.5	76.5	77	16	25	25	24	23	21
	8	4	12.7	62.6	163	51	92	92	90	85	81
	9	3	18.1	48.1	206	83	159	159	156	147	141
	10	2	22.3	32.7	229	108	212	213	209	198	189
	11	1	25.1	16.6	240	124	246	248	243	230	220
		12	26.0	0.0	244	129	258	260	255	241	230
	Surface daily totals				2074	892	1726	1736	1696	1608	1532
Oct 21	8	4	3.0	58.5	17	2	9	9	10	10	10
	9	3	8.1	44.6	122	26	86	91	93	92	90
	10	2	12.1	30.2	176	50	152	159	161	159	155
	11	1	14.6	15.2	201	65	193	201	203	200	195
		12	15.5	0.0	208	71	207	215	217	213	208
	Surface daily totals				1238	358	1088	1136	1152	1134	1106
Nov 21	10	2	3.0	28.1	23	3	18	20	21	21	21
	11	1	5.4	14.2	79	12	70	76	79	80	79
		12	6.2	0.0	97	17	89	96	100	101	100
	Surface daily totals				302	46	266	286	298	302	300
Dec 21	11	1	1.8	13.7	4	0	3	4	4	4	4
		12	2.6	0.0	16	2	14	15	16	17	17
	Surface daily totals				24	2	20	22	24	24	24

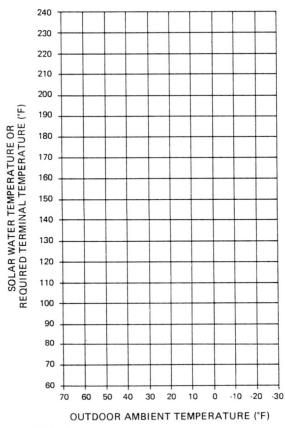

SOLAR WATER TEMPERATURE OR
REQUIRED TERMINAL TEMPERATURE (°F)

OUTDOOR AMBIENT TEMPERATURE (°F)

FIG. A–8. System evaluation chart

Line	Description	Source	Units	Data
1	Indoor Design Temp.	Heat Loss Calc.	°F	
2	Outdoor Design Temp.	Heat Loss Calc.	°F	
3	Design Temp. Difference	(1) - (2)	°F	

Line	Description	Source	Units	Data
4	Bldg. Design Ht. Loss; BTU/hr	$\frac{\text{Ht. Loss}}{1000}$	1000 BTU Per Hr.	
5	Daily Design Bldg. Heat Loss	(4) x 24	1000 BTU Per Day	
6	Bldg. Heat Loss BTU per Deg. Day	$\frac{(5)}{(3)}$	1000 BTU Per D.D.	

Line	Description	Source	Units	Data											
				J	F	M	A	M	J	J	A	S	O	N	D
7	Month			J	F	M	A	M	J	J	A	S	O	N	D
8	Day/Mo.			31	28	31	30	31	30	31	31	30	31	30	31
9	Degree Day Per Month	Climatic Atlas	$\frac{\text{D.D.}}{\text{month}}$												
10	Bldg. Heat Loss Per Month	$\frac{(6) \times (9)}{1000}$	Million BTU/Mo.												
11	Bldg. Heat Loss Per Day	$\frac{(10)}{(8)} \times 1000$	1000 BTU/Day												

FIG. A–9. Chart for estimating a building's daily, monthly, and annual heating needs

Determine insolation correction factor.

Line	Description	Source	Data		Line	Description	Source	Data
1	Clearness Factor	Clearness Factor Chart			3	Dirt, Etc. Factor		
2	Smog Factor				4	Insolation Correc. Factor	(1) x (2) x (3)	

Determine Daily collector insolation for month of_____

Line	Description	Source	Unit	Data													
5	Time		AM-PM	A.M.						Noon	P.M.						
6	Daily Time		Hour	6	7	8	9	10	11	12	1	2	3	4	5	6	
7	Available Insolation	ASHRAE Insolation Table	BTU/Ft^2 Per Hr.														
8	Corrected Insolation	(4) x (7)	BTU/Ft^2 Per Hr.														
9	ΔT_C	Fig. A-10	°F														
10	Glycol to Water HX approach ΔT	Design of HX if Used	°F														
11	Corrected ΔT_C	(9) + (10)	°F														
12	Fluid Parameter	(11)/(8)	$\frac{°F}{BTU/Ft^2Hr.}$														
13	Panel Efficiency	Use (12) w/Panel Eff. Chart															
14	Collectable Hourly Insol.	(8) x (13)	BTU/Ft^2 Per Hr.														
15	Total Daily Collectable Insol.	Summation Line (14)	BTU/Ft^2 Per Day														

FIG. A-10. Chart for estimating collectable insolation

Line	Description	Source	Units	Data														
1	Month			J	F	M	A	M	J	J	A	S	O	N	D			
2	Start Tank Temperature	System Evaluation Chart	°F															
3	Daily Heat Load	Line 11, Fig A-9	$\frac{1000\ BTU}{Day}$															
4	Tank Temp. Rise	$\frac{(3)}{Tank\ Cap\ (gal) \times 8.33}$	°F															
5	Final Tank Temp.	(2) + (4)	°F															
6	Mean Tank Temp.	$\frac{(2) + (5)}{2}$	°F															
7	Mean Ambient Temp.	Climatic Atlas	°F															
8	Base ΔT_C	(6) - (7)	°F															
9	Low Ambient Temp.	Climatic Atlas	°F															
10	Start ΔT_C	(2) - (9)	°F															
11	High Ambient Temp.	Climatic Atlas	°F															
12	Final ΔT_C	(5) - (11)	°F															
13	ΔT_C to 10 AM	$\frac{(10) + (8)}{2}$	°F															
14	ΔT_C 10AM-2PM	(8)	°F															
15	ΔT_C after 2PM	$\frac{(12) + (8)}{2}$	°F															

FIG. A–11. Chart for estimating ΔT_c

Line	Description	Source	Units	Data														
1	Month			J	F	M	A	M	J	J	A	S	O	N	D			
2	Day/Month			31	28	31	30	31	30	31	31	30	31	30	31			
3	Collector Area	Assume	Ft^2															
4	Collected Daily Insolation	Fig. A-11	BTU/Ft^2 Per Day															
5	Possible Monthly Coll. Insolation	$\frac{(2) \times (3) \times (4)}{1,000,000}$	Million BTU/Mo.															
6	Sunshine Factor	Climatic Atlas																
7	Probable Monthly Collection	(5) × (6)	Million BTU/Mo.															
8	Heat Load/Month	Fig. A-9	Million BTU/Mo.															
9	Solar Heat Used/Month	Smaller of (7) or (8)	Million BTU/Mo.															
10	Monthly % Solar	$\frac{(9) \times 100}{(8)}$	%															
11	Solar Heat Used Per Year	Summary of (9)	Million BTU/Yr.															
12	Total Heat Load Per Year	Fig. A-9	Million BTU/Yr.															
13	% Solar Heat	$\frac{(11) \times 100}{(12)}$	%															

FIG. A–12. Chart for calculating solar portion of heating load

INDEX

absorber coatings, 29
absorber plates, 27, 28
absorption, 21
acrylics, 22
active systems, 10–14
air vents, 81
aluminum absorbers, 34
Annual Cycle Energy System, 40
antifreeze, 81

balancing valves, 52, 53
baseboard heating, 98, 99
brazing, 59–65
brazing alloys, 60, 61

check valves, 52
Circuit Setter valve, 52
clearness factor, 18
cloudiness, 18, 19
coefficient of performance, 103
collector containers, 31–33
collector efficiency, 25–27
concentrating collectors, 10, 11
controllers, 74, 75, 95
cooling tower, 105–6
copper absorbers, 34
copper fittings, 50, 51
copper tubing, 47–75
cover plates, 30, 31

degree days, 109
design conditions, 109–10
design of piping systems, 65–69
domestic water heating, 83–89
dynamic head, 66

efficiency, instantaneous, 25–27
electromagnetic radiation, 17, 18
emittance, 21
ethylene glycol, 73, 74
evacuated collectors, 12

f-chart method, 112–13
fiberglass, 22, 30, 43, 44
fiberglass insulation, 36, 37
Filon, 22, 31
fittings, 50, 51
flash heaters, 87, 88
flat-plate collectors, 12–14
fluid parameter, 111
fluid passages, 28, 29
fluxing, 57, 62
forced-air heating, 99, 100
frictional resistance, 68, 69

gamma rays, 1
gate valves, 52
glass, 21
globe valves, 52
greenhouse effect, 23

heat exchangers, 81, 82, 84, 85, 92
heat pumps, 101–8

instantaneous electric heater, 88
insulation, 36, 37

Kalwall, 31
Kaptan, 22

laminar flow, 66
latent heat, 39

Mylar, 22

orbiting array, 14

passive systems, 5
performance curves, 71, 94
photovoltaics, 10
piping, 46–75
piping the array, 89–95
polycarbonates, 22, 31
polyethylene, 23, 30
power tower, 14, 15
preheat tank, 84, 85
pressure loss and velocity relationships, 67, 68
propylene glycol, 73, 74
pumps, 70–72
pump controllers, 74, 75
pumps in parallel, 72
pumps in series, 72

radiant heating, 99
radiation, 1
reflection, 21
reverse return, 79, 80
Reynolds number, 68

selective surface, 29
sensible heat, 39

silicone, 74
solar constant, 18
Solaris heating system, 39
solders, 54, 55
solder joints, 56–59
specific heat, 39
stagnation, 24
standby heat losses, 86
static head, 65, 66
storage temperatures, 98–100
stratification, 42
sun, 1
sunshine factor, 116

Tedlar, 23, 31
thermal-efficiency curve, 26, 27
thermal storage, 39–45
thermocirculation, 83, 84
Thermoflo, 52
Thermon, 36
tilt angle, 19
transmission, 21
Trombe wall, 6–10
turbulent flow, 66, 81

valves, 52, 53
vinyl, 23

X-rays, 1

Zero Energy House, 40, 41